The jeweller's directory of gemstones

The jeweller's directory of gemstones

A Complete Guide to Appraising and Using Precious Stones, From Cut and Colour to Shape and Setting

Judith Crowe

A QUARTO BOOK

First published 2006
A&C Black Publishers
38 Soho Square
London W1D 3HB
www.acblack.com

Copyright © 2006 Quarto Publishing plc

ISBN-10: 0 7136 7656 6
ISBN-13: 978 0 7136 7656 3

Designed and produced by
Quarto Publishing plc
The Old Brewery
6 Blundell Street
London N7 9BH

QUAR.DJG

EDITORS: Susie May, Karen Koll
ART EDITOR: Sheila Volpe
ASSISTANT ART DIRECTOR: Penny Cobb
COPY EDITOR: Fiona Robertson
DESIGNER: Tanya Devonshire Jones
PHOTOGRAPHERS: Paul Forester,
Juliet Sheath
ILLUSTRATOR: Kuo Kang Chen
PROOFREADER: Richard Emerson
INDEXER: Pamela Ellis
PHOTO RESEARCHER: Claudia Tate

ART DIRECTOR: Moira Clinch
PUBLISHER: Paul Carslake

Manufactured by Modern Age Repro
House Ltd, Hong Kong

Printed by SNP Leefung Printers Limited,
China

contents

FOREWORD 6

INTRODUCTION 8

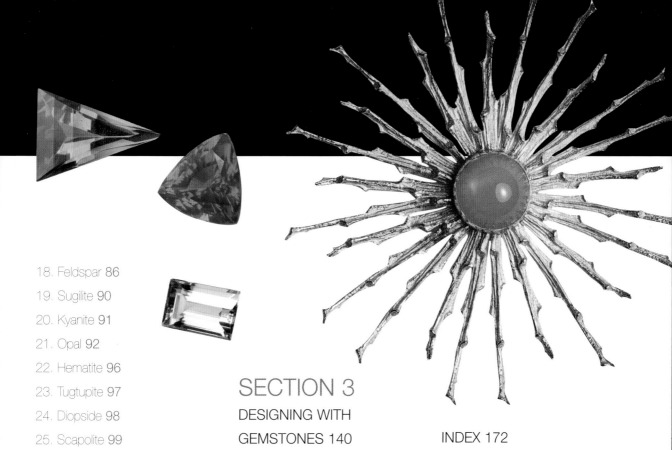

SECTION 3
DESIGNING WITH
GEMSTONES 140

PRACTICAL ADVICE 162

foreword

I am both a gem dealer and a jewellery maker, so when I look at

gemstones I not only get excited by a stone's gemmological attributes,

but I also find myself lured by its design potential – I immediately envision

the gemstone in a range of different jewellery settings. It is with this

approach that I wrote this book. I've aimed to provide an inspirational

guide to gemstones that supplies essential gemmological and practical

information and also encourages jewellers to produce imaginative and

distinctive jewellery designs that celebrate the qualities of stone.

The book is intended for jewellery makers and designers, students who work with gemstones and people who have a passion for stones and gem-set jewellery. It answers many of the questions I regularly get asked by students and jewellery makers and designers about gem usage and features a broad range of gemstone materials, some more challenging and rare than others. I hope it will excite and entice you.

Judith Crowe

Judith Crowe

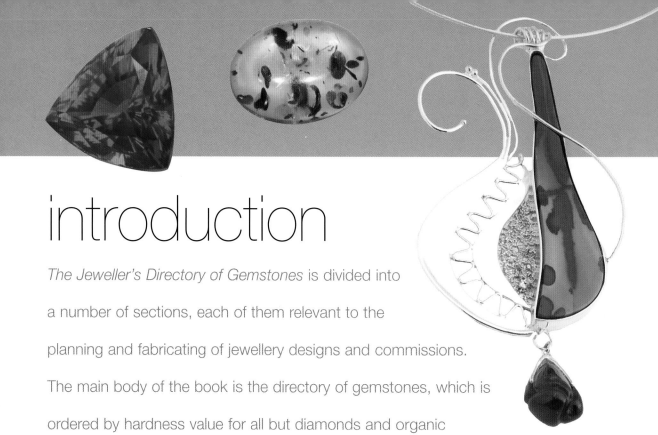

introduction

The Jeweller's Directory of Gemstones is divided into
a number of sections, each of them relevant to the
planning and fabricating of jewellery designs and commissions.
The main body of the book is the directory of gemstones, which is
ordered by hardness value for all but diamonds and organic
gemstones, which follow the rest. The directory covers the many
practical considerations around using a particular stone: its visual and
physical properties, colour treatments, availability and how it handles.

Further sections cover gem-related topics such as the mining, selection and usage of rough material and the designing and cutting of gemstones. A designing section explores how a gemstone's properties of colour, texture and scale can influence a design and discusses the use of delicate material and nonstandard forms. Practical advice takes the reader through the processes of gemstone appraisal and buying; it aims to give jewellery makers a better understanding of the gemstone trade so that they get greater value for their money.

creating gemstones

The earth's natural forces have created a wonderful array of gemstones, defined by their shape, colour and crystalline structure, for the jeweller to enhance. From this raw material, modern technologies allow the creation of a greater range of jewellery than ever before.

gemstone formation

Geologists divide rock types into three groups, depending on how they have formed. Gemstones can be found in all three types: igneous, sedimentary and metamorphic. Each rock type is formed as a result of different processes, which together comprise a continuous cycle of events – the rock cycle.

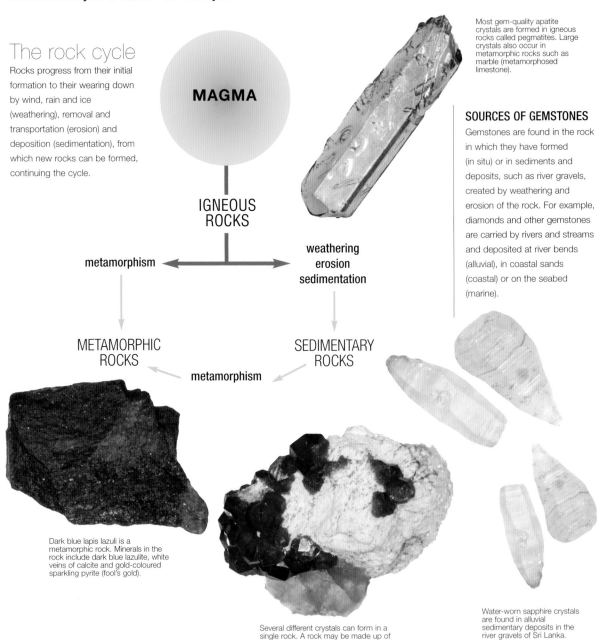

The rock cycle

Rocks progress from their initial formation to their wearing down by wind, rain and ice (weathering), removal and transportation (erosion) and deposition (sedimentation), from which new rocks can be formed, continuing the cycle.

MAGMA

IGNEOUS ROCKS

metamorphism

weathering erosion sedimentation

METAMORPHIC ROCKS

metamorphism

SEDIMENTARY ROCKS

Most gem-quality apatite crystals are formed in igneous rocks called pegmatites. Large crystals also occur in metamorphic rocks such as marble (metamorphosed limestone).

SOURCES OF GEMSTONES

Gemstones are found in the rock in which they have formed (in situ) or in sediments and deposits, such as river gravels, created by weathering and erosion of the rock. For example, diamonds and other gemstones are carried by rivers and streams and deposited at river bends (alluvial), in coastal sands (coastal) or on the seabed (marine).

Dark blue lapis lazuli is a metamorphic rock. Minerals in the rock include dark blue lazulite, white veins of calcite and gold-coloured sparkling pyrite (fool's gold).

Several different crystals can form in a single rock. A rock may be made up of many smaller crystals of other minerals, too small for faceting as gemstones.

Water-worn sapphire crystals are found in alluvial sedimentary deposits in the river gravels of Sri Lanka.

Igneous

The term *igneous* is from the Latin word *ignis,* meaning fire. It is named after the burning red volcanic lavas that cool to form igneous rock.

INTRUSIVE IGNEOUS ROCK

Rocks created from molten rock (magma) may take millions of years to form as the magma slowly cools beneath the surface of the earth or cools as it rises toward the surface. As temperatures and pressures change, crystals form within the cooling magma, eventually solidifying to produce solid rock. The slower the cooling, the larger the crystals that can form. Rocks formed in this way, such as granite, are called intrusive igneous rocks, formed inside the earth.

EXTRUSIVE IGNEOUS ROCK

Igneous rocks may also form as a result of magma reaching the surface, erupted from volcanoes or fissures as lava or ash. Olivine basalt is a volcanic rock that contains crystals of olivine, the mineral that gemologists call peridot. Zircon, ruby, sapphire, moonstone, topaz and the rare bixbite (red beryl) can also crystallize from lavas as they cool.

Peridot is formed in lavas erupted by volcanoes and also in metamorphic rocks. Good crystals of peridot have been found on the island of Zagbargad (formerly St John's Island) in the Red Sea, near Egypt.

PEGMATITE

Pegmatites are intrusive igneous rocks. They are created during the final stages of crystallization and solidification, and can form huge crystals and a wider variety of gemstones than in any other rock type. The most famous pegmatite region is that of Minas Gerais (Brazil), where large, clear crystals such as tourmaline, topaz, aquamarine and morganite are found. Other pegmatite areas include the Pala area of California, the Nuristan area of northeast Afghanistan, the Altai mountains of northwest China and the Yekaterinburg (formerly Sverdlovsk) region of Russia. Hot, mineral-rich fluids concentrated within cracks and fissures (hydrothermal fluids) may cool to form crystals such as amethyst, topaz, emerald and benitoite.

The best crystals of aquamarine, blue beryl, are formed in slow-cooling igneous rocks called pegmatites.

OBSIDIAN

Extrusive igneous rocks cool quickly, sometimes so quickly that crystals are too small to see without the use of a loupe (magnifier), or so fast that volcanic glass (obsidian) is formed.

Cooled so fast that a natural glass is formed, the fractured edge of obsidian makes a sharp blade used for knives, arrowheads and cutting tools. When polished, the glass may be used as a mirror.

Sedimentary

Sedimentary rocks are formed by the weathering, erosion and deposition of other rocks, and the evaporation, cooling or transportation of mineral-rich fluids. Gemstones created by sedimentary processes include turquoise, malachite, rhodochrosite, amethyst and agate. Opal forms from a silica gel, replacing bones and shell or filling small cracks and cavities.

The green bands of malachite form as crusts and layers of mineral-rich solutions are deposited in cracks and fissures within rocks. Malachite and azurite are coloured by copper in the solutions.

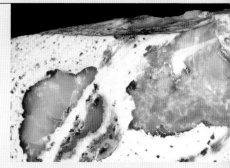

Opal is a silica gel that fills cavities in sedimentary rocks and cracks and fissures within igneous rocks. It may replace organic material in wood, shell and bone.

Metamorphic

Metamorphic rocks are formed as rocks are altered by temperature and/or pressure, creating new crystals and minerals. They may be associated with large mountain-building processes or with smaller, more local events such as faulting or folding. The rubies of Myanmar (formerly Burma) were formed as a result of the collision of the Indian subcontinent with Asia more than 65 million years ago, which pushed up the highest mountain range in the world, the Himalayas. Jadeite is found in metamorphic rocks and as river boulders and pebbles.

Ruby forms in metamorphic and igneous rocks. Weathering and erosion of rocks releases the rubies. Transported by rivers and streams, they can be found in alluvial sedimentary deposits as crystals and water-worn pebbles.

sourcing and availability

The continued exploitation of deposits, the development of modern mining technologies and the discovery of new sources has led to an increase in the availability of a wide range of gemstones. Diamonds, once found only in India, Borneo and Brazil, are now also sourced in quantity from many African countries, as well as Australia, Russia and Canada.

Tanzanite was first discovered in 1967. Cut as a cabochon and mounted in a plain silver ring, this blue stone can be worn by men or women.

With today's great choice of gemstones, jewellers need to know far more about the colours and sources of gemstones, the popularity and value of which are led by fashion, quality and availability.

Deciding whether you will source your material from an independent gemstone dealer, wholesaler, large retailer, auction house, small store or market stall will depend on your needs and experience. Consider the difficulties you may have, for example, in finding two matching gemstones for a pair of earrings or several for a ring, or many beads for a necklace. Ask yourself whether you need particular gemstones or features such as colour, size or shape, and also whether you want to have material identified or certified by a gemstone laboratory.

A gemstone dealer can be asked to source large pieces, or individual or matching stones for specific customers or designs. Some professional dealers gain their expertise through a knowledge of a particular area of the world or by specializing in a particular gemstone type. For instance, a ruby or sapphire buyer may have experience in dealing with Thailand and Sri Lanka, while another might only source coloured gemstones from Africa. However, many dealers carry a broad range of stock.

Diamond production is such that it is possible to source sufficient diamonds of similar size and shape to make intricate designs with matched stones.

Gemstone mining is often a highly industrial process.

Gemstone colour is no longer so dependent upon the source. It is now common practice for heat treatments and irradiation to be used to change or enhance colours. This enables sources that were once thought inferior to produce marketable gemstones, competing, for example, with the famous red "pigeon's blood" rubies of Myanmar (Burma rubies) or the cornflower-blue sapphires of Sri Lanka (Ceylon sapphire).

Supply and demand

Political instability and government regimes can affect the sourcing and availability of gemstones. In 1969, the famous Mogok ruby mines of Myanmar (Burma) were annexed by a military government, blocking the traditional source of rubies. The ruby mines of the Thai-Cambodian border were able to supply enough facetable material to meet the demand. Although the colours are inferior, modern heat treatments improve both colour and clarity and enable Thai and Cambodian ruby sales to dominate the market. However, the presence of the Khmer Rouge in Cambodia interrupted supplies from that country for a time, and today many mines in Thailand are exhausted.

Fashions affect the popularity of particular gemstones. Diamond, still the number one choice for an engagement ring, is now sought after in fancy colours (natural and heat treated), as celebrities opt for larger and more colourful diamonds.

Tanzanite, the blue gemstone first discovered in 1967, is mined from only one locality in Tanzania. As the source has diminished and replenishment becomes less likely, the rarity and perceived value of the stone has increased. The impending sense of "buy now or it will be too late" has become a powerful marketing tool.

Certification and marking of diamonds (for example by laser) to prove their source has been introduced to try to prevent fraud and to try to stop the sale of so-called "conflict diamonds" whose proceeds are used to finance conflict and war.

Black diamonds surround a blue tourmaline. Black diamond has gained popularity recently, and even industrial quality black diamond may be polished as spheres and sold as beads.

The "eye" of this ring is a faceted, off-white rose-cut diamond.

These cufflinks feature rectangular-cut sapphires ranging from colourless to pink. Rainbow and multicolored jewelry, with gemstones of similar shape but different colours, is widely available.

This oval brilliant-cut blue tanzanite is set in a ring with diamonds. Tanzanite, found in only one locality, is often heat treated to enhance its colour.

mining and collecting

Methods of mining and collecting gemstones range from the traditional means used for thousands of years, such as panning to search river gravels and waters, to highly complex technologies such as those employed in the modern diamond-mining industry.

Gemstones are mined throughout the world and are a valuable commodity, providing an important source of revenue and employment. They have also always been associated with conflict, from the ancient tales of murder and intrigue that surrounded famous gemstones to the contemporary use of diamond profits to fund guerrilla warfare and drug barons. It has become necessary for reputable suppliers to take measures to promote confidence in the diamond industry, and as a result De Beers has introduced diamond laser marking to accompany certification and encourage trade in "conflict-free diamonds". (See page 121 for more on ethics and the diamond industry.)

Diamond mining, shown right and above, is a high-tech industry. The process is highly mechanized and computerized and each stage is carefully monitored.

Open-pit mining

Mining generally starts at the surface, in a conventional open-pit mine. The surface is stripped to expose the rock, which is blasted, loaded onto trucks and taken to rock crushers before being transported to the main treatment plant for processing. Surface mining may continue for many years.

Underground mining

As mining continues, the mine becomes deeper, eventually leading to underground mining. Workers and machines follow the diamond-bearing rocks deep underground, excavating shafts and tunnels.

Secondary deposits

Diamonds may be mined from primary deposits – the volcanic rocks in which they are found – or retrieved from secondary (placer) deposits, for example river gravels and beach sands, where they have been transported as a result of weathering and erosion. Diamond-bearing sands are trucked to treatment and processing centres. Grooves and hollows in rocks underlying the sands are checked by hand for any remaining diamonds.

Vacuuming

Specially adapted ships are used to "vacuum" diamond-bearing sands off the seabed. The diamonds are retrieved and sealed in containers to be collected by helicopter, while the used sands are pumped back into the sea.

Traditional methods

Gemstones are generally heavier and more durable than the sands and gravels in which they may be found. Panning, sieving and jigging separate out the gem material, which can then be washed and sorted by hand.

The introduction of mechanized mining methods has increased the rate at which gemstones are retrieved but will also decrease the lifespan of the sources, as they will be mined out sooner. Some mines that are no longer producing sufficient material to be commercially profitable are kept open as tourist attractions.

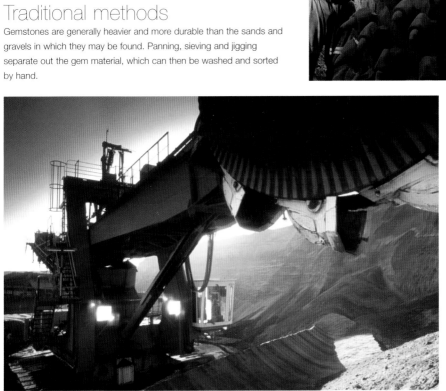

This bucketwheel dredge is in operation on the coast of Namibia. The giant machine scoops up large quantities of sand that is then sifted for diamonds.

usage and supply chains

The main criteria that decide the use of a gemstone are size, appearance and availability. Stones that do not make the grade in terms of size, colour and clarity may be put to industrial usage. There are a number of routes by which gemstones reach the customer; the journey that a diamond takes from the mine to the market is referred to as "the diamond pipeline" and is controlled principally by De Beers. The diamond pipeline is unique and not representative of trade in other gemstones.

Gem-quality diamond crystals may have flat or rounded faces. Crystal shapes include eight-sided octahedra, cushion shapes and twinned crystals. Some crystal faces may show triangular markings (trigons).

At one time, De Beers produced over 90 per cent of the world's diamonds and was the only major supplier of diamonds. Even now, more than half of all the diamonds mined in the world are handled or distributed through De Beers. The path taken by other gemstones from the mine or deposit to the consumer may have many more steps than the De Beers–controlled system. Gemstones may be traded at the mines and in local towns and cutting centres, or they may be exported to be traded, cut and set throughout the world before reaching the wholesaler, retailer and consumer.

The facets of a diamond are created using a rotating cast-iron disk coated or ingrained with a diamond compound.

A rough diamond is cleaved into two pieces to produce economical sizes and shapes for cutting and polishing. Saws and lasers are also used for this purpose.

Industrial usage

Diamonds of insufficient size, colour or clarity to be cut as gemstones may be used for industrial purposes. The ratio of gem-quality diamonds to industrial diamonds in a mine's output varies. The proportion of gem-quality diamonds found in alluvial deposits is higher than in mines, because the processes of nature make the first sorting as diamonds are weathered and eroded, and flawed diamonds seldom finish the journey. Other gemstones are also sorted by nature in this way and the stones concentrated in gem gravels are of sufficient quality to have survived the transportation.

The diamond pipeline

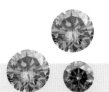

1 Although parts of the process are mechanized, the skill of sorting experts is needed to separate rough diamonds into as many as 16,000 different categories depending on combinations of size, shape, colour and clarity. In addition to its London offices, De Beers also has major sorting operations in Kimberley (South Africa), Windhoek (Namibia) and Lucerne (Switzerland).

2 Packages of diamonds (sites) are prepared for sale to a group of diamond manufacturers (site holders), who then offer these for sale through diamond bourses and other channels for cutting and polishing. Sales of sites take place 10 times a year in London. To accommodate the individual needs of different cutting centres, each site holder may request a certain combination of gemstones.

3 Manufacturers tend to specialize in particular markets. Smaller stones are generally required for cutting and polishing in India, medium to large stones are required by Asia and Europe, and the occasional very large diamond is sought after particularly in the Middle East, United Kingdom and United States. The world's main cutting and trading centres are Antwerp, Mumbai, New York, Tel Aviv and Johannesburg. Diamond cutting is increasing in Thailand, and China is investing in training and may soon be a formidable competitor.

4 Once polished, most diamonds are sold and traded in the 24 registered diamond bourses around the world.

properties of gemstone material

An understanding of the optical and physical properties of the material is a prerequisite to knowing the best ways of working with gemstones and to making the most of their inherent qualities.

Crystal form

Most minerals are crystalline; they grow atom by atom, layer by layer, into a regular 3-D atomic structure. In most rocks, the crystals are too small to be seen without the use of a microscope (microcrystalline or cryptocrystalline), or the crystals are too small or irregular to be used as gemstones. A few minerals are amorphous, which means that they have a weak crystal structure or lack one altogether. Crystalline material may form with an irregular shape (massive), but there will be an internal regular 3-D atomic structure, even though no crystal faces are visible. The physical properties of crystals (their hardness and durability, the way they break or fracture) and their optical properties (the way light is reflected off surfaces or travels through them) are all related to the atomic structure.

Crystal habits

The orientation of the flat faces of a crystal and their rate of growth control the final appearance of the crystal – its crystal habit. Most gemstones have a typical crystal habit, such as the acicular (needlelike) crystals of rutile found as inclusions within quartz, amethyst prisms, spinel octahedra and fluorite cubes. Others have a number of habits.

CRYSTAL HABITS

Diamond crystal habit: octahedron

Pyrite crystal habit: pyritohedron

Plane of symmetry

Beryl crystal habit: hexagonal prism

Quartz crystal habit: trigonal prism

Crystal systems

Geologists, mineralogists and gemmologists use symmetry to divide crystals into different systems. Diamond, for example, forms as a structure of carbon atoms, bonded in such a way that cubes, octahedra (bipyramids) and other cubic crystal habits are created. Diamond, like spinel and garnet, therefore belongs to the cubic system. There are seven main crystal systems, defined by their minimum symmetry.

CUBIC
Three four-fold axes.

TETRAGONAL
One vertical four-fold axis.

HEXAGONAL
One vertical six-fold axis.

TRIGONAL
One vertical three-fold axis.

ORTHORHOMBIC
Either one two-fold axis at the intersection of two mutually perpendicular planes or three mutually perpendicular two-fold axes.

MONOCLINIC
One two-fold axis.

TRICLINIC
Either a centre of symmetry or no symmetry.

Cleavage and fracture

A crystal can break along lines of weakness related to the atomic structure (cleavage) in such a way that a flat surface called a cleavage plane is left. Cleavage may be described as perfect (easy), distinct or indistinct. Where the break is not related to the atomic structure (fracture), the resulting surface will not be flat or smooth. Fracture may be described as uneven, splintery or conchoidal (the shell-like fracture of obsidian and many transparent gemstones).

PERFECT CLEAVAGE

Cleavage and fracture affect the strength of a gemstone and the ease with which it can be worked. Extra care must be taken when working with gemstones that have one or more directions of perfect cleavage. Topaz has three directions of perfect cleavage. Other gemstones with perfect cleavage include diamond, fluorite, calcite and spodumene (including kunzite).

Green tourmaline crystals have been partly polished to give beads of similar size while retaining the crystal shape. Tourmaline is pleochroic: crystals appear a different shade or colour from different angles.

Hardness

The strength and durability of a gemstone is dependent upon its structure – on whether it is fragile and can be chipped, or is tough and fibrous – and its hardness. There are a number of scales used to compare the hardness of gemstones. The scale most commonly used by gemmologists is the Mohs' scale of hardness. Mohs arranged 10 common minerals in order of their "scratchability" from the softest, talc, at 1, which could be scratched by all those higher on the scale, to the hardest, diamond, at 10, which could scratch all others.

Comparison of the Mohs' scale of hardness and the Knoop indenter hardness scale shows the dramatically greater hardness of diamond as compared with the nearly linearly related hardnesses of other minerals.

MOHS' SCALE OF HARDNESS

1	talc
2	gypsum
3	calcite
4	fluorite
5	apatite
6	feldspar
7	quartz
8	topaz
9	corundum
10	diamond

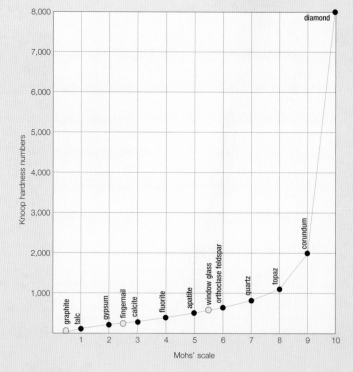

Specific gravity

The heaviness, or "heft", of a gemstone to be used in jewellery should be considered, as it may limit the usage of the final product. A very heavy piece may be uncomfortable or impractical to wear, while a piece that is too light may not sit or hang well. The heft of a gemstone is referred to as specific gravity and is measured as a comparison of the weight of a gemstone and the weight of an equal volume of water.

Colour orientation

Crystals seldom have a perfectly consistent and intense colour throughout. During their formation events such as changes in temperature, pressure or the behaviour of surrounding chemical ingredients may cause an alteration or interruption in the rate of growth. This can affect crystal habit and colour, forming growth features such as colour banding in agate or uneven colour zoning, for example in sapphire. The range of colour and patterns produced during growth can add to the interest of a gemstone. However, care should be taken when choosing rough material to view the crystal from all angles to check for colour variation.

PLEOCHROISM

Gemstones may also appear to be different colours or shades of colour when viewed from different directions. This is called pleochroism and is a result of the way light behaves in relation to the 3-D atomic structure of the crystal rather than a consequence of changes during growth. Gemstones that show two different colours or shades of colour are called dichroic; those that show three are called trichroic.

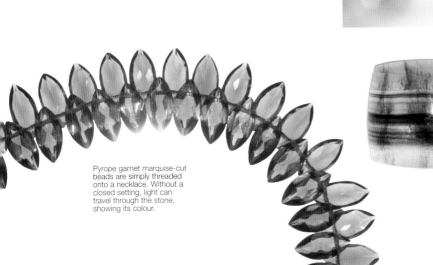

Pyrope garnet marquise-cut beads are simply threaded onto a necklace. Without a closed setting, light can travel through the stone, showing its colour.

inclusions and optical phenomena

Much of the beauty of gemstones is due to the way they react when light shines on them. Some gemstones exhibit special optical effects that add to their value; others may have inclusions that increase their appeal and rarity.

These pale blue turquoise beads feature copper inclusions of brown limonite or black manganese. They pattern the beads and make each one unique.

Lustre

The surface appearance of a gemstone is referred to as its lustre. Most transparent gemstones have a vitreous or glasslike lustre. Other terms used to describe lustre include adamantine, or diamondlike (diamond and demantoid garnet), metallic (hematite), waxy (turquoise), greasy (topaz), resinous (amber), silky and dull. Polishing, waxing and oiling can enhance the lustre of a gemstone.

Hematite has a metallic lustre and takes a high polish. It may be faceted, carved or polished as beads for jewellery or decorative items.

Green demantoid garnet has an adamantine (diamond-like) lustre. Characteristic "horsetail" inclusions are golden or brown crystal threads of chrysotile.

Inclusions

Gemstones may have inclusions that have formed before, during or after the surrounding (host) gemstone. They may be solid (for example crystals or fossils), liquid or gas. More than one phase may be present, for example Colombian emeralds may contain all three phases – salt crystal, liquid and gas. Inclusions may either add to the novelty, rarity and value of a gemstone, or be viewed as imperfections that detract from its beauty.

Golden-coloured rutile inclusions and black tourmaline needles within colourless quartz (rock crystal) beads add interest and value to this necklace.

The large polished cabochon at the top of this 18K gold choker has a high lustre because of its reflective surface.

Cat's-eyes

Gemstones with oriented inclusions such as fibrous or needlelike crystals or cavities may be cut as a cabochon, with a polished domed-top surface, to reveal a cat's-eye (with a single bright line) or star. Cat's-eye gemstones are also called chatoyant, after the French word for cat (*chat*). The cat's-eye is a result of light reflecting off internal structures, such as a single set of parallel inclusions. Cat's-eye gemstones include quartz, chrysoberyl and garnet.

Interference

Interference patterns, such as you might see on the surface of an oil spill on the road, are caused in gemstones by reflection off internal surfaces. Light is split into the colours of the rainbow, some or all of which can be seen on the surface of the gemstone without the need to cut it as a cabochon, though the features may be enhanced by polishing. The play of colour of precious opal, also called iridescence, is a result of light reflecting off patterns of spheres within the gemstone. The iridescence seen in labradorite, due to light reflecting off thin internal layers, is called adularescence, schiller or sheen. Other gemstones that show iridescence include hematite, iris quartz and quartz.

This star stone shows the four arms, or rays, of the star reflected on the surface of an opaque polished cabochon of diopside. Characteristically, two rays are straight and the other two are slightly wavy.

Star stones

As a result of the reflection of light off more than one set of parallel inclusions, a gemstone cut as a cabochon may reveal a star stone (asterism). Star stones with six rays (three sets of parallel features) are the most common, but they may have four (two sets of parallel features) or 12 or more rays. Star stones include quartz, corundum and garnet.

This citrine necklace features charming bubble effects – in this case they are not a natural feature of the stone but were carved by the designer. In the ring at top, colourless quartz (rock crystal) looks particularly interesting thanks to needlelike inclusions of black tourmaline crystals.

gemstone cuts

Behind every beautiful gemstone is a highly talented designer, but the skill of the lapidary (cutter) is often overlooked as the gem takes centre stage. The lapidary will choose the cut to show off a stone's best features, such as its colour, clarity, size or inclusions.

The next few chapters explore how gemstones are designed and created, from the shaping of faceted stones, cabochons and beads, to hand carving and the use of natural forms. Jewellers need to be familiar with the labour involved in producing gemstones in order to understand the strengths and weaknesses of a stone, and to be able to advise a customer on what is possible and practical.

The well-proportioned cut of this faceted pink spinel allows the stone's brilliance and colour to be fully appreciated.

Showcase

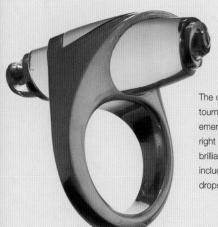

The collection of tourmaline and emerald jewellery at right uses a variety of brilliant-cut gemstones including pear shapes, drops and ovals.

This gemstone was hand-carved from a single heliodor crystal, which was bright and clear but pale. Heliodor is excellent carving material as it is tough, clean-cutting and polishes well. The rough material was maximized by the elegant design, which enhanced the pale yellow of the heliodor with the reflection of 22K gold.

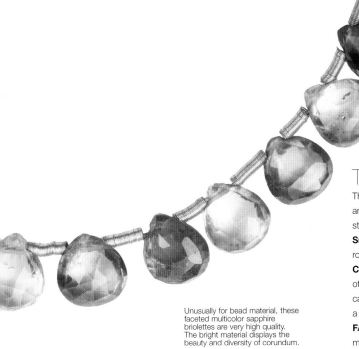

Unusually for bead material, these faceted multicolor sapphire briolettes are very high quality. The bright material displays the beauty and diversity of corundum.

Talk of the trade

The gemstone trade uses specific terminology to appraise a stone and assess its qualities. This long-standing terminology enables a stone to be described accurately without it actually being seen.

SHAPE The outline of a stone when seen in plan view, such as round, oval or pear shape.

CUT The proportion, symmetry, polish and finish of a stone – in other words, its overall appearance and not its shape. Sometimes called the "make", the cut describes the factors involved in creating a gemstone from rough material.

FACETING A method of shaping a gem by cutting the surface into many small, flat faces (facets) at varying angles, so that light travels through the stone and makes it brilliant.

Parts of a faceted gemstone

These are the terms for the different parts of a round brilliant-cut gemstone. Their varying proportions will affect the brilliance, beauty and colour of the stone.

GIRDLE The outer edge or perimeter of a gemstone, where the crown meets the pavilion.

CROWN The top portion of a stone, above the girdle.

PAVILION The lower part of a stone, from the girdle to the culet.

TABLE The flat surface on top of a stone; the largest facet or face.

CULET The lowest part of the stone, which appears as a point or ridge.

A perfect octahedral diamond crystal.

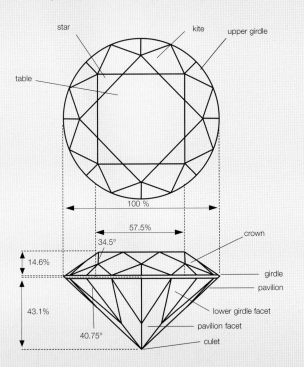

star

kite upper girdle

table

100 %

57.5%

34.5°

crown

14.6%

girdle

pavilion

43.1%

lower girdle facet

pavilion facet

40.75°

culet

faceted round cuts

There are two main categories of faceted stones: round shapes and straight-sided shapes. The cutting of curved gemstone shapes has been dictated by the development of faceted diamond cuts, with the terminology and cutting methods also applied to coloured stones.

Proportions of a round brilliant cut

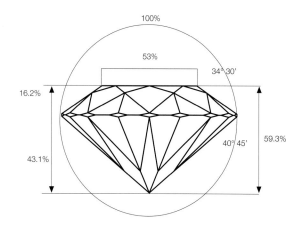

Usage and common faults

As the brilliant cut was originally designed for diamonds, it is typically used for pale, transparent material with a naturally high dispersion. Rose cuts were also designed for diamonds, but pyrites (marcasites) and garnets are frequently cut this way. Briolettes and drops can be cut in most gemstone material, whether transparent, translucent or opaque, and can be drilled vertically or horizontally. The mixed cut is used regularly on corundum (ruby and sapphire), because it will improve the colour of pale stones.

The most common problem with round brilliant-cut gems is poor proportions. The cut may be dictated by the shape of the rough material, or the position of flaws and inclusions. In the Far East the aim of cutting is usually to retain as much weight as possible, whatever the proportions. A gemstone's proportions will affect the intensity of colour; dark stones are sometimes cut shallow to brighten the stone, and pastel stones often need a deep cut for the best colour.

A brilliant cut or mixed cut will disguise irregular colour distribution much better than a step cut. If the colour is concentrated in the culet area of a deep pavilion, or a single plane of colour is run across the centre of the stone, the patchy colouring can appear perfect when viewed through the table. Flaws and inclusions can be successfully hidden under the upper girdle facets or around the outer edges of the pavilion facets, while the central area appears perfectly clean.

Careless cutting and poor proportions can be unsightly and leave a stone more vulnerable to breakage. Check that the girdle of a brilliant-cut stone is neither too thick (which will look ugly) nor too thin (which can make the gemstone fragile). Sharp culets are liable to damage and open culets can be seen through the table and will be reflected in the facets. An off-centre culet in a pale stone will be visible through the table, while darker colours may disguise lack of symmetry.

Weights and measures

Most small faceted gemstones are cut on machines that give exact calibration for their overall dimensions. The table at right provides the calibrated sizes of rounds with associated weights. As gemstones differ in specific gravity (density), the table gives the weights of a variety of gemstone types.

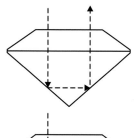

Ideal proportions of a brilliant cut. The crown should appear to be one-third of the depth of the pavilion.

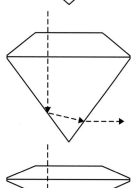

If the stone is cut too deep, light is reflected through the sides and the gemstone will have black spots and an uneven appearance.

If the pavilion is too shallow, light leaks through the bottom of the stone. The reflection will be dull and the gemstone will have a glassy "window" effect.

Brilliant cut

The brilliant cut has been developed as an ideal cut of mathematically calculated proportions (for the story of its development, see page 112). This cut maximizes a gemstone's natural light dispersion, bending light rays toward the centre of a stone and then reflecting them out again to produce "fire" and brilliance. Fire is the dispersion of white light into the colours of the spectrum that occurs as the light rays are bent.

The brilliant cut's angles and proportions have been adapted for a variety of other shapes, including the oval, antique cushion, pear shape (or pendeloque) and marquise (or navette). Various shapes are pictured in the emerald and tourmaline collection on page 26.

Marquise

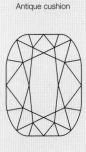

Antique cushion

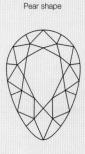

Pear shape

The round brilliant cut

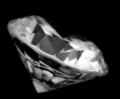

Briolette cut

The briolette cut is effectively a double rose cut, with an elongated cone-shaped upper crown and rounded pavilion covered with triangular or rectangular facets.

Briolette

Drop

Traditionally briolettes are transparent gem material, but the translucency of the carnelian also works well in this form.

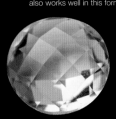

This yellow beryl is a modern variant of the double rose cut, called the checkerboard cut or chess cut.

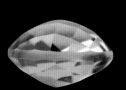

Mixed cut

The mixed cut is a combination of a brilliant cut and a step cut (the latter is used more often in straight-sided forms). In a mixed cut, the pavilion is step cut while the crown is brilliant cut.

A mixed-cut green tourmaline. The deep step-cut pavilion is typical, as it is designed to boost colour and retain weight.

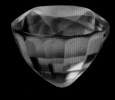

ROUND	CARAT WEIGHTS FOR GENUINE STONES							
Stone (mm)	2	3	4	5	6	7	8	10
Quartz	0.04	0.10	0.20	0.40	0.70	1.30	1.80	3.30
Aquamarine/Emerald	0.04	0.12	0.27	0.48	0.80	1.70	2.50	6.10
Garnet	0.05	0.13	0.30	0.60	1.00	1.60	2.50	5.75
Ruby/Sapphire	0.05	0.15	0.34	0.65	1.05	1.60	2.25	4.50
Blue Topaz	0.04	0.11	0.30	0.56	1.00	1.55	2.50	5.75
Diamond	0.03	0.10	0.25	0.50	0.75	1.25	2.00	3.50

faceted square cuts

The second group of faceted cuts includes straight-sided girdle shapes: squares, rectangles, octagons, triangles, trapeziums, hexagons and barrels. These forms are traditionally cut as a series of rectangular parallel facets that follow the shape of the girdle in a stepped arrangement – hence the term *step cut.*

Showcase

A gold ring with a mirror-cut, navette-shaped aquamarine

A gold ring set with a cross-cut pink tourmaline octagon

Fancy-cut asymmetric sapphire earrings

A pair of amethysts cut in a fancy isosceles triangle (below and at left)

Usage and common faults

A step cut can be used on all coloured stones. It may not have the brilliance of a brilliant cut, but its clean lines can create simplicity and elegance. Fancy cuts can appear in all types of material, but will tend to be one-offs and will not come in a choice of material and colour.

The depth of the stone can cause problems in straight-sided step cuts. A heavy base can make a gemstone look very dark, while a shallow stone can seem pale and have an obvious "window." The cross cut can inject life into a dull or poorly coloured stone. Inaccurate cutting sometimes means that the sides of step-cut stones are not parallel, which can make them difficult to set.

Baguettes and trillions are relatively easy to break if too much pressure is placed on a corner during setting. Mirror cuts frequently use flawed material with inclusions, as these contribute to the optical effect and provide real depth. However, such flaws can make mirror cuts fragile, and weak areas will result if the inclusions are close to the girdle or the stone is cut slightly shallow. Be careful if you are planning a rub-over setting. Buff tops are much stronger; the cut is suitable for softer material and the smooth polished surface is less vulnerable than a faceted crown.

Step cut

This very old cut was originally developed for diamonds, but is now used primarily for coloured stones, as it doesn't produce the sparkle and life of the brilliant cut. It does, however, show off colour very effectively. A rectangular step cut with corners cut diagonally to make an octagonal shape is an emerald cut, used to display the emerald's colour and protect the fragile stone from damage. In rectangular step cuts, the culet takes the form of a ridge rather than a point.

The simplicity of the rectangular step cut gives this pink topaz clean geometric lines and a modern look. Thinner, elongated rectangles are known as baguettes.

Cross cut

The cross cut (or scissor cut) is a modification of the step cut, in which the steps are divided into triangular facets that introduce more light and life into the gemstone. This cut is commonly used to improve weak or dark stones. The cross cut can also conceal flaws in the outer areas of the stone and will help hide a "window" in a shallow gem.

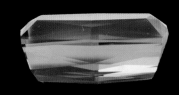

French cut

Another modification of the step cut is the French cut. It is used on small stones (less than ¼ in/6 mm) with rectangular, square and triangular shapes. Ruby, sapphire and emerald are often cut this way for channel setting or use in line bracelet and necklace designs.

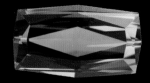

STRAIGHT-SIDED GEMSTONE CUTS

Step-cut trapeze baguette | Step-cut hexagon | Emerald cut with two crown steps | Square French cut with square table

French-cut equilateral triangle | Cross-cut rectangle | Cross-cut long hexagon | Cross-cut pillow (barrel)

This tourmaline is a cross-cut long hexagon. The cut emphasizes the gemstone's clarity and colour, and produces more brilliance than a basic step cut.

Fancy cuts

Fancy cuts were originally devised to retain maximum weight in irregularly shaped crystals or in material that had been cleaved from larger crystals. Nowadays, however, fancy cuts are design-led. They create different optical effects, such as mirror cuts and prism cuts, and may also be variations of existing cuts. For example, the crown of step-cut or brilliant-cut gemstones is frequently modified – the surface can be faceted with small squares in a low-domed chess cut or cut like a cabochon with a smooth buff top. Sometimes fancy cuts are used to disguise faults, so examine them closely.

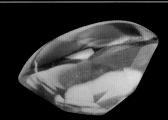

MODIFICATIONS TO THE CROWN

Flat top with step-cut pavilion (side view) | Buff top with brilliant-cut pavilion (side view) | Chess cut (plan view) | Bent top rectangle triangle cut (plan view)

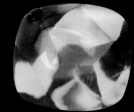

This peridot has a buff top and modified brilliant-cut pavilion.

cabochons

Attitudes toward cabochon-cut gemstones vary from country to country. The United States and Britain view faceted stones as the more desirable form of gem and attach much less value to cabochons. Germany, on the other hand, has a strong tradition of producing fine, well-cut cabochons, and jewelry buyers appreciate the qualities of colour, texture and light.

The choice of material in cabochon form is much wider and cheaper, and it is a less dominant form that offers greater flexibility in design. It is not really surprising, therefore, that contemporary jewellery designers elect to use cabochons more often than faceted stones.

The purity and colour of this pyrope garnet cabochon is exceptional. Cabochon garnets of this size (25.49 ct) would usually have to be hollowed out as carbuncles to prevent them from looking black. Such a stone would also normally be faceted, rather than cut as a single cabochon.

Showcase

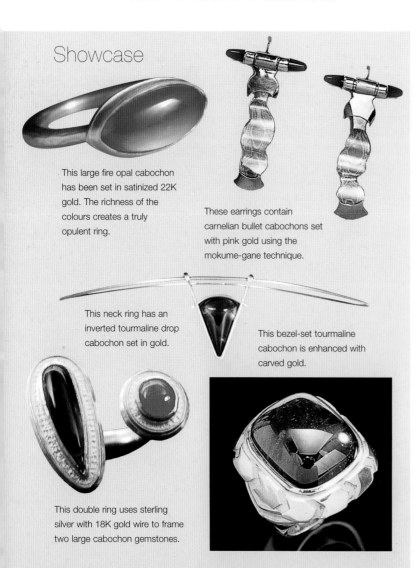

This large fire opal cabochon has been set in satinized 22K gold. The richness of the colours creates a truly opulent ring.

These earrings contain carnelian bullet cabochons set with pink gold using the mokume-gane technique.

This neck ring has an inverted tourmaline drop cabochon set in gold.

This bezel-set tourmaline cabochon is enhanced with carved gold.

This double ring uses sterling silver with 18K gold wire to frame two large cabochon gemstones.

Usage and common faults

The majority of gemstone types, from ruby and emerald to agate and quartz, can be found in cabochon form, including material that is too soft to be faceted, such as amber, apatite, rhodochrosite and fluorite. Low-grade material has traditionally been used for cabochons, but the quality is now improving. Obviously, the best gem material will still be kept for faceted stones.

Stars and cat's-eyes are always cabochon cut, as are the majority of stones with interesting optical effects, such as opals and moonstones. The gem material has to be oriented correctly and the cut itself will affect the quality of the effect – a low buff top will display better iridescence and schiller than a high domed cut.

The most common problems with cabochons are cracks and surface abrasions, flaws that are too close to the surface (which are unsightly and might cause the stone to break), poor finish and polish, lack of symmetry and muddy or dark colour. Check that the slope from the base of the cabochon is sufficient for the stone to be bezel-set or mounted. If it slopes too sharply there is a risk of the girdle chipping while it is being set, and the stone may not be gripped securely by the setting. High, elongated bullets need to be set with care as the top of the stone can snap under pressure. Check a hollowed-out carbuncle for any cracks or major flaws that could make it fragile. Carbuncles are often backed with a foil reflector to increase brilliance.

Range of cuts

Cabochon cuts can vary in both outer girdle shape and the convex curve of the surface. The shapes – such as the marquise, pear shape and cushion – are the same as those of faceted stones and they are cut in the same calibrated sizes, but the weights are different. The surface profile can range from a flat slab to a high-domed bullet. The base can be flat, or rounded as a double cabochon to increase colour density in lightly coloured transparent stones. Cushion cuts are always popular; they can either have a plain, smooth dome or be cross-vaulted, with ridges that intersect on the diagonal.

CABOCHON CUTS

Low dome

High dome

Cone

Bullet

Double beveled

Hollow/carbuncle

Double

Flat cut/slab

Buff top

Buff top
(cross-vaulted)

CABOCHON SHAPES

Round

Square

Octagon (square)

Oval

Rectangle (cushion)

Octagon (rectangle)

Pear

Oblong

Cushion antique

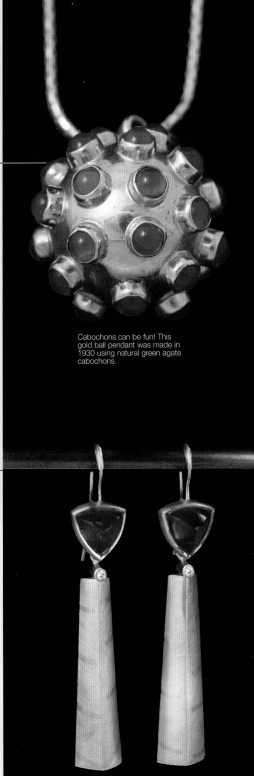

Cabochons can be fun! This gold ball pendant was made in 1930 using natural green agate cabochons.

These earrings are set with hot pink tourmaline trillion cabochons and white brilliant-cut diamonds in 18K gold.

cutting to order

Sometimes it's not possible to find what you want among available gemstones. You may have a design in mind that requires a specific material or type of cut that is simply not available, or you might have sold a piece of jewellery that used a particular stone and want to repeat the design. Your only option then would be to have the stone cut to order.

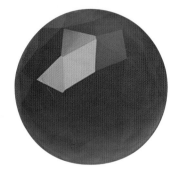

This blue chalcedony was rose cut to a customer's specifications. The idea was to facet a gemstone material that is traditionally cut *en cabochon,* to experiment with the combination of translucency and the faceted surface.

This rhodochrosite cabochon was cut in Germany and measures 0.5x1.6 in. (13x41 mm). It's a one-off piece, as rhodochrosite rough of that size and quality is not easy to source.

Obviously, cutting to order will be more expensive than buying a ready-cut stone, which may have been cut as part of a large consignment, possibly in the Far East. But don't let that put you off. Having your stones cut to order is very satisfying for a designer, and perfectly achievable as long as you understand the parameters of what is possible.

GRADING ROUGH MATERIAL

Gemstone rough comes in a range of qualities and prices. The best material accounts for only 5 per cent of the total mined and will always be sold at high faceting prices. The grades of rough gem material are usually described as:

A+ Exceptional colour and clarity

A Top grade/clean

B Good/eye clean

C Medium/some inclusions

Getting stones cut to order

You'll need to find yourself a knowledgeable dealer who can access the necessary rough material, has good lapidary contacts and is willing to listen to your ideas. Cutting and material costs will be priced per carat, not per piece. Generally, the larger the cutting order is, the better the value. Cabochons are a cheaper option as the rough material and cutting charges will be less. However, faceted gemstones can still be cost-effective, especially for a design that needs a large number of small stones of the same size in matching material.

Consider what type of material is suitable for your design. Hardness, cleavage and durability are important considerations and your first choice of material might not be the right one. Crystal shape, size and colour range will have to be taken into account; some gemstones only occur in small sizes, for example. You also need to think about design practicalities, such as the weight of the stones. Earrings, for example, should weigh no more than 7 grams or they become uncomfortable to wear. The different density of gemstones means that a certain size of turquoise stones might be suitable for earrings, while earrings using the same size of garnet, topaz or corundum may be unwearable.

Rough material can be very deceptive and may not give an indication of the stone's final appearance. Fine planes of colour may be removed with just a small amount of grinding, resulting in a significant loss of colour intensity. To obtain a matching pair of stones, the lapidary might have to cut as many as five stones.

Certain gemstones are remarkable for their colour, size or properties and it may not be possible to find a similar stone quickly – or at all. Some stones become unavailable as the source is mined out.

The dandelion cut is rarely seen these days. The author came across this stone in South Africa and had it reproduced in Germany. The cut combines a faceted pavilion and a domed crown that is ground with flat disks.

Showcase

The component parts of this nephrite jade bracelet were blocked out and drilled in Germany according to the designer's detailed drawings. The designer then shaped the pieces and cut the inlays. The bracelet folds open on springs and is secured by an internal catch.

This gold and silver necklace features an unusual gemstone cut. The fluorite was specially hand-carved to make it an integral part of the pendant structure.

The high-dome navette cabochons were designed in tandem with the ring. To keep within budget the designer chose the gem material for availability and price, using natural blue topaz, amethyst and rose quartz for the cabochons.

These elongated pendeloques are cut in maw-sit-sit (jadeite). The material was selected as it is tough enough to use for such slender drops yet also light to wear.

An 18K gold brooch with fancy-cut pink and blue sapphires. The sapphires were cut to order.

beads

Beads are believed to be the earliest of jewels – their simple form could be carved easily out of soft gemstone material. The increase in bead manufacture over recent years has been phenomenal and today the market offers a huge range of styles and qualities. Jewellery designers now include bead-based designs in their work alongside traditionally cut stones.

Multicolored
tourmaline beads

Showcase

Drilled faceted nuggets of rock crystal and aquamarine have been used singly as ring stones; the designer has created an original and effective means of "setting" the beads.

Drilled crystal beads have been used to create this distinctive gold and aquamarine brooch.

The rough unpolished labradorite of this necklace contrasts with the randomly placed gold beads. The schiller of labradorite is just as effective in an unfinished state as when it is polished.

These made-to-order beads are hand-carved using white and green nephrite jade and red coral. The customer wanted a long, delicate necklace without a clasp, specifically for day wear. The white nephrite beads were hollowed out and inlaid with a funnel hole in pale green jade to reduce the weight and prevent dirt from accumulating inside.

Usage and common problems

Precious beads made of emerald, ruby and sapphire will come in several grades of colour and clarity and a range of calibrated sizes starting from about 2.5 mm in diameter. Typical bead shapes are buttons, rounds and rondelles (plain and faceted). The rows are usually graduated. Wholesale semiprecious beads are sold by gram weight and then priced per strand to buyers. Fine-quality beads are sold by carat weight rather than per row. The length of a row is normally 16 inches (40 cm); briolettes can be found in half-rows.

Cheaper beads come in a huge range of shapes and sizes, but don't expect a particular design or cut to be available in different sizes. It is possible to find rows of drilled natural crystals, but some will require work to neaten ends or remove traces of matrix rock. This can be done using a diamond needle file or diamond burr on a pendant drill.

The quality of beads is variable. The most common problems are damaged material (chips, cracks or scuffing), irregular hole sizes that make beads difficult to string, and uneven drilling that prevents them from lying straight on the row. Holes can be opened up with a diamond-impregnated bead reamer, but this is tricky to use on hard material. Holes in softer gem material can be drilled out. Beads such as rondelles, buttons and rounds should have an even profile of the same thickness and a consistent colour, and should lie straight. It is possible to find beads of high-quality material with a good cut, but they will cost you much more.

Treat soft gemstones such as apatite, rhodochrosite, opal and turquoise with care. Check beads for damage before buying a row, to avoid cracking and breakage when you start to string them. Ideally, fragile stones should be knotted between beads to prevent them from rubbing against each other. Store delicate rows of beads individually in protective wrapping.

Thread used for stringing should be thick enough to fill the bead hole snugly, otherwise the strand can look sloppy and the beads may be damaged. Gimp will protect the ends of the necklace, preventing the metal clasp from wearing through the cord. Cable is a plastic-coated stainless steel cord that comes in many thicknesses – some can be knotted. If you are using metal beads, if the beads are very heavy, or if the gemstone is faceted and sharp, string on cable rather than silk.

Common cuts of beads

OVALS

Flat ovals always lie well when worn. Check turquoise beads before you buy for cracks and damaged drill holes. Not all turquoise beads are natural; check for reconstructed or imitation material.

RONDELLES

These emerald rondelles are evenly shaped, well drilled and well polished. This is good-quality material for beads.

TUBBY BRIOLETTES

Briolettes like these are often called "tubbies" because of their shape. These stones have a good cut and shape – the translucent chalcedony suits the flat cut.

FACETED BUTTONS

Cheaper diamond beads such as these are usually cut as faceted buttons in order to maximize the sparkle. These stones have been laser drilled with very small holes that are uneven in size, making them difficult to string. Diamond beads have sharp edges, so a strong thread or fine cable is needed.

FACETED NUGGETS

Large irregular beads such as these nuggets have become very popular. This heavy type of bead needs to be checked for cracks and surface abrasions.

FACETED DROPS

Ruby-in-zoisite faceted drops. The lapidary has used the natural patterning of the gemstone to great effect in this beautiful and imaginative row of beads.

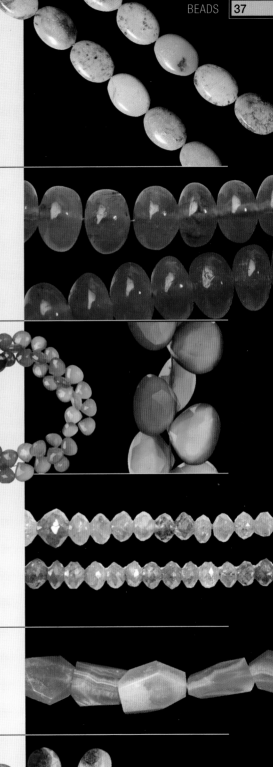

natural crystals

Many jewellery designers choose to avoid traditionally cut gemstones, instead using natural forms that require minimal cutting. Gemstone crystal clusters, slices and pebbles can all be transformed into precious gems simply by trimming the overall shape, grinding the base flat or polishing a surface.

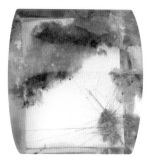

The inner world of a gemstone

Crystalline drusy surfaces from the linings of agate geodes, grape-like botryoidal crusts and pyrite layers will give a design brilliance, sparkle and texture. Fossilized coral and wood can provide decorative abstract patterns, while opalized wood and shell or baroque pearls can add structure and form to a unique piece of jewellery. Crystal shapes from a range of materials can be used in jewellery – try aquamarine, heliodor, tourmaline, quartz or diamond.

Usage and common problems

Some natural crystal forms are collectables or mineral specimens, which can make them more expensive. This is the case with perfect, fully terminated crystals, material with unusual inclusions or colour banding, and some crystal formations. Any diamond, tourmaline or beryl crystals that might be used for faceted stones will have a higher price.

Polished crystal slices can be found in many materials. Tourmaline is wonderful for its bi- or tricoloured cross-sections, but has become quite expensive. Quartz can be sliced to display interesting inclusions of hematite leaflets, rutile and tourmaline needles and iron or manganese staining, as well as colour zoning. Beryl has a suitable crystal shape for slicing, although emerald is a little too fragile (and expensive). Sliced agate can provide beautiful coloured banding and dendritic inclusions, and is a good value.

The outer edge of the crystal should be undamaged, otherwise it might break when you are burnishing the surrounding wall. Drusy and botryoidal crusts are slightly fragile and need to be treated with care. Ideally, they should have a flat base and slightly beveled sides so they can be given a protective setting that is flush with the surface. Check for cracks and avoid pieces of drusy that have very thin areas.

Drilling can be problematic with certain crystal forms, so take advice first. A hand drill or power rotary tool with flex-shaft attachments may be used. A high-speed twist drill bit will make holes in softer stones, such as shell, amber, malachite, marble, sugilite and lapis. For material with a hardness between 5 and 7 Mohs you will need to use tungsten carbide drill bits with embedded diamond grit. Diamond needle files or diamond-impregnated burrs will allow you to shape material and tidy up the crystal ends. Cool the gemstone with water to prevent it getting too hot and becoming damaged.

Natural crystal forms require special settings. Flat slabs or slices of crystal can be held with walls of burnished soft gold or silver, to allow light to travel through the piece. Work gently with the burnisher to avoid overstressing the slices, as thinner material or material with a large surface area will be vulnerable to pressure. Small individual crystals can be capped, wire wrapped, caged or drilled as a briolette. Drilling a diamond crystal requires specialist equipment; ask a diamond cutter for help.

The lapidary has only partially faceted this beryl, allowing the natural crystal to remain on the underside. The gem has been shaped as a marquise and the crown has been faceted as a mirror cut, so that the natural forms can be seen.

The natural surface texture of hematite has been retained, while the sides and underside have been ground flat.

Showcase

This cross has been cut from pink cobalt calcite drusy, a soft, delicate material that would not be suitable for rings. The gem is protected by a 22K gold wall, which has been burnished over the edge of the stone. Its wonderful texture and colour make it look delicious!

These sweet earrings use polished aquamarine crystal slices and 18K gold.

This polished amethyst slice contains black acicular (needle) inclusions that contrast with the oxidized silver of the brooch. The stone has been set without backing so that light passes through the stone as through a stained-glass window. The edges are beveled to enable the flat, wide claws to hold the stone securely while exposing its geometric outline.

This large rutilated quartz cabochon has been hand-carved and combined with drusy quartz and natural driftwood to create a necklace of contrasting textures and forms.

This ring has been designed around a rare belemnite opal – an opalized ink sac from a squid. A rich 22K gold wall enhances the gem and protects it from damage.

carving your own

Gem carving and engraving has been performed since ancient times – jade has been carved decoratively in China for the last 3,000 years. Today, the main producers of gem carvings are India, China, Hong Kong, Thailand, Italy and Germany.

The base of this aquamarine cabochon has been engraved, as well as its top surface, so you see two images when looking into it. This gives the piece a good depth.

The carving of gemstones has traditionally focused on cameo and intaglio work, although it is also possible to find decorative designer work. The lapidaries of Germany have a strong tradition of carving. Their work is very fine, using high-grade material, but the pieces are rather expensive. Carvings from the Far East are cheaper due to lower labour costs, and much more traditional in design.

The carving of freeform gemstones is currently practised by a relatively small number of lapidaries and jewellers. Large-scale work requires machinery such as flat laps, drum sanders, diamond grinding wheels and polishing machines, which can be expensive. It is possible, however, to carve on a small scale, using silicon carbide and diamond drill bits and burrs in conjunction with a flex-shaft hand piece and power rotary tool. The diamond polishing compounds can be used on felt buffing wheels and mops.

Elaborately carved pieces of quartz (top) and beryl (above)

SAFETY PRECAUTIONS

Remove jewellery, tie hair back and use protective goggles and a dust mask when carving. The dust of certain materials, such as mother-of-pearl, beryl, quartz and malachite, can be harmful if inhaled.

Choosing the right material

Carving material should ideally have a tightly knit granular structure, as found in jade, agate and chalcedony. If the material is crystalline, it should be tough, free of internal stresses and easy to polish, like heliodor (beryl). The material's hardness and cleavage will affect the polishing of a stone – polishing on a cleavage plane is very difficult because portions of the crystal will be lifted as you work. Other important factors are the material's fracture, porosity and ability to cope with heat and chemicals.

Pleochroism has to be considered as it will dictate how the material is oriented. You also need to assess the number, type, position and colour of any inclusions, as well as colour distribution and zoning. Furthermore, if a gemstone has been treated by staining, stabilizing or fracture filling, it could lose colour or crumble when being carved.

Carving tips

• Keep the gemstone material wet to avoid overheating it. Don't push too hard or for too long with the rotary tool drill bits and don't let them dry out. Heat can affect the colour and clarity of the stone, or cause breakage.

• Don't skip the polishing process. Taking time to gradually "step down" in the grits and grades of diamond pads or paste will make a superior finish.

• Joints should be glued with a good-quality synthetic epoxy resin. This will retain a small degree of flexibility that instant adhesives don't possess – superglues can become brittle with age and the bond will eventually break. Work with the epoxy resin while it can be applied thinly and sparingly. Remove excess with a scalpel.

These modern pink tourmaline cabochons show typical Indian carving.

Showcase

The flowing structure of this beautiful necklace contains a carved section of rutilated quartz. Ribbons of 18K yellow gold enhance the shape of the carving and complement the golden needlelike inclusions in the quartz.

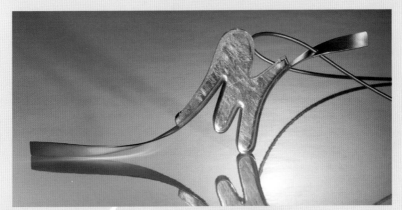

This brooch has been carved from a slab of monochrome print jasper and then set in 18K yellow gold. The orange bezel-set spessartite garnet (2.43 carat) terminates the form and provides this dramatic design with brilliance.

Enhanced with a backing of foil, this bright pink-red tourmaline makes a real statement. The internal tensions of tourmaline make it a difficult stone to work; try carving a part of a crystal or a crystal with inclusions, in which the tension will be lessened.

The rainbow obsidian (natural glass) has been hand-carved and combined with a natural ammonite and green tourmaline cabochon. The purple and green iridescence of the obsidian contrasts well with the tourmaline, and its glassy lustre is offset by the natural texture of the ammonite.

This 19th-century emerald ring, created in India, is decorated with diamonds and enamel work, and inlaid with gold. The use of emerald is remarkable, as this material is usually brittle and far from ideal for carving. The ring would have been carved with very basic tools, using abrasives such as quartz sand or corundum.

types of gemstone

Knowledge is the key to working with different types of gemstone. Understanding their unique properties, and those that they share with others, will enable you to make the most of the inherent qualities of each gemstone. Being aware of possible treatments and their effects on the material is also essential when choosing, working with and trading gemstones and jewellery.

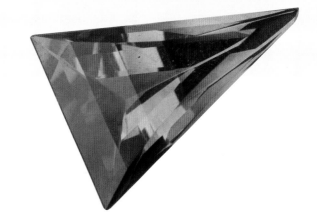

gemstone treatments

The majority of gemstones on the market are routinely enhanced using a range of treatments. You should be aware of the effects these may have on the way you use the gemstones and also on how you can advertise and sell your jewellery.

Apatite may be heat treated to improve its appearance by removing yellow or brown colouration while retaining the blue, or to deepen its colour giving it a more attractive blue.

If you advertise or sell jewellery, the claims you make about your products must be accurate. Products must be described truthfully and any information about gemstone treatments disclosed to customers. It is advisable to buy your material from a reputable source and know how to recognize some of the treatments. Commonly used treatments include: heating, dyeing and staining, bleaching, coating, irradiating, impregnating, fracture filling and diffusion treatments.

There are a number of organizations, such as the Federal Trade Commission (FTC) and the World Jewellery Confederation (CIBJO), that offer guidelines for the disclosure of treatments, describe the treatments and outline what is currently considered acceptable practice in the gem and jewellery trade.

Silver rings with yellow citrine. Citrine may be heat treated to improve its colour. Purple amethyst may be heat treated to change its colour to yellow citrine.

DISCLOSING TREATMENTS

The FTC states that "sellers should tell consumers about gemstone treatments ... if the treatment is not permanent or if the treated stone requires special care", and even when this is not the case, you should "tell consumers about the treatment if it significantly affects the value of the gemstone". The FTC recommends the following disclosures:

• If the colour of a treated gemstone will fade over time, tell the consumer that the gemstone has been treated, that the treatment is temporary, and that the stone's colour will fade over time.

• If ultrasonic cleaners or solvents should not be used to care for a treated stone, tell the consumer that the gemstone has been treated and the cleaners or solvents to avoid.

• If a diamond has been laser drilled to improve its clarity – but is then less valuable than a comparable diamond that has not been treated – tell the consumer the diamond was laser drilled.

Turquoise may be waxed, oiled or treated with resins to improve its appearance and keep it from drying out. It may also be stained to improve its colour.

Surface treatments

Surface treatments, including waxing and inking, are not permanent and may be rubbed off. The stone's surface may also be covered with a thin film or foil to enhance its appearance. A dye, stain or bleach may colour the surface leaving the centre unchanged, may follow along cracks and flaws, or may diffuse throughout the whole gemstone, changing colour, clarity and appearance.

Colourless and coloured waxes, oils, resins, plastic and glass are used to impregnate gemstones, filling cracks and flaws and improving appearance, which adds to the value. Turquoise is often waxed. Oiling of emeralds is such common practice that it is seldom disclosed. This is acceptable where colourless oils and resins are used, but all coloured treatments should be disclosed. Natural oils and resins may "leak" over time, and emeralds should be reoiled regularly to avoid drying out and cracking.

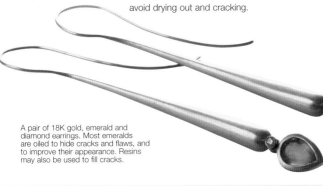

A pair of 18K gold, emerald and diamond earrings. Most emeralds are oiled to hide cracks and flaws, and to improve their appearance. Resins may also be used to fill cracks.

Topaz may be irradiated and heat treated to improve its colour. Opaque brown topaz can be changed to a range of attractive blue-coloured gemstones for use in jewellery.

Heating, irradiating and the use of lasers

Heat treatments are common practice in the gem and jewellery trade, so much so that you can assume all material has been heat treated in some way, unless it is described otherwise. Heating is used to change, lighten or darken the colour of a gemstone or improve its clarity. Heat treatments are generally permanent.

Irradiation treatments bombard gemstones with electrons or gamma rays to alter their colour. Diamonds can be irradiated to remove the yellow tinge and increase the colour grade and therefore the value. Topaz may be heat treated and irradiated to change brown opaque crystals to the bright blue topaz so popular in jewellery. Laser drilling is used to remove dark inclusions from diamonds, improving the clarity of the stone.

Pearls

• You should tell customers whether the pearls you are selling are natural, cultured (cultivated) or imitation (artificial or simulated).

• The origin of the pearls should be included in the description wherever possible, specifying for example, akoya cultured pearls or cultured freshwater pearls.

• If you know whether the pearls are nucleated (cultured around a bead or nucleus) or non-nucleated, add this information to the description.

• Both natural and cultured pearls may be dyed or irradiated to change or improve their colour. You are required to tell consumers whether either of these treatments has been carried out.

These two pieces make use of various freshwater pearls. The types and any treatments they have had should be identified to customers.

gemstone family tree

Gemstones with the same or similar chemical composition are placed together in groups or families. Ruby and sapphire, for example, share a chemical composition and are members of the corundum group. Jewellers can tell them apart by their colour, which is caused by the addition of minute amounts of trace elements. Chromium gives ruby its red colour, and iron and titanium colour blue sapphire. This chart shows the family tree of the main gemstone groups that are used in jewellery, excluding organics.

Diopside

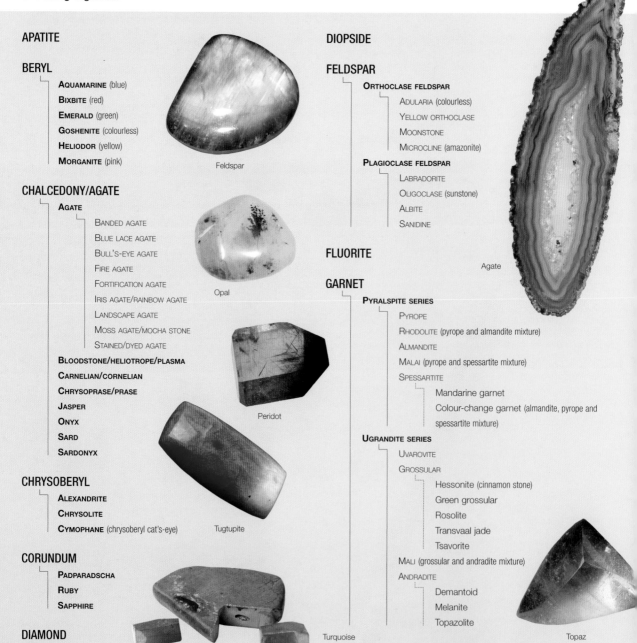

APATITE

BERYL
- AQUAMARINE (blue)
- BIXBITE (red)
- EMERALD (green)
- GOSHENITE (colourless)
- HELIODOR (yellow)
- MORGANITE (pink)

Feldspar

CHALCEDONY/AGATE
- AGATE
  - BANDED AGATE
  - BLUE LACE AGATE
  - BULL'S-EYE AGATE
  - FIRE AGATE
  - FORTIFICATION AGATE
  - IRIS AGATE/RAINBOW AGATE
  - LANDSCAPE AGATE
  - MOSS AGATE/MOCHA STONE
  - STAINED/DYED AGATE
- BLOODSTONE/HELIOTROPE/PLASMA
- CARNELIAN/CORNELIAN
- CHRYSOPRASE/PRASE
- JASPER
- ONYX
- SARD
- SARDONYX

Opal

CHRYSOBERYL
- ALEXANDRITE
- CHRYSOLITE
- CYMOPHANE (chrysoberyl cat's-eye)

Peridot

Tugtupite

CORUNDUM
- PADPARADSCHA
- RUBY
- SAPPHIRE

DIAMOND

Turquoise

DIOPSIDE

FELDSPAR
- ORTHOCLASE FELDSPAR
  - ADULARIA (colourless)
  - YELLOW ORTHOCLASE
  - MOONSTONE
  - MICROCLINE (amazonite)
- PLAGIOCLASE FELDSPAR
  - LABRADORITE
  - OLIGOCLASE (sunstone)
  - ALBITE
  - SANIDINE

FLUORITE

GARNET
- PYRALSPITE SERIES
  - PYROPE
  - RHODOLITE (pyrope and almandite mixture)
  - ALMANDITE
  - MALAI (pyrope and spessartite mixture)
  - SPESSARTITE
    - Mandarine garnet
    - Colour-change garnet (almandite, pyrope and spessartite mixture)
- UGRANDITE SERIES
  - UVAROVITE
  - GROSSULAR
    - Hessonite (cinnamon stone)
    - Green grossular
    - Rosolite
    - Transvaal jade
    - Tsavorite
  - MALI (grossular and andradite mixture)
  - ANDRADITE
    - Demantoid
    - Melanite
    - Topazolite

Agate

Topaz

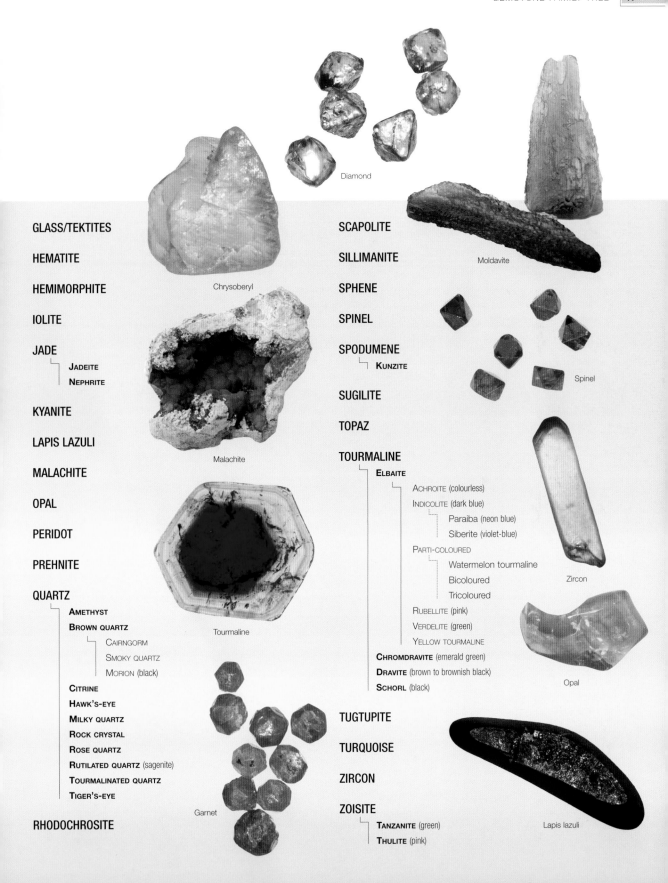

Diamond

GLASS/TEKTITES

HEMATITE

HEMIMORPHITE

IOLITE

JADE
    JADEITE
    NEPHRITE

KYANITE

LAPIS LAZULI

MALACHITE

OPAL

PERIDOT

PREHNITE

QUARTZ
    AMETHYST
    BROWN QUARTZ
        CAIRNGORM
        SMOKY QUARTZ
        MORION (black)
    CITRINE
    HAWK'S-EYE
    MILKY QUARTZ
    ROCK CRYSTAL
    ROSE QUARTZ
    RUTILATED QUARTZ (sagenite)
    TOURMALINATED QUARTZ
    TIGER'S-EYE

RHODOCHROSITE

SCAPOLITE

SILLIMANITE

SPHENE

SPINEL

SPODUMENE
    KUNZITE

SUGILITE

TOPAZ

TOURMALINE
    ELBAITE
        ACHROITE (colourless)
        INDICOLITE (dark blue)
            Paraiba (neon blue)
            Siberite (violet-blue)
        PARTI-COLOURED
            Watermelon tourmaline
            Bicoloured
            Tricoloured
        RUBELLITE (pink)
        VERDELITE (green)
        YELLOW TOURMALINE
    CHROMDRAVITE (emerald green)
    DRAVITE (brown to brownish black)
    SCHORL (black)

TUGTUPITE

TURQUOISE

ZIRCON

ZOISITE
    TANZANITE (green)
    THULITE (pink)

Chrysoberyl

Malachite

Tourmaline

Garnet

Moldavite

Spinel

Zircon

Opal

Lapis lazuli

1/corundum

The most important of the gem families, corundum provides us with two of the best-known stones: ruby and sapphire. The popularity and price of these gemstones remain strong due to the beauty, durability and versatility of the material. Unfortunately, however, the ongoing development of synthetics, imitations and enhancement treatments has made the task of choosing and buying sapphire or ruby complex and sometimes risky.

This polished gem-quality Burmese sapphire crystal displays the colour concentrations that typically occur in corundum crystals.

Jewellery makers and buyers should assume that the vast majority of corundum they see is enhanced in some way. Since the 1960s, heat treatment has been a common practice. Sadly for those on a budget, natural untreated rubies and sapphires carry a significant price premium: in terms of cost and rarity, a natural Burmese ruby of 10 carats is now on a par with natural coloured diamonds.

Burmese blue sapphires are usually a uniform blue, without any colour zoning. Burmese rubies often contain silk and possess a bright violet-red colour. The stones pictured here are natural (unheated). The sapphire weighs 5.02 ct and the ruby 6.24 ct.

The colour zoning commonly seen in corundum relates to the growth layers of a crystal, and appears as a series of concentric hexagons parallel to the prismatic crystal faces. Ruby exhibits strong pleochroism, showing yellow-red and deep carmine red when viewed from different angles; this optical effect can also occur in sapphire. Corundum can be transparent to opaque and have a vitreous to dull, greasy lustre. When transparent, the material is moderately brilliant.

Pricing corundum

• Sapphires and rubies are priced according to colour, clarity, size, cut and proportions. When pricing blue sapphires the purity and intensity of blue is critical. Ideally, it should possess a violet overtone with no sign of grey or green. The lightness or darkness of a stone, colour zoning and clarity all need to be considered; irregular colour zoning detracts from a stone's value and beauty. Inclusions are not necessarily bad – they can indicate whether or not the stone has been treated or identify its origin. Larger gems are more expensive, but small stones with good colour and clarity can still have a reasonable value.

• Rubies should be viewed in different light conditions as the spotlights in a shop make the colour intense and "hot", while daylight cools the colour down. Dark stones can appear nearly black in incandescent light.

• Origin has a direct impact on price, so make sure your receipt states the country of origin, especially if the gem is Burmese. If you are planning to buy an expensive natural ruby or sapphire, it is important to obtain a laboratory report before spending your money – the majority of reputable gem dealers would agree to this.

• Colourless sapphire is sometimes used as a cost-effective alternative to diamond; if cut well the stones can be brilliant and even contain some fire. It is a tougher stone at small sizes than white topaz and quartz, which have a tendency to break when being gypsy set.

SPECIFICATIONS

HARDNESS 9 Mohs

SPECIFIC GRAVITY 3.97–4.05 (ruby) 3.95–4.03 (sapphire)

REFRACTIVE INDEX 1.762–1.778

CRYSTAL FORM Trigonal. Ruby crystals occur as hexagonal prisms, tables and rhombohedrons. Sapphire crystals occur as barrel-shaped, double-pointed hexagonal pyramids and tabloid shapes. Corundum is found in igneous and metamorphic rocks and also in alluvial deposits.

SOURCES OF RUBY

Afghanistan, Australia, Cambodia, India, Kenya, Myanmar (formerly Burma), Pakistan (Kashmir), Russia, Tanzania, Thailand, United States (North Carolina), Vietnam.

SOURCES OF SAPPHIRE

BLUE SAPPHIRE Africa (Tanzania, Nigeria, Madagascar, Kenya, Malawi), Australia, Brazil, Myanmar (Burma), Pakistan (Kashmir), Sri Lanka, Thailand, United States (Montana).

PINK SAPPHIRE Madagascar, Myanmar (Burma), Sri Lanka, Tanzania.

PADPARADSCHA Sri Lanka.

YELLOW/GREEN/PURPLE SAPPHIRE Australia (Queensland, New South Wales), Myanmar (Burma), Sri Lanka, Tanzania, Thailand, United States (Montana).

COLOURLESS SAPPHIRE Sri Lanka.

COLOUR-CHANGE SAPPHIRE Tanzania.

Sapphire can be found in a range of crystal shapes.

Working with corundum

- Most large, fine sapphires are oval, emerald or cushion cut – the smaller stones have a greater variety of shape. You should examine the cut of rubies and sapphires carefully. Stones that have been cut deep to retain weight can be difficult to set in jewellery and should cost less per carat because they are overweight for their size. A shallow cut will sacrifice brilliance for lightness of colour and the gemstone will contain a noticeable "window". Corundum has to be repolished following heat treatment to remove the damaged exterior layer and, if this is not done with care, the gemstones can end up with a double girdle and/or pockmarks. Rubies and sapphires are often recut in the West to correct proportions, but the subsequent loss of weight and size will result in an increase in the carat price of the stone.

- Corundum is a durable gemstone – it is the hardest material after diamond and is used as an industrial abrasive. However, although it has no cleavage, it does have preferred directions of parting, which means that the material can be brittle despite its hardness value. It has a conchoidal fracture, and the many internal flaws or cracks found in rubies and sapphires can weaken a stone. The frequent twinning that occurs with ruby crystals can also make the material liable to damage. These factors have to be taken into account when cutting, polishing and setting corundum. However, ultrasonic and steam cleaners will not harm the stones.

- The hardness of corundum does give the gemstones longevity, making them ideal for jewellery that will take a lot of wear and tear over many years. Rubies and sapphires might suffer some scratches or lose a little sharpness on the facet edges over time, but the metal work is more likely to fail first. Prongs and settings loosen up with continual use and the tips of claws can become brittle, crack or wear down. To prevent the loss of an expensive sapphire or ruby, check the stone for movement and inspect the settings from time to time.

Types of corundum

RUBY

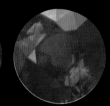

Ruby is corundum that has a purplish-bluish red to yellow-red colour. The finest colour is pure red with a hint of blue, as seen in glowing coal or the red of a traffic light. Burmese "pigeon's blood" rubies possess this fine colour and are the most sought after and expensive of rubies. As the mines in Mogok have been under the strict control of the Myanmar government since 1963, and are leased to nationals of Myanmar only, it is virtually impossible to travel there as a trader. Instead, individuals bring material over the border into Thailand, where towns have been established to accommodate the gem trade.

Matching pairs of rubies over 2 ct are hard to find and carry a price premium. This pair of Burmese rubies have been recut to ideal proportions, which has increased their value.

Vietnam and Tanzania have produced rubies of a similar colour to the pure red of Burmese rubies, but most of them are heated violet and brownish red material. Tanzanian rubies are usually opaque, occurring with green zoisite, and used for decorative carvings. Sri Lankan rubies tend to be light red to raspberry red in colour. Thai rubies were once dismissed by the trade because of their similarity to garnet, but there is now more Thai than Burmese material produced. The gem-quality Thai rubies have a slightly darker purplish red colour but are "cleaner" stones overall, having less rutile needle inclusions and more lustre than Burmese rubies.

The colour of rubies can be slightly uneven and it is normal for them to have minor inclusions, such as minerals, growth structures, canals and cavities. The inclusions will often indicate the country and area that the ruby came from. For instance, Burmese rubies typically contain rutile, calcite, apatite, olivine, sphene and spinel inclusions. Discoid fractures around natural mineral inclusions often occur and are a sign of heat treatment. Some rubies, in particular Burmese stones, fluoresce under ultra-violet light and good gemstones will even fluoresce in sunlight. However, a useful indicator of synthetic rubies is their very strong fluorescence.

This star ruby has the typical colour zoning and hexagonal banding of corundum. This is not ideal in a star stone, but is compensated for by the clear and sharp quality of the star.

When the rutile needles in a ruby are aligned, asterism occurs in the form of a six-ray star. Ideally, star rubies should be a good translucent red rather than the opaque brownish purple colour usually available. The rays should be sharp silvery white lines that extend to the base of the stone. Rubies may also have a cat's-eye effect, but this is very rare. Trapiche rubies are mainly sought after by collectors and consist of a wheel-like growth of several prismatic ruby crystals. When cut or ground flat, trapiche crystals have the appearance of a wheel with black spokes.

The cutting of rubies usually occurs in the country where they are mined. Pleochroism dictates the orientation of the material, with the table aligned so that the stone has the best red colour. The ruby is then cut, as a step or mixed cut, to yield the greatest weight but not necessarily the best proportions.

Rubies often suffer from being cut at their point of origin. Gem crystals frequently take the form of worn-down hexagonal pyramids, which can result in very shallow cuts or cuts with the culet off-centre (as pictured here).

Continued on page 51 ▶

Imitations

• Prior to the 1800s, red spinel, red garnet and ruby were all thought to be one gemstone (ruby) because of the similarity of colour. Thus a variety of misnomers appeared: almandine ruby (garnet), Australian ruby (garnet), balas ruby (spinel), Bohemian ruby (garnet) and Cape ruby (garnet).

• Composite doublets are manufactured by gluing a pale or colourless corundum crown to a synthetic blue sapphire pavilion. Alternatively, cobalt blue glass is given a crown of garnet, or a low-grade sapphire crown and pavilion are simply glued together with a coloured epoxy to create a sapphire of an expensive colour. Numerous doublets are sold to travellers in the Far East; they are difficult to spot when set in jewellery and do not always show up in gemmological tests. Blue star sapphires can also be manufactured: a star rose quartz often has blue enamel painted on its flat base, or a six-ray star may be engraved on the back of a synthetic cabochon.

Showcase

This ruby pendant was formerly a hair ornament that was made in the early 20th century in northern India. It uses Burmese ruby cabochons (foil-backed), faceted emeralds and old brilliant-cut diamonds, set in 18K yellow gold against an enamelled background. The necklace is made from modern freshwater pearls.

These earrings have suspended, faceted pear-shaped pink sapphires surrounded by small pavé-set pink sapphires. The cufflinks use baguette-cut sapphires in various hues of apricot, lilac and rose-pink. Corundum is hard enough to withstand the wear and tear that cufflinks receive.

An 18K yellow gold and sapphire necklace with inlaid platinum. The sapphires are cut asymmetrically, using blues, pinks, reds and lavenders. The material is slightly included, which gives the stones strength of colour while keeping the cost down. The rub-over settings emphasize the different shapes of cut, as does the segmentation of the necklace.

Treatments

• There are several ways in which the colour of corundum is enhanced. One is fracture filling, a common practice in the industry that reduces the visibility of flaws by making the fractures nonreflective. The colour of the gem is not diminished and the white patches around the fractures are lost. Oil, wax, paraffin, glass and epoxy resin are all used as fillers.

• Heating corundum lightens or intensifies colour, improves uniformity and enhances clarity by melting some of the silk that commonly occurs. The process is permanent. The inclusions may show evidence of heat treatment, as the heat can cause small crystals to melt or change, but if there are no inclusions it is difficult to tell whether the gemstone is natural or not. Irradiation is occasionally performed on sapphires, but is not an accepted treatment as the colour is not permanent and will fade.

• There has been much discussion over diffusion treatment. Unlike traditional heat treatment, this colours the surface of the gemstone only, while the centre remains colourless. The procedure involves introducing chemicals (the colouring agents of ruby and sapphire) into the upper surface of a colourless or pale stone and then heating it over a prolonged period of time. The effect is permanent, but the surface colour could be removed if the stone were badly chipped and needed repolishing. However, it is possible to repeat the process and restore the colour. The practice is acceptable as long as it is disclosed and the price of the gemstone reflects the fact that it has been treated. The diffusion treatment can also induce asterism in sapphires and rubies.

• Sapphires and rubies are also diffusion treated in the presence of beryllium. Low-grade corundum is heated alongside chrysoberyl to achieve intense orange and padparadscha colours, while Vietnamese and Tanzanian (Songea) rubies that normally have the colour of red garnet are beryllium treated to bright red-orange colours. However, the beryllium diffusion treatment doesn't always work and some stones end up with purple-black blotches (or explosions) within the material. There has been tremendous controversy regarding this process, with many fearing it would affect the sale of natural rubies and sapphires, but that has not been the case. Instead, nontreated stones have become more desirable and valuable. Standard gemmological tests cannot detect this type of treatment, which requires microscopic analysis of the inclusions. It is proposed that these stones should be labelled as "heat treated with additives (including beryllium-bearing substances)", and that there should be a warning that the resulting colour could be removed if the stone is damaged or repolished. There is disturbing evidence that suggests the beryllium treatment poses a health hazard to the workers who process and cut the gemstones and to the merchants who handle them.

The vibrant red-orange colour of the ruby on the right is indicative of beryllium diffusion-treated material. The stone on the left is a Burmese ruby that has been traditionally heated.

Types of corundum

SAPPHIRE

Sapphire is more abundant than ruby because its colouring agents (impurities) are more common than those of ruby. The most valuable colour is blue, and Burmese and Kashmir blue sapphires are the most sought-after gemstones. Kashmir sapphires are mined on the borders of India and Pakistan; the gems are a deep velvet blue that is sometimes described as cornflower blue. No new material from Kashmir is appearing on the market as the deposits are virtually worked out. Burmese blue sapphires are an intense, bright blue (royal blue) with a hint of purple.

The colour range of sapphire is extensive and, aside from the blue and pink colours, the prices are extremely reasonable.

Sri Lankan blue sapphires have become very popular and range in colour from mid-blue with a tinge of violet to pastel blue. The material often has irregular colour distribution and the Sri Lankan cutters take advantage of this to ensure that some colour is always in the stone's culet. This makes a stone appear to have a good colour, even if it is mostly colourless when viewed from the side. Since the 1970s, Sri Lankan geuda – or colourless – sapphire has been heated in a secret process to produce bright, lustrous blue sapphires that are sometimes sold as natural.

Thai blue sapphire, which tends to be rather dark in colour, is produced in huge quantities by the lapidaries who operate in partnership with the Thai miners. Australian sapphires can appear inky in artificial light, so material is sent to Thailand for cutting and heating to lighten and clarify the material. Unfortunately, this can result in the sapphires gaining a green tint.

African blue sapphires are variable in colour. Nigerian stones are often very dark, but Tanzania produces good-quality coloured sapphires, including fine blue crystals. Gem sapphires from Montana are usually pastel violet-blue to steel blue. The colour can be irregular with strong zoning and the material can be included. In general, American sapphires are quite small, rarely over 1 carat, but they are usually natural. However, Western mining techniques and labour costs make the production of Montana sapphires expensive.

This Tanzanian sapphire has a beautiful velvet blue colour and costs much less than a sapphire from Myanmar (Burma) or Kashmir.

Fancy sapphires are found in any colour other than blue. Pink sapphire has become very popular and appears regularly in jewellery designs. The colour can range from soft baby pink to hot bluish pink. Ideally, it should be a uniform, intense pink with no lavender or brown tones. Natural hot pink sapphires have risen in cost significantly and are selling at prices similar to medium-grade blue sapphire. Yellow sapphires are quite common and range from pale yellow to intense amber – they used to be called oriental topaz. Pure golden yellows are quite rare, so many sapphires are heated to a golden colour.

Padparadscha – which is Sinhalese for a type of lotus flower – is a rare and very expensive sapphire that shows pink and orange simultaneously. The source is Sri Lanka. Buyers need to be wary as orange sapphire is frequently offered in place of padparadscha, and pink sapphire is treated with beryllium to create the same effect.

Colourless sapphire is free from any impurities and easy to find in small sizes. Large pieces of colourless sapphire are traditionally heated to blue. Green sapphire used to be called oriental peridot, and often consists of very fine alternating bands of yellow and blue. Unfortunately, the colour can be quite dark and somber. Violet or purple sapphires are coloured by vanadium and occur in pale lilac to deep purple colours. They should resemble fine amethyst, but be slightly redder. Smaller stones are good value, but larger purple sapphires can be expensive.

As with rubies, sapphires have inclusions that denote their origin. For instance, Thai sapphires often contain tiny liquid drops that resemble fingerprints. Rutile needle inclusions in sapphire not only provide "silk" (a silk-like appearance), but also asterism. Ideally, star sapphires should have an intense, translucent blue colour (not grey or black, as is common), with minimal hexagonal banding and well-defined and centred stars. Cracks, pits and an uneven base are common failings and devalue the stone. There is a practice among Thai and Sri Lankan lapidaries of gluing the base of star sapphires together if a section breaks off during cutting. This might make the stone appear tidy and make it easier to set, but over time the glue will stain the sapphire yellow, spoiling its appearance.

Star sapphires can occur in a range of colours. This lilac-blue stone has good clarity and a reasonable star, but it has been cut very deep to create weight, which will affect its value.

Colour-change sapphires are a rare phenomenon. The gemstones can simply show different shades of blue depending on the light source, or they can change colour completely from blue-violet in daylight to red or reddish violet in artificial light.

Synthetics

• In the early 20th century the market was flooded with synthetic rubies, causing widespread apprehension as sales of natural rubies decreased and their value dropped. The synthetic rubies were manufactured by the Verneuil method, in which powdered aluminium oxide and colouring agents were exposed to a flame. A synthetic colourless sapphire, called diamondite, was also produced this way.

• Nowadays, highly developed flux-grown synthetics are manufactured for gem use, and sell in four inclusion-based grades and several size or weight categories. These Chatham and Ramaura rubies and sapphires are far from cheap. Synthetic star rubies and sapphires, called Linde stars, have been sold since 1947 and have been extremely popular. Synthetic colour-change sapphires are also manufactured.

This synthetic star ruby, with a perfect six-rayed star wrapped around the surface of the stone, looks almost too good to be true! Note that these stones, unlike natural star rubies, are cut quite shallow.

2/chrysoberyl

The chrysoberyl species consists of three very different gemstones that bear no resemblance to one another. Each stone possesses a quality that makes it desirable and valuable: one changes its colour, another is chatoyant (with a cat's-eye effect) and the last is a brilliant transparent gem. Together, they provide jewellery makers with an interesting and challenging choice of stones.

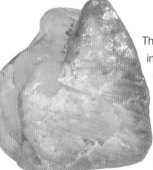

The chrysoberyl crystal's wedge-shaped end is partially visible.

The chrysoberyl family includes two of the most important gemstones: alexandrite and chrysoberyl cat's-eye. Alexandrite was discovered in Russia in 1831 and named after the Czar, Alexander II. It is considered a stone of good omen by many cultures, especially those in the Far East. Chrysoberyl cat's-eye is also thought to have mystical properties, and is used by some as a charm to ward off evil spirits and protect its owner against ill-health and loss of wealth.

Chrysoberyl is the third (and rather forgotten) member of the chrysoberyl group. It has several good qualities, being a large, durable and "clean" stone that comes in attractive colours and costs a fraction of the price of its two relatives. It is an excellent stone for jewellery makers.

Treatments and imitations

• As alexandrite requires such a financial investment it is important to be aware of synthetics and imitations. Prior to the 1970s, the synthetic spinel and corundum offered as alexandrite were relatively easy to spot as fakes. In 1973, however, a very good synthetic alexandrite was developed, which had properties identical to natural alexandrite and fooled many buyers for some years. It was created using the flux-melt process and the colour change was greenish blue to purplish red. It is more than likely that some of these synthetics are still on the market, having been bought unwittingly as natural alexandrite. If you're purchasing alexandrite, have the stones tested no matter who the dealer is.

• Synthetic corundum also has a colour-changing effect and is widely used to imitate alexandrite. The colour change is from grayish green to grayish purple and its correct name is synthetic alexandritelike corundum. Natural colour-change corundum has properties very similar to alexandrite, but with a different colour change (from blue to reddish violet).

• Synthetic spinel produces the same colour-changing effect as alexandrite.

• The only chrysoberyl cat's-eye imitation is quartz cat's-eye, which is an opaque to semiopaque grey-brown colour. The term *cat's-eye* always refers to chrysoberyl cat's-eye – not to stones such as quartz cat's-eye, tiger's-eye or hawk's-eye. These other chatoyant stones are much cheaper and lack the distinctive optical effect of chrysoberyl cat's-eye.

• There are no specific imitations of chrysoberyl, but it could be confused with yellow and brown topazes, yellow and green beryl, peridot, green tourmaline and andalusite.

SPECIFICATIONS

HARDNESS 8.5 Mohs
SPECIFIC GRAVITY 3.70–3.78
REFRACTIVE INDEX 1.746–1.763
CRYSTAL FORM Orthorhombic system. Crystals typically have wedge-shaped ends. Good cleavage and conchoidal fracture. The inclusions are similar to those of corundum: fine rutile needles all pointing in a single direction. Inclusions also consist of fingerprints and parallel lines of repeating twins.

SOURCES OF THE CHRYSOBERYL FAMILY

ALEXANDRITE Brazil, Russia, Sri Lanka, Southern Tanzania (where a stone of an exceptional 14 carats was found).
CHRYSOBERYL CAT'S-EYE Very few locations. Brazil, Russia (the Urals, which are nearly mined out), Sri Lanka (the best stones), Tanzania.
CHRYSOBERYL Brazil, Madagascar, Myanmar (formerly Burma), Sri Lanka, Tanzania, Zimbabwe.

Pricing the chrysoberyl family

- There are numerous average to poor specimens of alexandrite on the market, small stones containing flaws, with rather murky colours and a mediocre colour change. Even these stones go for high prices, as alexandrite is rarer than corundum. Alexandrite usually comes in small sizes, and gemstones are, on average, between 1 carat and 1.5 carats in weight. Stones over 2 carats in weight are scarce and extremely expensive. Be suspicious if you are offered a large alexandrite, and have it tested at a laboratory.
- The price of chrysoberyl cat's-eye is dependent on the size, colour and quality of the optical effect. Large stones are expensive and quite rare, but smaller stones are readily available and much cheaper to buy.
- As chrysoberyl doesn't have the price tag of alexandrite and chrysoberyl cat's-eye, it is excellent value for the money and worth checking out.

Working with the chrysoberyl family

- Alexandrite is sensitive to impact and pressure, and its colour-change ability can be affected by exposure to great heat.
- Alexandrite gemstones are frequently small, so the jewellery designer has to find a way of setting that allows the colour change to be seen and fully appreciated – which is quite a challenge!
- The setting of chrysoberyl cat's-eye is also critical. The stone has to be oriented and seated accurately, so that the "eye" sits centrally. It is quite common for these stones to have uneven bases, which require a certain amount of work to get them to sit straight.

Types of chrysoberyl

ALEXANDRITE

Alexandrite is a transparent gemstone with a remarkable colour-change property: it appears leaf green in daylight and red or red-brown under artificial incandescent light. This is influenced by the different colours in light sources; daylight contains blue light while incandescent light has a red tone. The best colour change can be seen in thick stones.

Alexandrite is a hard, durable stone and normally faceted. Some cat's-eye alexandrites exist in cabochon form. These are usually quite small, but they will have colour-change properties.

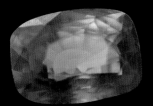

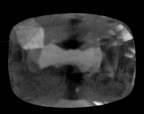

In daylight the faceted alexandrite is blue-green, but in artificial light the same stone is red-brown.

CHRYSOBERYL CAT'S-EYE

Chrysoberyl cat's-eye is very different from alexandrite. It is cut as a cabochon and has a pronounced silver-white cat's-eye effect, which moves from side to side when the stone is rotated. The colours range from honey yellow and honey brown to yellowish green and nearly bright green. The ideal colour for chrysoberyl cat's-eye is a light golden brown with a darker shadow that produces the stone's "milk and honey" or cat's-eye effect. The stone should be translucent and possess a beautiful velvet to silk-like lustre.

Another name for chrysoberyl cat's-eye is cymophane, which is Greek for "waving light", a reference to the optical effect caused by the light-refracting properties of the rutile needle inclusions and the chrysoberyl. The white line of the "eye" should be placed down the centre of the stone. If the domed surface is not smooth or not symmetrical, the eye will sit off-centre or the line will be broken, and the value of the stone will be reduced. The finer, straighter and more distinct the band (or eye), the better the quality of the stone.

This stone has good clarity, an attractive milk-and-honey appearance, and a cat's-eye running down the centre of the stone.

CHRYSOBERYL

The least well known of the chrysoberyl group, chrysoberyl is a brilliant, clear, transparent gemstone that is very durable. The colour ranges from yellow and yellow-green to golden brown, greenish brown and green. The most highly prized colour is golden brown.

This faceted chrysoberyl is a good size (6.83 ct), and the delicate greenish yellow colour means it is inexpensive. It would be a good stone for a designer who wanted to work with reasonably priced large stones.

3/spinel

Beauty, rarity, brilliance and value for money make spinel a great gemstone for jewellers and designers. Despite its good looks and the fact that it is nearly as durable as ruby and sapphire, spinel is not that well known as a gemstone. This makes it an affordable alternative for budget-conscious jewellery makers – for now.

In the past spinel was often called rubicelle because until the 1850s it was thought to be the same material as ruby. The reasons for the confusion were quite simple: spinel is found among sapphire and ruby deposits, its colour can be similar to Burmese and Thai rubies and, like ruby, red spinel will fluoresce under ultraviolet light.

Typical inclusions are tiny spinel octahedral crystals, rutile needles and zircon "halo" crystals. It is rare to find large spinels of over 4 carats and the majority of faceted stones are quite small, weighing between 0.5 carat and 2 carats. The rarity of large stones is probably the reason why spinel is not better known. It is a good stone for cutting as it isn't brittle and the facet edges stay sharp over time. With the right proportions, a faceted spinel can produce the brilliance and fire of a diamond.

This set of spinel crystals displays the gemstone's crystal form and colour range.

SPECIFICATIONS

HARDNESS 8 Mohs
SPECIFIC GRAVITY 3.54–3.63
REFRACTIVE INDEX 1.712–1.762
CRYSTAL FORM Spinel belongs to the cubic crystal system, usually appearing in octahedral form. It is found as perfect crystals or as stream pebbles. It has an indistinct cleavage and a vitreous lustre.

SOURCES OF SPINEL

The most important sources are Cambodia, Myanmar (formerly Burma), and Sri Lanka. Also found in Madagascar, Tanzania, Nigeria, Afghanistan, Pakistan, Thailand, Brazil, Russia.

Showcase

This impressive Indian neckpiece dates from the 19th century. Matching faceted pink spinels and natural pearls have been window set in a wire frame to form an intricate and delicate floral pattern.

A bright red spinel has been set with a pair of brilliant-cut diamonds in simple rub-over collets, below. The intense colour of the spinel is enhanced by the contrasting whiteness of the diamonds.

Bright red octahedral spinel crystals have been set in 22K gold to make this charming pair of earrings. The crystals are open-backed to allow light to travel through them and bring out their full colour.

Colours of spinel

Spinel comes in a huge range of colours depending on the impurities or colouring agents it contains.

The most popular and sought-after colour of spinel is bright red-orange, like that of a poppy or a flame. Stones with this colour are sometimes called flame spinel and their price tag is far higher than for spinel in other colours. The spinel varieties gahnite and gahnospinel are a blue-violet colour and can be confused with blue sapphire. Green, yellow or colourless spinel is very rare, as are star spinels.

This glorious red-orange flame spinel weighs 3.52 ct; it is the most sought-after and expensive colour of the species. The gemstone is Burmese.

This Burmese spinel has an attractive blue colour with lilac tones. It could be used as an alternative to blue sapphire because it is durable, brilliant and affordable. Spinels also occur in a cobalt blue colour.

This matching pair of Russian rose pink spinels has been faceted with a brilliant cut to bring out the natural high dispersion.

Treatments and imitations

• Unlike other gemstones, spinel is rarely heat treated or irradiated to change or improve its colour. However, synthetic spinel has been in production since 1920. Powdered raw material is melted at a high temperature and heavy metals are then added to achieve colours very close to that of other gemstones, such as aquamarine and tourmaline.
• Spinel can be confused with other gemstones such as ruby, sapphire, zircon, red, pink and blue tourmalines, amethyst and garnet.

Pricing spinel

Barring the expensive red-orange variety of spinel, the price is similar to that of aquamarine or tourmaline. Larger sizes are more expensive because of their scarcity. Unfortunately, as public awareness grows, the price of spinels will increase.

Working with spinel

• Spinels can frequently be found in antique Asian jewellery. The hardness of the stone gives it longevity so it remains intact over time.
• Spinel is a good material for small faceted stones, especially if they are being gypsy set. Its hardness prevents the stone from crumbling or splintering when pressure is applied onto the girdle. Spinel is also excellent for engagement rings or any piece of jewellery that is going to be worn every day.

Small octahedral spinel crystals exhibiting the typical red colour

• As more and more corundum is heated or treated, spinel can be bought knowing that it is in its natural state. This is an important selling point for jewellery makers and designers.
• The most common colour of spinel is soft red, like the small crystals in the picture below. If you are looking for cabochons or beads in spinel, you will most likely find them in this colour. Only occasionally are beads produced in other colours.
• Black spinel is relatively cheap and polishes well. It is a good alternative to softer materials such as dyed black onyx or jet.

4/topaz

To many people, the word *topaz* brings to mind an inexpensive stone that is either a heat-treated bright blue or a brownish yellow colour (the latter case usually turns out to be citrine).
A genuine precious topaz, however, is much rarer, more expensive and an altogether more beautiful gemstone than people first imagine.

This 3.5 ct precious pink topaz has great depth of colour for an unheated stone. The step cut is traditionally used on pale gemstones because it displays the colour best.

This freeform natural blue topaz cabochon displays typical topaz inclusions. Despite the inclusions, the natural material has produced an attractive blue stone that is more affordable than aquamarine cabochon material.

When faceted, white topaz produces lively bright gemstones, and the abundant supply of material makes the stones great value.

Topaz is a transparent gemstone that commonly contains inclusions. They can be two-phase inclusions, consisting of characteristic tear-shaped cavities containing a gas bubble and liquid, or three-phase inclusions, consisting of gases, liquid and small crystals together. They might have cracks, streaks and veils. This is a durable stone that has a reasonable hardness and is impervious to most scratching. Topaz crystals are often very large and can weigh up to several pounds – in 1964 blue topaz crystals were found in Ukraine weighing 220 pounds (100 kg) each.

As the colour of topaz is rarely vivid, cuts such as step cuts or scissor cuts are used to display it to best effect. Topaz has a high brilliance and vitreous lustre, so colourless or weakly coloured material is often faceted as a brilliant cut in order to provide a lively gemstone that is a cheaper alternative to corundum or diamond.

SPECIFICATIONS

HARDNESS 8 Mohs
SPECIFIC GRAVITY 3.49–3.57
REFRACTIVE INDEX 1.609–1.643
CRYSTAL FORM Orthorhombic system. Most topaz crystals are prismatic and one end of the crystal is usually terminated by dipyramids (wedge-shaped ends). They have characteristic eight-sided cross-sections with striations parallel to the length.
TOPAZ DEPOSITS are found in igneous rocks, such as pegmatites and volcanic lavas, or as alluvial stream pebbles. They are often associated with gold deposits.

SOURCES OF TOPAZ

PINK TOPAZ Brazil, Pakistan, Russia.
LIGHT BLUE TOPAZ United Kingdom (Cornwall, Northern Ireland, Scotland).
Topaz can also be found in Afghanistan, Australia, Myanmar (formerly Burma), Nigeria, Sri Lanka, United States (California).

Treatments and imitations

• Topaz is commonly confused with citrine (yellow quartz) and smoky quartz. Many traders from the Far East continue to refer to quartz as topaz and the following names are used in error: Rio topaz, Madeira topaz, Spanish topaz, Caribbean topaz, Palmeira topaz.
• Sherry and imperial topaz could be confused with zircon as both gemstones possess a good brilliance. Blue topaz can resemble aquamarine, apatite and treated blue zircon.
• Pink topaz can imitate pink tourmaline, pink kunzite, pink spinel and pink sapphire.

IRRADIATION

Irradiation changes colourless topaz to blue, intensifies yellow and orange shades and even creates a neon turquoise similar to that of paraiba tourmaline. Colourless rough material can be found throughout the world in plentiful supply, but the best commercial rough for irradiating comes from Sri Lanka. The material remains radioactive for a relatively short time (a few months) following irradiation, enabling dealers to sell it quickly. White topaz material from Nigeria and Brazil stays

Showcase

A precious sherry topaz is the focal point of this intricate and original ring design. Two diamond-set bands arch protectively over the top of the sometimes fragile gemstone, while a decorative dragonfly perches on the side.

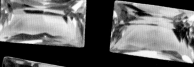

This pale yellow topaz came from Africa and is described as champagne topaz. The unheated material has produced lively, bright stones.

Colours of topaz

True precious topaz is rarely seen in jewellery stores despite being a beautiful and versatile gemstone. It is a hard and brilliant stone that comes in a range of gentle colours that depend on the impurities, or colouring agents, present. The most common natural colours are yellow, yellow-brown, orange-brown, pinky brown, light to medium red, blue and colourless. More rarely, topaz can be found in light green, pink, pink-red, light greenish yellow and violet. The most expensive and desirable colours are found as sherry topaz (a reddish orange colour that is occasionally confused with citrine), precious imperial topaz (a fine apricot-orange colour) and pink topaz (which can vary from pale pink to violet-pink).

The natural pink topaz has a slight peachy imperial colour on one end. Most stones would be heated to lose orange tones such as this, but I prefer to have an unheated stone with minor colour variation.

This irradiated Swiss blue topaz material has been cut into a fun stone in which the concave-cut table creates an interesting optical effect.

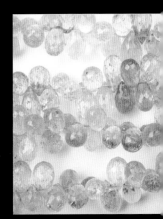

Topaz is commonly treated; for example, natural pink stones are rare, so yellow material is heat treated to pink. As a result, natural pink stones carry a higher value. Treated topaz provides colours that are more intense and usually free of inclusions. Irradiated material comes in a light sky blue (which is sometimes confused with aquamarine), a vibrant Swiss blue and a dark grey-blue called London blue topaz. The colours of diffusion-treated topaz are deep green and blue-green.

It is unusual to find precious pink topaz in bead form. Imperial topaz is mixed with the pink in these beautiful, brilliant briolettes.

radioactive for a longer period due to the impurities in the rough, and the stones have to "cool" for up to several years before they are free of dangerous radioactivity.

Stories about "hot" topaz being released onto the market led the authorities in the United States and Europe to demand a certificate of origin for irradiated topaz. The purpose of the certificate is to control the distribution of treated stones and ensure that they are free from dangerous levels of radioactivity. In addition, producers are legally required to label their goods with details of the irradiation process. In the United States, deep blue (London blue) treated topaz has to be tested for radiation levels. The Gemological Institute of America (GIA) provides this service to individuals.

Initially, in the early 1980s, the prices of irradiated blue topaz were high, but the flood of material onto the market led to a reduction in value. Demand for irradiated topaz remains high despite concerns surrounding the treatment process, but the abundance of material keeps the price relatively low.

DIFFUSION TREATMENT

Diffusion involves heating topaz over a prolonged period of time with a chemical contact. The resulting colour change occurs only over the surface of the stone, while the centre remains untouched and retains its original colour. Diffusion treatment creates green and blue-green topaz.

HEAT TREATMENT

Prior to heat treatment, brown-coloured topaz is partially cut as a gemstone. It is then heated to 840°F (450°C) until it loses its colour, and then cooled gradually until it becomes pink (with various degrees of saturation). The length of the heating process and the speed at which

the stones are heated and cooled is critical; if the process is rushed the colour can become turbid or the stones can lose their colour altogether. A stone that has undergone this treatment is known as a pink topaz, and the process is commonly called pinking. Heating is a legitimate process as long as the colour is stable and no dyes are used.

Pricing topaz

• Topaz can be found in large sizes, but it has a high specific gravity and, like garnets, weighs in heavier than other gemstones of the same size. It is worth bearing this in mind if you are looking for a large stone as it will have a noticeable effect on the price.

• The prices of pink and imperial topaz are relatively high, and a pink stone known to be a natural pink will carry a premium. The prices of yellow, brown-orange, blue and colourless topaz are much lower, making them good value for the money.

Working with topaz

• Topaz has one perfect cleavage and a conchoidal, uneven fracture. As a result it can be cleaved perpendicular to the crystal's longitudinal axis and a slight blow along the stone's length could cause it to divide. Special care needs to be taken during setting. It is advisable to use a protective setting if making the topaz into a ring, to guard the girdle and edges of the stone from accidental bumps.

• Not all colours of topaz are stable. Some irradiated brown-yellow topazes lose their colour after just a couple of days' exposure to the sun, and some natural yellow-brown stones gradually fade in sunlight. It might be worth keeping topaz-set jewellery out of direct sun or heat.

• Topaz is not resistant to hot sulfuric acid, so care must be taken when soldering or working on jewellery. You should also try to avoid overheating the stone during soldering and polishing.

5/beryl

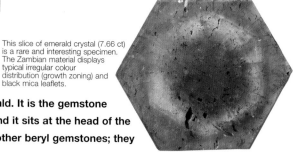

This slice of emerald crystal (7.66 ct) is a rare and interesting specimen. The Zambian material displays typical irregular colour distribution (growth zoning) and black mica leaflets.

Few people can resist the glamour and intensity of the emerald. It is the gemstone that made Cleopatra's mines famous throughout the world and it sits at the head of the beryl family tree. But don't let this diminish your view of the other beryl gemstones; they are by no means the poor relations.

These two emerald crystals from Pakistan are 3 x 9 mm.

The beryl species offers a rich mix of gemstones and includes, in addition to the emerald, the sparkling aquamarine, the vibrant heliodor and the delicate morganite. They should all be viewed as valuable precious gems, which can be used to great effect when designing jewellery. The critical factor in judging and pricing beryl is its intensity of colour and this has meant more material being treated in some way to improve the colouring.

SPECIFICATIONS

HARDNESS 7.5–8 Mohs
SPECIFIC GRAVITY 2.69–2.80
REFRACTIVE INDEX 1.57–1.59
CRYSTAL FORM Beryl has a hexagonal, prismatic structure and occurs in granites and pegmatites as well as in alluvial deposits of gravel. It has a vitreous lustre.

SOURCES OF BERYL

EMERALD Best sources are Colombia, Zambia and Brazil. Also found in Australia, India, Pakistan, Russia, South Africa, United States.
AQUAMARINE Brazil, Mozambique and Afghanistan produce the best sky blue aquamarine. Dark blue material is found in Nigeria and Madagascar.
HELIODOR The finest material comes from the Russian Urals and Brazil. Also found in Madagascar, Namibia, United States.
MORGANITE Madagascar and Brazil produce fine-grade material. Also found in Mozambique, Namibia, Pakistan, Zimbabwe.
GOSHENITE Brazil, Canada, Russia, United States.
BIXBITE United States.

This water-worn aquamarine crystal comes from an alluvial deposit in Afghanistan.

These heliodor crystals have an elongated hexagonal shape.

Types of beryl

EMERALD

The chromium and vanadium present in emerald produce its vibrant colour, which is stable against light and heat and so will not fade. The colour of emerald varies according to its source or location, the most desirable colour being a strong, slightly bluish green.

Colombian emeralds are pure green with a faint tint of blue. They are dichroic, which means the colour has two axes and will vary in appearance depending on the angle from which you look at it. Colombian emeralds have dominated the market for many years, but their extraction methods are thought to be causing long-term damage to the mine sites. The explosives and giant tractors used to accelerate the mining process are potentially harmful to the emeralds, which are very sensitive to shock.

Brazilian emeralds are slightly lighter in colour and contain more yellow than Colombian stones. They often have a slight cloudiness, but are mostly free of larger inclusions.

Zambian stones are a fine, deep emerald green and their clarity is good.

Very few emeralds are absolutely "clean". They often have inclusions of fibers or tremolite rods, internal cracks or irregular colour distribution, and can appear cloudy or "sleepy". The resulting internal stresses make emeralds very sensitive to pressure. The emerald cut (or step cut/octagon) was specifically designed to maximize the valuable stone and to intensify its colour. This cut, in which the corners are removed to avoid chipping or breaking, also protects the somewhat brittle material

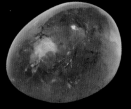

This Zambian emerald cabochon weighs 11.08 ct. This beautiful stone contains liquid-filled cavities surrounded by a gas bubble.

The vibrant colour of emerald comes from the presence of chromium and vanadium. It is stable against light and

Aquamarine can be found in sea green, sky blue and dark blue. In the 19th and early 20th centuries, sea green was preferred but since then sky blue and dark blue have become more desirable and the most valuable colours. Some of the best aquamarine comes from Brazil and Mozambique; the blue is intense, the material is clear and the crystals are large. Aquamarine is dichroic, so the intensity of colour changes depending on the angle it is viewed from and the material is usually cut according to best colour angle as opposed to greatest size. The step cut or emerald cut is frequently used with aquamarine in order to intensify its blueness.

Aquamarines have a much better clarity than emeralds. It is far easier to find clean stones at a good size, and fewer inclusions and cracks mean there is less internal stress and the material is less brittle. Flawed material that is cloudy and nearly opaque does exist, but is normally used for beads and cabochons, where it can sometimes produce a cat's-eye effect.

natural blue green.

This step-cut octagon has been cut from sky blue Afghan material.

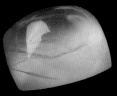

Dark blue is the most sought-after colour of aquamarine. This gemstone is from Nigeria.

This large aquamarine cabochon contains typical milky veil-like inclusions.

HELIODOR (YELLOW OR GOLDEN BERYL)

Heliodor is a yellow form of beryl, which was linked with the sun by ancient civilizations and so acquired its name. It often forms alongside aquamarine in granite pegmatites. The colour ranges from pale lemon yellow to yellow-green to a rich, warm gold. Heliodor may contain fine tubelike inclusions that can create a cat's-eye effect when cut in cabochon form.

The flat table of this mirror-cut beryl clearly shows off the tiny crystal inclusions and slender tubelike voids within.

This heliodor stone comes from Namibia.

MORGANITE (PINK BERYL)

The majority of morganite is a soft peachy pink colour that can be made more intense by using a closed setting of white metal. The first morganite was found in California, alongside deposits of tourmaline. Depending on the levels of manganese impurities, morganite can be pale pink, rose-pink, peach, apricot/salmon and even violet in colour. Like aquamarine and emerald, it is dichroic and so shows two shades of colour if viewed along the two different axes. Sometimes crystals contain both pink morganite and blue aquamarine.

The majority of morganite is a pale pink colour, although stronger colours do occur. It can be made to look more intense if it is set in a closed collet of white metal.

GREEN BERYL

The majority of green beryl is transformed into blue aquamarine by heating the material at high temperature. The depth and intensity of colour and the hue generally dictate whether a stone is called green beryl or emerald, and the two should not be confused. Emeralds should have a strong or deep green, bluish green or slightly yellow-green colour. Green beryl should be pale green or pale yellow-green. It can often contain inclusions similar to the fibres, rods or cloudiness found in emeralds.

The stone on the left is green beryl. The intensely green stone on the right is emerald.

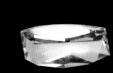

Faceted bent-bar cut green beryls

GOSHENITE

Goshenite is named after the town of Goshen in Massachusetts, where it was first found.

It is the pure variety of beryl, with no colouring agents. Needlelike inclusions can occur in the crystals. When faceted, goshenite has a good brilliance and could be confused with white topaz or white sapphire; backed with silver foil in a closed setting it has even been

BIXBITE (RED BERYL)

This is a very rare form of beryl. Usually only small gem-quality crystals are found, so cut gemstones normally weigh less than 1 carat. Larger stones do exist but they tend to be heavily included. Red beryl is not easy to source and is so expensive that it is not really

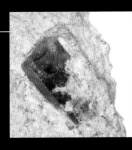

This is red beryl crystal

Treatments and imitations

• Emeralds are frequently "oiled" to fill and disguise whitish flaws and improve the overall colour. It is a practice that has been carried out since early Greek times and is accepted in the trade as long as the oil that is used is not dyed green. With time the emerald will "dry out", exposing the original cracks and poor colour. It is possible to have the stone reoiled.

• The modern practice of "filling" emeralds using vacuum and heat technology involves introducing epoxy resin, which becomes an integral part of the stone. However, when the treated emerald is subjected to a degreasing procedure, such as an ultrasonic cleaner, and the resin (or oil) is removed, previously hidden flaws become visible and a considerable loss of colour results. Most Colombian and Brazilian emeralds are automatically treated this way; Zambian material does not normally go through a vacuum-filling process but traditional oiling might still occur.

• A great deal of aquamarine is heat treated to intensify the colour and change it from green-blue to sky blue. Unless it is specified otherwise, it is wise to assume that the stones you buy are heat treated. The colour of aquamarine can also be improved with neutron and gamma irradiation, but the change is not permanent and the colour is unstable. Morganite can be heat treated in order to achieve a pure pink colour without any yellow or orange tone.

• Synthetic emerald has been successfully produced for some time, the first synthesis being made using the flux-melt technique in 1848. In this process, powdered ingredients are melted and fused in a solvent (flux) and kept at a very high temperature for months before being left to cool very slowly. It used to take up to a year to obtain a crystal of sufficient size to produce a stone of 2 carats. Synthetics can be identified by characteristic veil- or featherlike, liquid-filled inclusions.

• Pale, low-grade emeralds and beryl are sometimes coated with a layer of synthetic emerald, which crystallizes over the cut stone in a hydrothermal container. The layer is thin (approximately 1 mm), so that the polished stone possesses the desirable emerald-green colour but the natural inclusions can also be seen. If viewed through a loupe, the surface of the stone will have telltale cracks that crisscross each other and cannot be polished out.

• Emeralds can also be coated with a layer of a substance that looks like green nail polish. Scratching the stone with a sharp point or wiping over it with a solvent like acetone will indicate if it has been coated this way.

A lot of bead material is low grade, but these Indian emerald beads have an intense colour and the inclusions are not unsightly.

• Lannyte, soudé and mascot emeralds are emerald doublets. Two genuine pale stones, which could be rock crystal, aquamarine, beryl or pale low-grade emerald, are cemented together with emerald green paste. The upper segment often contains inclusions to fool people into believing the stone is genuine, but the cemented area can be seen if viewed from the side.

• Aquamarine has been successfully imitated using synthetic flame-fusion spinel. It is worth testing the aquamarines in mixed parcels as they often contain some synthetics. Synthetic morganite also exists.

• Green glass has even been used to imitate emerald. At one time, green traffic lights in Zambia were regularly smashed and the pieces taken to mix into parcels of emerald rough. Glass can be identified by its air bubbles or clouds of small bubbles.

• Emeralds can be confused with other natural gemstones of similar colour, in particular chrome tourmaline, chrome diopside, demantoid garnet and tsavorite garnet.

Pricing beryl

• The most important criterion in pricing beryl is colour intensity, and as a result treatment to improve colour is considered standard practice. Emeralds are often oiled to disguise flaws; you should be informed of this process by the dealer and the price should reflect the fact that the stone has been treated.

• Because of the rarity of large, clean, deep green emeralds, their prices can nearly reach those of diamonds. Ideal colour dominates the pricing of emeralds: if a stone is darker or lighter than the ideal colour, the price will be reduced. Clarity and size are the other pricing factors. Lower-grade emerald material is used for cabochons or beads.

• It is relatively easy to mistake aquamarine for blue topaz. The countries that mine aquamarine often produce blue topaz as well and parcels can get mixed (accidentally or not!). Blue topaz is a much cheaper, less valuable stone and is usually irradiated. Aquamarine is a precious gemstone that, depending on the intensity of colour and size, can have a considerable value.

Working with beryl

• Because so much aquamarine is heat treated to improve the colour, great care needs to be taken not to overheat the stone when polishing or soldering jewellery with aquamarine in situ.

• Even if an emerald looks flawless and transparent there are often minute cracks crossing the stone, which can open up under certain harsh conditions including stone setting, polishing and cleaning, and an emerald with inclusions will be particularly brittle. Extreme care should also be taken during work that involves applying heat to the emerald.

• When it comes to setting emeralds, certain faceted cuts are more prone to breakage than others. If you wish to use emerald baguettes and trillions, try to find material that is as clean and free of cracks or flaws as possible.

Showcase

This simple ring design (left) focuses on the unusual green beryl cabochon. It displays a cat's-eye effect caused by the fibrous nature of the material.

The design of this ring (right) is like an eternity ring but uses emeralds in place of diamonds. The channel setting protects the fragile stones.

6/sillimanite

For some time, this tough, durable gemstone has been either considered a collector's stone or used industrially (in the manufacture of spark plugs!). It is finally becoming available to jewellery makers, who will, no doubt, appreciate the subtle colours and optical effects that sillimanite has to offer.

SPECIFICATIONS

HARDNESS 7.5 Mohs
SPECIFIC GRAVITY 3.25
REFRACTIVE INDEX 1.65–1.68
CRYSTAL FORM Orthorhombic, occurring as long slender crystals in metamorphic rocks.

SOURCES OF SILLIMANITE

Myanmar (formerly Burma) (blue and violet), Sri Lanka (greenish gray). Also Brazil, Germany, India, Italy, Kenya, United States (Idaho).

Treatments and imitations

In its massive, noncrystalline form, fibrolite can resemble jade; "gemmy" faceted sillimanite can resemble iolite or pale sapphire.

Pricing sillimanite

Aside from the sought-after faceted blue gemstones, sillimanite/fibrolite is relatively inexpensive. Faceted material is still quite rare, but cabochons and cat's-eyes have become much more available.

Working with sillimanite

• Sillimanite is a relatively tough and durable gemstone; it is resistant to mechanical shock and chemicals and fairly tolerant of heat. However, one single good cleavage runs parallel to the length of the crystal, so if pressure is applied in the wrong place the stone can split in two.
• The fibrous material is slightly softer than the crystalline variety and has an uneven, splintery fracture. It is suitable for carvings and cabochons.

Types of sillimanite

Named after Professor Silliman of Yale University, sillimanite is very much a stone of two parts. When faceted, it is a lively, brilliant gem with a glassy to diamond lustre that comes in a range of subtle transparent colours: grey, blue, violet-blue, blue-green and brown-gray. The most sought-after colour is blue, which comes from the ruby-rich Mogok region in Myanmar (formerly Burma). Sillimanite is pleochroic, particularly so in the blue stones, which show yellowish pale green, dark green and blue from three angles.

The other face of sillimanite is very different and even has a different name – fibrolite. The name derives from the long slender sillimanite crystal prisms, which can occur in parallel groups that resemble fibres. This fibrous nature is more common in the massive opaque form of fibrolite, but traces of the perpendicular fibres can also often be seen in the translucent to transparent cat's-eye material. Fibrolite possesses a silky lustre, which is common to chatoyant stones, and can display a razor-sharp white "eye".

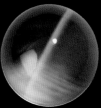

This faceted sillimanite shows flashes of colours caused by the stone's pleochroic properties.

A white cat's-eye stands out clearly in this subtly coloured grey-mauve stone.

Showcase

These faceted sillimanite beads graduate in colour from transparent near-white to semiopaque dark grey. Although the beads have an irregular cut, the row is valuable for its rarity.

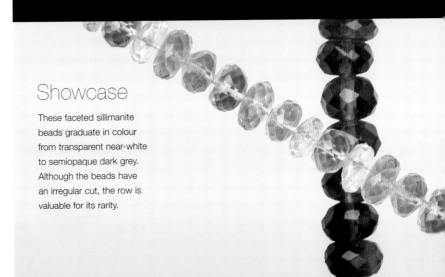

7/tourmaline

Tourmaline is a favoured gemstone, offering a variety of fabulous colours – sometimes several in just one stone. In a world where fashions change more quickly than ever, tourmaline can be adapted to suit new trends and will look great in a diverse range of designs. It is truly the gemstone of modern times.

This faceted rubellite weighs an impressive 17.36 ct and comes from Tanzania.

This cross-section of a tourmaline crystal displays the different tones of colour that can occur in a single crystal.

The Western world got its hands on tourmalines in 1703 when the Dutch began to import them from Sri Lanka. These gems were given the name *turamali,* meaning mixed colours. Tourmaline has now become an essential ingredient in Western jewellery design. Its versatility and appeal lie in its colours: pastels, intense neons, unique bi- and tricolours, which can sit side by side or stand alone. Designers love working these stones and buyers love wearing them. The prices for the most sought-after colours have at least tripled over the last few years.

Members of the tourmaline family share the same crystal structure but, depending on the impurities present, occur in different colours. These gemstones are dichroic to varying degrees; different colours or shades of colours can be seen depending on the viewing angle. In some, the effect is quite conspicuous; for instance, indicolite shows very dark blue from one angle and light blue from another. Red tourmaline shows dark red and light red, while green tourmalines are either dark green and yellow-green, or yellow-green and blue-green. Indicolite can often appear very dark, so needs to be faceted carefully to allow the lighter tone to dominate. The table facet is cut along the length of the crystal (the direction showing the lighter blue colour) and the pavilion facets are cut nearly perpendicular to the table to prevent the blackening of the stone through the dark blue colour axis. Pale stones need a table that is perpendicular to the long axis to get the strongest depth of colour. Tourmaline has a glassy to vitreous lustre.

Common inclusions in tourmalines are cracks that run parallel to each other at 90 degrees to the length of the crystal. They are highly reflective and frequently occur in pink to red stones or where colours change within the crystal. Thornlike fluid inclusions also occur. Many faceted tourmalines have step cuts or scissor cuts to display the best colour and to bring light into a potentially dark stone. The profile of the crystal means the stones are often rectangular or octagonal in shape.

SPECIFICATIONS

HARDNESS 7–7.5 Mohs

SPECIFIC GRAVITY Pink and red tourmaline: 3.01–3.06; brown, green and blue tourmaline: 3.04–3.11; black tourmaline: 3.11–3.20

REFRACTIVE INDEX 1.614–1.666

CRYSTAL FORM Trigonal system. The crystals look like hexagonal rods and the cross-section is either rounded triangular or completely triangular with pyramidal terminations. There are pronounced striations along the crystal length. Unicoloured crystals are quite rare; most tourmaline crystals have different tones or colours within one crystal. Tourmaline occurs in granite pegmatites, where it is often found with topaz, quartz, spodumene and beryl.

SOURCES OF TOURMALINE

Africa (Namibia, Nigeria, Tanzania, Zambia), Brazil, Myanmar (formerly Burma), Pakistan, Russia, United States (California).

These bicolour tourmaline crystals come from Pakistan. They are in perfect condition and show striations along the crystal length.

INDICOLITE

Indicolite includes tourmaline of all shades of blue, from the blue of a sapphire to a bright blue-green turquoise colour. Much blue tourmaline tends to be dark and inky, which is not popular with jewellery buyers. As a result, indicolite is often heat treated to lighten it.

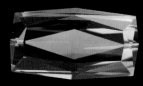

This scissor-cut indicolite gemstone has highly desirable blue-green colour.

This polished drop displays typical inky blue indicolite colour.

RUBELLITE

This is one of the most desirable and valuable of the tourmaline family. *Rubellite* translates quite simply as "red", and true rubellite should be an intense hot pink to red colour with a violet to blue tone and no muddying yellow or brown tones. The popularity and value of rubellite has increased enormously over the last few years, due to the major jewellery houses using it in their designs. Good rubellite deposits exist in Tanzania and Nigeria. Lower-grade rubellite is often heat treated to intensify the colour.

The hot pink rubellite cushion cabochon comes from Africa.

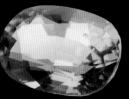

This faceted rubellite gem comes from Tanzania and weighs 5.08 ct.

VERDELITE

Most people associate bottle green or yellowish green with verdelite (green tourmaline). While these might be the most common shades of green, they are by no means the finest. Emerald green, bright leaf green and chrome green are the most sought-after colours and the hardest to find; consequently, their value is high. Although it is possible to find such colours in small sizes or to find stones that have inclusions or are that bit too dark or too pale, it is quite a challenge to find a clean, green tourmaline of over 5 carats. They simply don't appear that often.

Bright yellow tourmalines are not plentiful or easy to source. Often, yellow crystals have a green rind that gives the inner yellow core a greenish tinge, or the yellow is a golden peachy colour rather than the ideal sharp, citric yellow.

This beautifully cut tourmaline is a fine forest green colour.

This yellow tourmaline has a fresh citrus colour.

PARAIBA NEONS

In the 1980s the José de Batalha mine in the Brazilian state of Paraiba began producing a type of tourmaline that was like no other. It was to be the most important find of tourmalines in the 20th century. The colour range consisted of intense and vibrant greens, turquoise blues and lilacs, which became known as the neon tourmalines. The world went wild over them and their price shot up way beyond that of other tourmalines. There was speculation that some of these neons might be the result of a special heating process, but that has never been confirmed. Demand for the paraibas was huge and now that the original deposit is mined out there is only a small (and dwindling) supply left on the market, and consequently prices remain high.

The intense turquoise colour of this paraiba tourmaline cabochon makes it highly desirable despite inclusions.

BI- AND TRICOLOUR TOURMALINES

Many tourmalines consist of two, three or more colours. The best-known combination of colours is the watermelon tourmaline, in which the crystal has a pink centre and a green rim, or rind, so that it looks like a watermelon in cross-section. The variation of colour combinations is large and some crystals have a very definite colour contrast while others have just a tonal difference that creates a more subtle effect. These multicoloured tourmalines are cut specifically to show off the colour combination; cutters usually use a step-cut octagon or baguette cut. The better the colour contrast and cleaner the stone, the more expensive it becomes – a true watermelon will fetch a high price. These gemstones are extremely popular with buyers as each one is unique in the number of colours and shades it contains. The best pink and green watermelon crystals can be found in South Africa, East Africa and Brazil.

An unusual combination of deep blue and pink makes this tourmaline striking.

DRAVITE

Dravite is normally yellow-brown to orange-brown in colour; its colouring agent is magnesium and it often appears alongside yellow tourmaline in gem gravels. It has strong dichroism, showing two different colours when viewed from different angles. The colour of dravite is sometimes lightened using heat treatment.

The mirror cut of this cinnamon-coloured dravite gemstone gives it a metallic appearance.

SCHORL

Schorl, or black tourmaline, is rarely used as a gemstone except as bead material. It is in plentiful supply, with crystals measuring several feet (metres) in length. Black tourmaline was widely used in Victorian England to make mourning jewellery as it was much tougher and more enduring than jet.

Continued on page 64 ▶

from page 63

ACHROITE

Naturally occurring colourless varieties are rare, so light pink tourmalines are heated until they lose their colour.

TOURMALINATED QUARTZ

This stone belongs both in the section on crystalline quartz (see page 66) and in this section. Tourmalinated quartz occurs when black tourmaline needles form as an inclusion within clear quartz. If the quartz is crystal clear and free from cloudiness, the resulting appearance is abstract and rather dramatic, offering an interesting design opportunity for jewellery makers. It is not always easy to find clean examples with a good spread of black needles, so quality material has a fair value as a collector piece.

Black tourmaline needles are well defined within this quartz.

CAT'S-EYE TOURMALINE

Chatoyancy, or a cat's-eye effect, occurs from time to time in tourmaline, and is particularly strong in the pink and green colours. Tourmaline can have an almost fibrous habit when it contains a large quantity of needles. If the needles are ordered in a parallel manner, and the base of the stone is oriented parallel to the needles, the stone will take on a cat's-eye effect. Good examples fetch collector prices.

This chatoyant green tourmaline has excellent colour.

The blue tourmaline has a very fibrous nature, making it slightly dark with a white cat's-eye.

Treatments and imitations

• Tourmaline is commonly heat treated to lighten the darker shades, especially the blues and greens. Dark green stones from Namibia undergo a special heating process, which results in a brighter green colour that is close to emerald.

• Some tourmaline is irradiated to intensify the pink, red and purple shades, and also to turn white and pale pinks to a strong pinky red colour. The effects of irradiation can fade over time, so if you're buying dark pink to red tourmalines it is advisable to check which processes, if any, have been applied.

• Synthetic spinels are sometimes used to imitate tourmaline and, because of their high value, imitation paraibas are being produced. If you plan to spend a large sum of money on a neon paraiba, it is crucial that you have the stone tested to check that it is genuine.

• Pink and green tourmalines could be confused with green-yellow chrysoberyl, emerald, pink kunzite, pink topaz and morganite.

Pricing tourmaline

• The most desirable and expensive tourmalines are red-pink rubellite, blue indicolite, chrome green and the neon paraibas. Demand for the dwindling stock of paraibas in particular remains high, and as a result they are the most valuable of the tourmalines, fetching prices on a par with top-end sapphires and rubies. This looks unlikely to change.

• The value of the material is dependent on the quality of the colour; a large, crystal-clear blue-green indicolite tourmaline will fetch a considerable price while a darker navy blue stone will cost much less. Red rubellite decreases in value as the colour pales toward pink or the red becomes too dark.

• The yellow-brown to orange-brown of dravite is an inexpensive colour of tourmaline, and so represents good value for the money.

Working with tourmaline

• Tourmaline's indistinct cleavage and uneven, brittle fracture make the stone vulnerable to pressure; care needs to be taken during setting as there is a risk of the stone breaking. Some setters actually refuse to work with tourmaline because of the stone's fragility! As it is not the hardest of stones, it is important to incorporate some protection into the design of any ring setting.

• Tourmaline is one of the most difficult stones to match up into pairs as the colour range is extensive, especially with the greens, and the dichroism adds to the problem. It is more effective to cut a matching pair from one piece of rough than to try to hunt for a match to an existing stone. Cutting a pair will ensure that the stones can be oriented in the same direction and will match completely. Obviously this means that you will need a large piece of rough to accommodate two stones, which will have an impact on cost, but it will save wasted effort looking for a match or cutting a stone that will probably end up a different colour from the original.

• If tourmaline crystals are rubbed or heated they become electrically charged and as a result attract dust, fluff and dirt. Because of this, tourmaline jewellery needs to be cleaned more frequently than designs using other gemstones.

Showcase

The gold and green tourmaline ring was designed in the early 1970s. Its fluid lines and organic structure are reminiscemt of Art Nouveau jewellery designs of the early 1900s.

The two neckrings are set with navette-cut green tourmalines. The placement of the stones gives the illusion that they are precariously balanced on top of the main pendant.

8/iolite (cordierite or dichroite)

What most people don't realize is that top-quality iolite rivals the best tanzanite in both colour and saturation. If it were mixed with blue sapphire or tanzanite rough, the iolite would be difficult to distinguish. The most desirable, blue-violet colour is simply stunning.

The view through the table of a faceted iolite should provide an intense blue colour, while the side view should be light grey to colourless. The best blue colour is always shown down the length of the prismatic crystal.

Although it is rarely seen in jewellery stores, iolite is gradually gaining in popularity. It is one of very few blue gemstones available, and on the whole it is affordable. The name derives from the Greek word for "violet", and sometimes the terms *water sapphire* or *lynx sapphire* are used (normally by traders who are trying to talk the stone up).

Iolite is a transparent gemstone that can be found in dark violet-blue, light grey-blue, yellowish grey, green and brown. Most of the available iolite is a medium violet-blue; the intense violet-blue described above is not produced in large quantities. Iolite has a glassy lustre, and it is fairly durable and moderately brilliant. Although this is not a particularly lively stone, the fact that it is trichroic makes it an interesting one. It shows different colours when viewed along three different axes: pale greyish blue, yellowish to colourless and dark violet-blue.

Lower-grade iolite is often included and usually cut as cabochons. Dark fibrous inclusions are the most common, but small platy hematite and goethite inclusions also occur and create a reddish sheen or aventurescence. It is rare to find large pieces of iolite that are free of inclusions.

Treatments and imitations

No treatments have been found to successfully lighten the colour of iolite or remove the frequent inclusions.

SPECIFICATIONS

HARDNESS 7–7.5 Mohs
SPECIFIC GRAVITY 2.53–2.78
REFRACTIVE INDEX 1.522–1.578
CRYSTAL FORM Orthorhombic. Iolite appears as rhombic crystals (short prisms). It occurs in metamorphic rocks as well as in gneisses and schists. Gem-quality crystals are also found in alluvial deposits as small water-worn transparent pebbles.

SOURCES OF IOLITE

India, Madagascar, Myanmar (Burma), Sri Lanka, Tanzania, United States.

Pricing iolite

• Medium-grade iolite with a nice blue colour and good clarity is moderately priced, in plentiful supply and very good value. AA-grade iolite with the exceptional blue-violet colour is close to the cost of good-quality faceted tourmaline. When you compare the materials, you will understand why there is such a large price difference.

• There have been reports that the lapidaries of Idar-Oberstein in Germany are buying a great deal of high-grade iolite rough, apparently in readiness for an expected surge in the popularity and price of iolite.

Working with iolite

• The hardness of iolite makes it suitable for jewellery, but it does have a distinct cleavage in one direction and a conchoidal fracture. Bear this in mind when you are polishing and setting, as problems such as chipping can occasionally occur. Iolite is neither heat-sensitive nor particularly vulnerable to chemicals.

• Iolite is commonly faceted as a step cut because this enhances the colour. In the case of dark inky blue material, however, the stone is often slightly windowed or left shallow, to lighten the tone. The pleochroic properties of iolite require accurate orientation of the gemstone when it is being cut.

Showcase

In this Coffee Bean Choker, iolite was hand-carved in the shape of a coffee bean in order to bounce light through the iolite layers and get a good blue colour. The lack of large iolite rough meant that smaller pieces had to be glued together. The seams were then inlaid with silver dust. Finally, an emerald was set into the bean and the choker constructed with blued-steel chain mail.

9/quartz

Quartz is the biggest gemstone species of all, and one of the most widely used in modern jewellery making. This is an extremely versatile family of stones that includes a wide range of affordable coloured gems, with some remarkable inclusions.

Metallic-looking rutile needle inclusions have formed into an unusual star arrangement and the stone has been cut as a half-moon to display the effect fully.

This citrine crystal displays a hexagonal rod and hexagonal pyramidal termination.

This trigonal quartz crystal shows typical three-fold symmetry.

Inclusions in quartz can take many forms. This stone contains rutile needles, pyrite inclusions and iron staining.

The abundance and beauty of quartz has meant that it has been used as a gemstone since the dawn of history. Beads of quartz have been found in caves in Israel that were occupied between 5,000 and 6,000 years ago, and quartz of different types has been honoured and worshipped through the ages and worn as an amulet to protect against bad luck and poor health.

This section deals with the crystalline variety of quartz, which is found as a single crystal, rather than with cryptocrystalline quartz, which is a giant grouping that appears as a solid mass. Please see "Chalcedony and agate" on page 74 for cryptocrystalline quartz.

The colour range of crystalline quartz is wide, and colour zoning is a common feature that identifies the material. Quartz can vary from transparent to opaque and, although it is not hugely brilliant, it is an attractive stone. It can produce optical effects, such as stars and cat's-eyes.

Typical inclusions of crystalline quartz are small crystals, needles, delicate veils and internal cracks that give a rainbow effect. Quartz can often include mica crumbs and hematite flakes that flash when the stone is moved in the light; mica produces a silvery flash while hematite causes a red flash.

SPECIFICATIONS

HARDNESS 7 Mohs
SPECIFIC GRAVITY 2.65
REFRACTIVE INDEX 1.544–1.553
CRYSTAL FORM Crystalline quartz appears as single crystals in a trigonal system; the crystal habit is hexagonal rods with hexagonal pyramidal ends. The faces of the crystals often have horizontal markings.

SOURCES OF CRYSTALLINE QUARTZ

ROCK CRYSTAL, CITRINE AND SMOKY QUARTZ Africa, Australia, Brazil, Japan, Myanmar (formerly Burma), Spain.
AMETHYST The Russian Urals produce some of the best amethyst. Also found in Namibia and Zambia.
ROSE QUARTZ Africa, Brazil, India, Madagascar.
QUARTZ CAT'S-EYE Sri Lanka.
TIGER'S-EYE AND HAWK'S-EYE The best material comes from South Africa and Namibia.
DUMORTIERITE QUARTZ Namibia and Madagascar

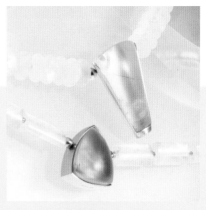

Showcase

The mirror-cut rock crystal in this pendant features Iodolite inclusions within its clean lines. The polished setting reflects light back through the stone; the lack of colour contributes to the very modern design.

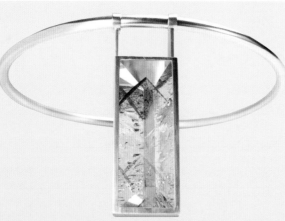

Frosted rock crystal cabochons have been set in rich yellow gold and suspended on necklaces of rock crystal beads. Over time, the rock crystal will lose its frosted appearance and become discoloured from the oils and dirt of the skin. It is possible, however, to retexture the stones.

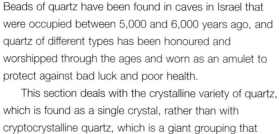

Types of quartz

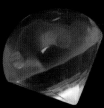

COLOURLESS QUARTZ (ROCK CRYSTAL)

High-quality rock crystal looks like a transparent mass of ice. An abundant gemstone, it was frequently faceted as beads and stones in antique jewellery. It is also used a great deal in the manufacture of lamps and lenses.

Although jewellery makers and buyers usually want gemstones that are free of inclusions and "clean", quartz often possesses inclusions that are decorative and can be used in the cutting and design of the stone. Sometimes the inclusions are very prominent and reflected in the stone's name, for instance tourmalinated quartz or rutilated quartz. Each stone is unique in its inclusions, offering great design opportunities.

Rock crystal is a brittle, difficult material to work with, so dandelion-cut stones like this one are a real challenge.

SMOKY QUARTZ

Unfortunately, smoky quartz is rather ignored at times and the full potential of the material is not always appreciated. It can appear in a range of soft, subtle colours including gentle yellowish brown, rich chocolate, dark charcoal-brown and nearly black. The stone is sometimes named after the Cairngorm and Morion mining areas in Scotland, which produce smoky quartz. It also often gets given the misnomer smoky topaz. Natural smoky quartz is in plentiful supply and is available in large sizes, making it extremely economical to use. When set in white metal, smoky quartz can be very chic in its simplicity.

This yellowish brown material displays a very clear six-ray star, caused by three sets of fibres.

TOURMALINATED QUARTZ

In tourmalinated quartz, black or green tourmaline needles pierce the clear quartz and create a striking and attractive pattern.

RUTILATED QUARTZ

This quartz contains yellowish brown or gold-coloured needles that sometimes sweep hairlike through the stone, which gave rise to the old name of Venus-hair stone. The inclusions in tourmalinated and rutilated quartz look best when the quartz is completely clear without any "foggy" veils.

The golden rutile needles have aligned to create a strong cat's-eye.

STRAWBERRY QUARTZ (HEMATITE QUARTZ)

Needles or particles of hematite often appear in clear quartz as red fibres. This type of material is sometimes called strawberry quartz.

This piece displays red hematite particles.

AMETHYST

Amethyst has been – and still is – one of the most popular crystalline quartzes, and a great deal of 19th- and 20th-century jewellery contains the stone. Russian material has always been considered the best, because it develops a reddish colour in artificial light. However, amethyst can be found in all shades of purple, from light lavender (or rose) amethyst to the intense Siberian amethyst that displays highlights of magenta when faceted. The name Siberian is used for any rich purple material, wherever it comes from. A deep uniform purple colour is more expensive than the pale lavenders. However, if the colour is too deep then the material can appear almost black and that is undesirable.

It is possible to find ametrine crystals, which are part amethyst and part citrine and often contain many inclusions where the colours change. Aside from colour zoning, amethyst can contain a number of inclusions, in particular parallel liquid-filled canals that look like serrated zebra stripes when seen through a loupe. Amethyst is also slightly dichroic, meaning that its colour has either a bluish tone or a reddish tinge when viewed from different angles.

The slight colour zoning in this amethyst makes it paler at the top point.

YELLOW QUARTZ (CITRINE)

Like smoky quartz, citrine often gets called the misleading name of topaz or quartz topaz. Not only is citrine much less expensive than topaz, it is in plentiful supply and, unlike precious topaz, is available in large sizes. Citrine ranges in colour from pastel lemon yellow to deep reddish brown and amber. The most common natural colour is golden and tends to be quite pale. However, naturally dark citrines do occur; Palmeira citrine has a bright orange-amber colour and Madeira citrine a beautiful deep brandy colour. The names relate to the source of the material. A relatively small amount of darker citrine is produced, making it quite scarce and much more valuable than the other colours of citrine. The darker the colour, the more expensive the material becomes. A sharp lemon-lime citrine is available, achieved by heat treating pale amethyst or smoky quartz.

Palmeira citrine has a beautiful tawny colour. Beads of this size (4 mm in diameter) are relatively inexpensive, unlike larger sizes.

The pale colour of this large golden citrine is natural. Colour zoning has been hidden by the lapidary.

The fresh, treated colour of lemon citrine is very distinct. Rough material is available in large sizes; this stone is 16.15 ct.

Continued on page 69 ▶

Treatments and imitations

• Irregularly colored or very pale amethyst is heated to 750–930°F (400–500°C), at which point it changes to a brownish yellow or brownish red colour – a dark citrine. (If the amethyst is heated above 1067°F/575°C it will lose its colour completely.) The majority of dark citrine is actually heated amethyst and it can resemble quality Brazilian topaz. Some of this material is marketed under the name topaz quartz. Deep brown to red quartz is sold as Madeira or Spanish topaz. Amethyst and smoky quartz are also heat treated to create a lemon-lime citrine. Some heated amethyst becomes green and is sold as prasiolite. Tiger's-eye quartz is heated to produce a red tiger's-eye.

• It is difficult to detect traces of heat treatment in burned citrines, and the depth and tone of colours produced tend to vary, making them hard to judge. Normally the price will tell you if you have natural material; heat-treated citrine is cheaper. Some heated amethyst does not have a stable colour and, after a couple of years of exposure to the sun, its colour will change and fade.

• Quartz is also coloured with different materials to improve its existing colour or to create imitations of natural stones. Quartz crystals are sometimes immersed in a green plastic dye to imitate emerald; they are then introduced into parcels of rough emerald to serve as the "leading stone". The leading stone is considered to be the most valuable or desirable stone in the parcel and determines the parcel price. Mixed with other stones, coloured quartz is difficult to spot. Often the pointed termination of the quartz crystal is broken off to leave just the hexagonal crystal body, which then looks similar to an emerald crystal. If quartz has been treated in this manner, you would be able to scratch the coating with a hard metallic point and peel off the colour.

• Quartz is also coloured red to look like ruby and then cut as cabochons in order to make reading the refractive index difficult. Quartz stones are also sometimes boiled with red-dyed oil, to resemble rubies. These are very difficult to spot, but if they are rubbed with acetone or alcohol some of the red dye will come off.

• Aventurine is often sold as green jade to unsuspecting tourists in the Far East. Good glass imitations of aventurine quartz are on the market.

• It was discovered that the colour of smoky quartz was influenced by the natural radiation underground. As a result, colourless quartz is now commonly irradiated to turn it a mediocre grayish brown.

Pricing quartz

On the whole, crystalline quartz is inexpensive. It has always been an affordable stone, accessible to many people who are unable to purchase more valuable gemstones. Siberian amethyst with an intense, even colour is more valuable, as is clear peachy pink rose quartz. Madeira and Palmeira citrines are the most valuable types of crystalline quartz, as they are naturally produced and mined in limited quantities.

Working with quartz

• Quartz is a versatile, wearable gem that is available in plentiful supply, in large sizes. It is fairly brilliant and moderately hard; however, care needs to be taken during setting to avoid damaging the stone. It does not have a great lifespan; if you look at antique quartz jewellery you will see a considerable wearing of facet edges and lots of scratches. Rose quartz's many internal fractures make the stone quite brittle, so included rose quartz is best avoided as it may break when being set or worn. The softness of quartz makes it suitable for engraving and carving.

• Care needs to be taken when soldering and polishing as sometimes heat can fade the material. It is also advisable to avoid wearing jewellery in intense sunlight, as this can also make the colour fade.

Showcase

Dramatic necklaces make use of rutilated quartz in a strong, angular design.

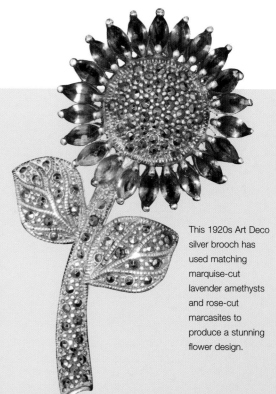

This 1920s Art Deco silver brooch has used matching marquise-cut lavender amethysts and rose-cut marcasites to produce a stunning flower design.

◀ Continued from page 67

The faceted rose quartz beads are of a better than usual grade.

ROSE QUARTZ

Rose quartz can be a beautiful gemstone with colours ranging from pale pink to a deep peachy pink colour. Most rose quartz is quite included or cloudy and has a translucent appearance. Clear "gemmy" material is limited and can be more expensive, especially the deeper colours. The lower-grade material is brittle and can be full of cracks and flaws, so be careful when buying cheaper material as cracks may open up when it is being set or worn. Despite its brittleness, a great deal of rose quartz is used in carving and beads. It is possible to find star rose quartzes, which exhibit asterism due to rutile inclusions. If the colour and star are good, such stones have a reasonable value.

Clear, gem-quality rose quartz is hard to find, and the colour tends to be slightly paler than included material.

BLUE QUARTZ

There are two blue quartzes available to jewellery makers. Quartz containing blue asbestos, called crocidolite, occurs naturally, but has quite a somber tone. The other blue quartz is naturally impregnated or stained with chrysocolla. It has the hardness of quartz (as opposed to the softness of chrysocolla), with a brilliant blue-green translucent colour. The latter stone is very beautiful and would be extremely popular if it were easier to obtain. It is also quite expensive.

PRASIOLITE

Prasiolite is a pale green transparent to translucent variety of quartz that is achieved by heating amethyst or citrine. Prasiolite can only be produced by heating material from certain locations. Initially it all came from mines in Brazil but other sources have since been found, bringing a greater quantity into the marketplace. Prasiolite is faceted, cut as cabochons and made into beads. It could be confused with yellow or green precious beryl.

AVENTURINE

This stone has a lovely medium to dark green colour, and is semitranslucent with tiny sparkling flecks of green fuchsite mica. It also occurs in a metallic orange-brown colour with brassy hematite inclusions. Aventurine is an affordable stone and makes attractive cabochons and beads.

Aventurine quartz is beautiful when it has this intense blue-green colour.

AMETHYST QUARTZ

This is an opaque variety of amethyst with marked colour zoning in white and purple. The material is a rougher, more compact form of amethyst and is layered with milky quartz. It is highly decorative and used for beads and cabochons.

MILKY QUARTZ

Milky quartz has a cloudy, whitish colour and can be translucent to transparent. The milky colour is caused by inclusions of gas and liquid bubbles, and the degree of milkiness depends on the number and size of the inclusions. Commercially, milky quartz has little value, so is used for cheap jewellery. When polished it can look a little like moonstone.

DUMORTIERITE QUARTZ

This is quite a rare stone with a beautiful violet-blue to denim blue colour. Dumortierite quartz sometimes has a slightly pitted surface when polished as a cabochon. It is not available in large quantities.

This cabochon weighs nearly 50 ct; it is quite unusual to find dumortierite quartz in this size and with this quality of colour.

QUARTZ CAT'S-EYE

Quartz cat's-eyes are unusual. They can be found in green to yellowish green, grey-green, yellow-brown and deep grey, and have a sharp white cat's-eye streak down the centre of the stone. This streak is a result of the presence of parallel wavy fibrelike inclusions of asbestos. In order to get a cat's-eye, the stone has to be cut so that the fibres are parallel to the cabochon base. It has a soft, silky lustre and is very good value compared to chrysoberyl cat's-eyes.

Quartz cat's-eyes can be sensitive to some acids, so need to be treated with care and protected from household chemicals.

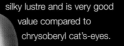

The navette shape here maximizes the tiger's-eye visual properties because the ridge aligns with the stripe.

TIGER'S-EYE AND HAWK'S-EYE

Tiger's-eye comes in brownish yellow, golden yellow, reddish brown and greenish to brown colours. The yellow-brown tiger's-eye stripes are a result of iron oxide staining. Hawk's-eye is similar in appearance, but with a much darker bluish to black colour. These stones have a striking optical effect that results from the replacement by quartz of closely packed blue asbestos fibres, the fibrous quartz structure making the surface appear to shimmer when a stone is rolled from side to side. The material is usually cut quite flat, into slabs or plates, in order to show off the optical effect. It is inexpensive.

The silky lustre and chatoyant stripes evident here occur because of the shape of the crocidolite fibres.

10/zircon

It is hard to understand why zircon is not more popular with jewellery makers. Its hardness and fracture are no worse than in gemstones such as garnet or tourmaline and it has numerous qualities in its favour: an adamantine lustre, strong double refraction, attractive colours and affordability.

These green low zircon crystals have a typically stubby shape.

Zircon is a brilliant transparent stone that comes in a number of natural colours: yellow, brown, orange, violet, green, blue and red. The most common are grey-brown to red-brown, while the most popular is golden brown. Colourless zircon is quite rare and when cut as a gemstone could easily be confused with diamond, because of its strong brilliance and fire. Like diamond, zircon has an adamantine lustre.

Some confusion exists between zircon and cubic zirconia; jewellery makers and buyers may think that zircon is not natural, that it is a synthetic stone or that zircon and cubic zirconia are the same stone. This mix-up is probably due to the similarity in names, the lack of awareness of zircon and the fact that some of the colours of treated zircon (the vivid blues and yellows) resemble the colours of cubic zirconia.

SPECIFICATIONS

HARDNESS 6.5–7.5 Mohs

SPECIFIC GRAVITY 3.93–4.73

REFRACTIVE INDEX 1.81–2.024

CRYSTAL FORM Tetragonal. The crystals are stubby four-sided prisms with pyramidal ends. Sometimes they appear as water-worn stream pebbles in alluvial deposits. Zircon has a lustre that ranges from resinous to adamantine, depending on the type of material.

SOURCES OF ZIRCON

HIGH ZIRCON Cambodia, Thailand, Vietnam.

LOW ZIRCON Sri Lanka. Also found in Australia, Brazil, Cambodia, France, Madagascar, Mozambique, Nigeria, Russia, South Africa, Tanzania.

These crystals are good examples of the zircon crystal's form: prism shape and pyramid ends.

Showcase

These pretty gold earrings use bright blue treated zircons. The intense colour of the gems is offset by the rich colour of the metal, resulting in an eye-catching design.

Types of zircon

Zircon contains traces of uranium and thorium, both of which are radioactive, and as a result can differ in hardness, specific gravity, refractive index and colour. There are two distinct types of zircon. High zircon is yellow-brown and the harder, more desirable stone. Low (decayed) zircon is greenish yellow to greenish brown, and is softer as a result of radioactive deterioration.

Zircon has medium to distinct differences in colour when observed from different directions. The strength of this dichroism depends on the type of zircon and the intensity of colour; high zircon with a dark colour will produce the strongest dichroistic effect. Another feature of zircon is its uneven colour distribution, which can be useful in identifying the stone.

The colour of these two brown zircons is sometimes called hyacinth, an old term. The material is from Russia and is untreated.

This gemstone is a diamond and shows the similarity between brown zircon and cognac or brown diamonds. The liveliness and brilliance of zircon gives it the appearance of diamond, but zircon is much more fragile than diamond.

Treated blue zircon has a very distinct turquoise-blue colour that is not easily confused with other stones. Its brilliance, fire and intensity set it apart from stones such as topaz or aquamarine.

Treatments and imitations

• Zircon has been heat treated for hundreds of years. This is an accepted practice that can change the colour of zircon to red, blue, orange or green, but some colours are not stable and will revert back or fade. Because of the scarcity of natural colourless zircon, reddish brown stones are heated to make them colourless; with prolonged exposure to sunlight or UV radiation, however, they can become dark brown again. Brown material can also be heated to a vibrant blue colour, and if the blue colour fades the stone can be reheated to regain its colour. Alternatively, reheating blue stones in the presence of oxygen will turn them golden yellow.

• Zircon is sometimes imitated with colourless glass and synthetic spinel. Green and yellow varieties of zircon could be confused with sapphire, demantoid garnet, chrysoberyl, hessonite garnet, topaz or tourmaline. Zircon has been used in place of diamonds in some antique jewellery. Look at the stones through a loupe to spot the scratches and scuffs on the facet surfaces and chips on the facet edges; this will distinguish them from diamonds.

Working with zircon

• Unfortunately, heat treatment affects the properties of zircon, making a stone more susceptible to wear and tear. A heat-treated gemstone will not only wear down more quickly over time, but also become more fragile at the junctions of the faceted surfaces.

• Zircon has a conchoidal fracture, which makes it a naturally brittle material. Despite being moderately hard, it will chip if knocked, so care needs to be taken during setting and polishing. Zircon is better used for pendants and earrings; if you are contemplating using it as a ring stone try to use an unheated stone and design a protective setting.

• Zircon possesses strong double refraction, which means that you will see a doubling of the back facets when you look into the stone through the table. The zircon cut was designed to show off this special property. This cut is a development of the brilliant cut that maximizes the light entering and leaving the gemstone, to display the full dramatic impact of double refraction.

11/garnet

Garnet is a far more exciting and versatile stone than people may think. Although the word *garnet* usually conjures up the low-priced dark red stone that is available in abundance, recent discoveries mean that garnet now comes in almost every colour and can cost nearly as much as a sapphire.

Spessartite garnet crystals displaying the symmetry of the cubic system.

We have a long association with this gemstone: beads of garnet turn up in prehistoric graves and red carbuncles (cabochons) have been appearing in jewellery for the last 500 years. Sadly, this has meant that people now think the stone somewhat old-fashioned and dull, leaving the full potential of garnet unrealized. It is to be hoped that the gemstone's durability, versatility, colour palette and price range will see it win back favour among jewellery makers and buyers in the not-too-distant future.

SPECIFICATIONS

HARDNESS 6.5–7.5 Mohs
SPECIFIC GRAVITY 3.49–4.16
REFRACTIVE INDEX 1.69–1.89
CRYSTAL FORM Garnet is a group of structurally and chemically related mineral species that crystallize in the cubic system. This system has the highest symmetry, and crystals can take the form of a cube, octahedron or pentagonal dodecahedron; spherical crystals also exist. Garnet has a vitreous, glasslike lustre. It is possible to find star garnets, which have a red/purple colour with faint four- or six-rayed stars that are much fainter than those on a star ruby or sapphire.

SOURCES OF GARNET

Argentina, Brazil, Germany, India, Kenya, Madagascar, Mali, Namibia, Pakistan, Russia, Scandinavia, South Africa, Sri Lanka, Switzerland, Tanzania.

Treatments and imitations

• It is possible to confuse pyrope with ruby and spinel, and imitations are made from red glass. Almandite can also be confused with rubies, especially Thai rubies, as the optical properties and specific gravities are similar. Tsavorite can be confused with emerald and chrome tourmaline.
• Convincing synthetic colour-change garnets were produced in the early 20th century, and can be found in some antique jewelry.

Pricing garnet

• Garnet has a high specific gravity, which gives it a heavy weight. This makes its cost slightly higher than for other gemstones of the same size and carat price.
• There is low public awareness of the tsavorite, demantoid, colour-change and mandarin garnets. Unlike pyrope and almandite garnet, they are extremely valuable and can be used for high-quality jewellery. They are also very collectible for enthusiasts.
• Mid-priced in the garnet group are rhodolite and spessartite garnets. Their colours are really intense and they are usually valued higher than pyrope and hessonite garnets.

Working with garnet

• Garnet is a hard wearing and durable gemstone, suitable for most types of jewellery. However, because it has no cleavage and an uneven fracture, it can be slightly brittle. When setting faceted stones, extra care must be taken to avoid chipping the girdle.
• Tsavorite and demantoid garnets can be a viable alternative to emerald, as they have better clarity and are more durable. They also have more brilliance and fire than an emerald and are less expensive.
• Pyrope and almandite garnets are still used for antique jewellery restoration, especially that of Victorian jewellery. It is also possible to find rose-cut garnets in antique jewellery; paler stones were often cut like this and then backed with coloured foil to improve and intensify the colour.
• The lustre (degree of surface polish) of garnets can range from adamantine (like diamond) to vitreous (like glass) to resinous (like amber). Demantoid garnet has an adamantine lustre, pyrope has a vitreous lustre and hessonite has a resinous lustre.

Showcase

This beautiful, tactile necklace is gold covered in drusylike uvarovite garnet crystals. Textured gold provides contrast.

This silver ring uses tsavorite garnet in three different shades. The placement of the claw-set gemstones creates a fluid and colourful design.

Types of garnet

PYROPE

Pyrope has a blood red colour with few inclusions. It was very popular in Bohemian jewellery during the 18th and 19th centuries. The best stones have a fiery red colour that does not darken too much once set. High-quality pyrope garnets have been mined in large quantities from the diamond pipes of the Kimberley and De Beers mines in South Africa.

ALMANDITE

This ranges in colour from deep red to violet-red or even black. Cabochons are often hollowed out on the underside to let more light filter through the stone. Almandite can be brittle and may chip when faceted. Occasional asterism (starlike effect) occurs. It is usually included or semiopaque and the inclusions take the form of black mineral clusters, rounded crystals and rutile needles.

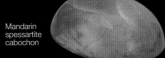

Do not confuse pyrope garnet with ruby or spinel.

RHODOLITE

Rhodolite has a beautiful bright violet-red colour with few inclusions. Its composition is between that of pyrope and almandite garnets but it is viewed as superior to both, as its colour is brighter than pyrope and it has fewer inclusions than almandite. High-quality material is found in Sri Lanka, Tanzania and Kenya.

Rhodolite stone

SPESSARTITE

Spessartite has a rich orange-red colour and feather- or lacelike inclusions, which are actually clouds of minute drops. It has a high lustre, but "clean" gem-quality material is rarely found. Spessartite garnet can easily be confused with hessonite garnet, but differences between the inclusions can be seen on close examination.

Spessartite cabochon

SPESSARTITE – MANDARIN

This variety of garnet, a pure form of spessartite garnet from Namibia, has the most fantastic bright orange colour. Gem-quality mandarin garnet is very rare and valuable.

Mandarin spessartite cabochon

HYDROGROSSULAR GARNET

Hydrogrossular garnet has a distinctive gooseberry-green colour. Translucent to opaque, it is usually made into cabochons or beads. Pink hydrogrossular garnet can also be found. Often there are black inclusions of magnetite, which give a speckled appearance. In South Africa the stone is called Transvaal jade or garnet jade, because it can resemble green jade.

Hydrogrossular garnet samples

GROSSULAR GARNET – HESSONITE

As a result of its brown-orange to brown-yellow colour, hessonite garnet is called cinnamon stone in Africa. The stone has distinctive swirling molasseslike inclusions, most of which are small crystals of apatite. The ancient Greeks and Romans frequently used hessonite in their jewellery, making faceted stones, cameos and cabochons.

A grade-faceted hessonite

GROSSULAR GARNET – TSAVORITE

This is the transparent lime-green to emerald-green variety of grossular garnet. Tsavorite was first mined in Kenya in 1968 and is also found in Tanzania. It is nearly always faceted as a gemstone, but the emerald-green crystals only produce small stones of 2 carats and under. As a result, the emerald-green colour is more expensive than lime-green. Tsavorite has a high lustre and inclusions in the form of golden-yellow needles, corrosion tubes and black graphite flakes.

Faceted tsavorite grossular garnets

GROSSULAR GARNET – MALAY

Gem-quality grossular garnet has been found in Mali relatively recently. The colours are beautiful, ranging from golden brown to yellow-apricot to peach-pink and sometimes green. It is also called Mali garnet.

DEMANTOID

This is the bright green variety of the andradite group of garnets. It is very rare and there are few stones greater than 1 carat in weight. The traditional source is the Ural mountains in Russia. Demantoid garnet has higher light dispersion and brilliance than a diamond, which results in lively fire (colour flashes). However, the facet edges can become worn down as the stone is only 6.5 Mohs hardness. Demantoid garnet has characteristic "horsetail" inclusions, which are yellow-brown hairlike pieces of asbestos. This is the most valuable type of garnet.

Demantoid garnets

COLOUR-CHANGE GARNET

These garnets can appear green-blue in daylight (fluorescent light) and magenta-red in incandescent (artificial) light. Others change from red-purple to yellow-red. The stones are a mix of pyrope and spessartite garnets, and are very rare.

12/chalcedony and agate

This polished slice captures the beauty of agate. The colouration would make an unusual and decorative brooch or pendant.

Beautiful in its simplicity, the luminous pure colour of chalcedony makes it a truly versatile stone to work with. Agate, on the other hand, provides an infinite number of patterns and textures that mesmerize, fascinate and are totally unique.

Chalcedony is the name given to a group of compact microcrystalline (or cryptocrystalline) quartzes in which the crystals are so tiny that they appear as a solid mass. The quartzes have fibrous and granular varieties; the fibrous type is the most common and it appears as solid-coloured stones (such as chalcedony) or has banding or dendritic inclusions (as do the agates).

Chalcedony and agate are highly regarded stones, worn in many cultures as protection from the "evil eye". They have also been used for many years as ornamental gems by makers of jewellery, such as the Art Nouveau and Arts and Crafts designers who employed these colourful cabochons as an antidote to the heavy diamond-set jewellery of the Victorians. Working with chalcedony and agate requires great skill; the German lapidaries of Idar-Oberstein excel at it and create true art forms in stone.

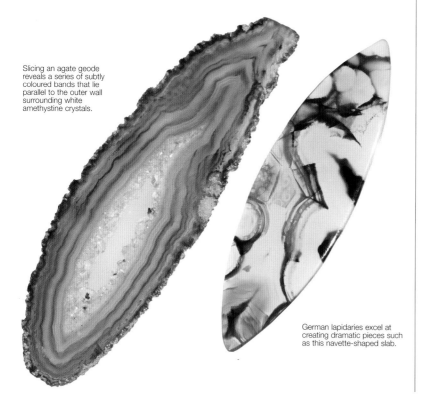

Slicing an agate geode reveals a series of subtly coloured bands that lie parallel to the outer wall surrounding white amethystine crystals.

German lapidaries excel at creating dramatic pieces such as this navette-shaped slab.

SPECIFICATIONS

HARDNESS 6.5–7 Mohs
SPECIFIC GRAVITY 2.58–2.64
REFRACTIVE INDEX 1.53–1.54
CRYSTAL FORM Trigonal – mainly fibrous aggregates with a porous nature. Chalcedony and agate both have a waxy, dull lustre.

SOURCES OF CHALCEDONY

CHALCEDONY The best material comes from Brazil and Uruguay. Also found in South Africa, Indonesia and Turkey.
CARNELIAN The primary source is India, where it is placed in the sun to change the brown tints to red. Brazil and Uruguay also produce good material.
CHRYSOPRASE The primary source is Australia, but also found in Brazil, India, Madagascar, the Russian Urals, South Africa, Tanzania, and the United States (California).
SARD Found worldwide.
ONYX Found worldwide.
BLOODSTONE The primary source is India, but also found in Australia, Brazil, China and the United States.
JASPER Red jasper comes from India and Venezuela; orbicular jasper comes from California; striped jasper comes from France, Germany and Russia.

SOURCES OF AGATE

AGATE The famous agate mines at Idar-Oberstein in Germany are now exhausted, but there are huge deposits in Brazil and Uruguay. Also found in Egypt, Italy, Madagascar, Mexico and Scotland.
MOSS AGATE China, India, United States.
DENDRITIC AGATE Brazil, India, United States.
FIRE AGATE Mexico, United States (Arizona).
FOSSILIZED WOOD Africa, Argentina, Canada, United States (Arizona).

Types of chalcedony

Chalcedony often occurs as translucent greyish to honey-yellow material. It is quite porous, so can be dyed and stained. Natural chalcedony should have even colour with no banding.

BLUE CHALCEDONY

This can be a really beautiful stone, offering floral tones ranging from delicate lilac to periwinkle blue to smoky lavender. The best material is translucent; lower-grade chalcedony can have some clouds. The enormous increase in the popularity of blue chalcedony over the last few years has pushed up its prices and top-quality intense blue material can be moderately expensive.

This blue chalcedony has a beautiful intense colour and is free of clouds, so is very desirable.

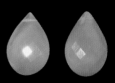

Lilac-coloured chalcedony

Banded blue chalcedony is often called blue lace agate. It is cut into cabochons and beads.

CARNELIAN

Carnelian (also called cornelian) has been a popular stone for many years, its warm tones attracting jewellery buyers and makers alike. The colours range from a pure, intense red-orange to softer brownish oranges and reds. High-quality material is semitransparent with an intense colour that seems to glow. The colour of carnelian can be enhanced by heating and dyeing; sometimes the stones are actually agates that have been dyed or heated. Natural carnelian should have a cloudy distribution of colour, without any faint banding or colour zoning. Carnelian has a long history and can be found in antique jewellery as carved or engraved cameos. Many Muslims revere the stone as it is said that the Prophet Muhammad wore it in a ring. Except for the best red-orange material, it is relatively inexpensive.

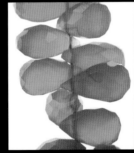

Good carnelian possesses an intense fiery glow that is a result of the colouring agent iron.

CHRYSOPRASE

The best chrysoprase should have an intense apple-green colour and be translucent with no clouds. However, chrysoprase often varies in colour depending on its nickel content and can be pale green, emerald green or even dark green. The stone's translucency will also vary and at times it can appear almost opaque. Colour tends to be uniform and evenly spread without any zoning or banding. Inclusions in the form of black or brown speckled deposits can occur and give a jadelike appearance. Some deposits produce chrysoprase that fades in sunlight, but the better Australian material maintains its intensity of colour. Be careful when buying chrysoprase as it is often dyed to improve or enhance its colour. Dyed chrysoprase has lower value.

This is an ideal material for jewellery makers. It has been used for centuries as a decorative stone because it is attractive, durable and readily available. The popularity of the intensely coloured chrysoprase has made it more expensive, but the lower-grade colours are moderately priced.

The pure apple-green colour of chrysoprase is unmistakable. Its colour is derived from the presence of nickel.

SARD AND SARDONYX

Sard is reddish brown to orange in colour. Sardonyx is banded sard, with apricot and brown stripes. This material is often carved for cameos and is excellent for inlay work.

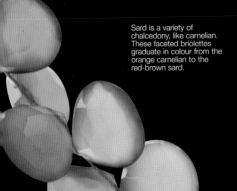

Sard is a variety of chalcedony, like carnelian. These faceted briolettes graduate in colour from the orange carnelian to the red-brown sard.

ONYX

In its natural state, onyx has straight bands of white and earthy brown colours – it is used a great deal in cameo and carving work. Black onyx is not onyx but dyed black agate or chalcedony; it does not exist naturally. Agate is sometimes soaked in a sugar solution and then heated in sulphuric acid to carbonize the sugar particles, which turns it black. Dyed black onyx has been used in jewellery for many years and was very popular with designers of the Art Deco period; they created geometric designs using slabs of black onyx set with marcasites.

Art Deco jewelry designers regularly used black onyx in their monochrome designs, cutting slabs and setting them with white diamonds or paste.

Continued on page 77 ▶

Treatments and imitations

• Few imitations of agate exist. There have been attempts at reproducing the landscape "scenes" of dendritic agate using silver nitrate. Moss agate doublets have also been manufactured.

• Buyers need to exercise caution when purchasing chalcedony and agate because of the amount of dyeing that goes on. Agate has been dyed since the 1820s at Idar-Oberstein, the centre for cutting and polishing agate. The dyeing process requires the use of special inorganic pigments, because organic colours fade in sunlight and are generally less intense. It is a complex procedure because the absorption of the dye depends on the degree of porosity of the different layers in the agate.

• The colours of many dyed agates are so subtle that they are not obvious to the naked eye, so don't assume a piece is natural just because there are no bright blues or greens. Although agate dyeing is seen as routine in the gemstone trade, the process should be disclosed to buyers. Natural-colour agates are more expensive, while low-grade, cheaper material is normally used for dyeing.

• One indicator of dyed material is that agates kept in a plastic bag or plastic box will "sweat" in warm weather, leaving visible deposits or traces of the dye.

Pricing chalcedony and agate

Although the supply is plentiful, it would be wrong to think that chalcedony and agate are commonplace and inexpensive. Good-quality chrysoprase can sell for high prices and certain varieties of agate with special "scenes" (markings) are extremely valuable.

Working with chalcedony and agate

• The colour of chrysoprase can fade when heated, so care needs to be taken during soldering and polishing. Colour can sometimes be restored by keeping the stones or rough material in damp conditions.

• On the whole, agate and chalcedony are tough materials and resistant to chemicals. However, certain types of agate need to be treated with more care than others and should be protected from knocks. Jasper can separate along the layers within the stone, so banded or patterned material should be handled gently during cutting, polishing and setting.

• The inclusions of dendritic agate lie at different depths within the stone, which is ground to bring them closer to the surface. As a result the stone can have an uneven surface form and some areas will be thinner than others. It is a good idea to check for any weak points before beginning to work with the stone.

Showcase

Translucent blue chalcedony briolettes have been wired with silver to create elegant drop earrings. The spiraling wire adds texture and interest to the design.

Hand-carved blue chalcedony has been set in silver with five white diamonds and a chalcedony cabochon. The pendant is strung along with blue chalcedony beads.

The inventive neckring at left contains a stone of two halves: chalcedony and drusy.

◀ Continued from page 75

BLOODSTONE (HELIOTROPE)

Bloodstone is an opaque dark green colour, with specks of red jasper. It is more attractive when the green is not so dark that it appears black and when the red flecks show up well. The material is readily available and inexpensive. Traditionally, it has been used for men's rings.

JASPER

Jasper is a granular, opaque variety of chalcedony. It is fine-grained and often strongly marked with orbicular or striped patterns. The more popular jasper is opaque red (coloured by iron oxide), and yellow, green and brown colours also exist. Jasper has a striking range of patterns that are quite modern in appearance and offer numerous creative opportunities for young jewellery makers.

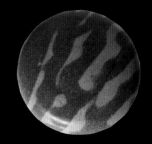

Jasper rarely has a uniform colour. This cabochon is made of what is sometimes called zebra jasper or print jasper.

Types of Agate

Agates occur as nodular masses that, when spilt open, reveal a fascinating variety of colours and patterns.

BANDED AGATES

Banded agates have distinct colour banding in rounded layers of different thicknesses and often contain white quartz crystals. Both features distinguish the stones from chalcedony. The band colours depend on the impurities present, and, being porous, the material is frequently stained and dyed.

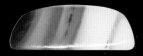

This banded agate is cut as a deep cabochon so the colours and pattern show from the sides and top.

DENDRITIC AGATE (LANDSCAPE AGATE)

This is wonderful material: the translucent, pure white agate contains amazing "scenes" of black or dark brown dendritic (treelike) inclusions, caused by iron oxides and hydroxides. The black dendrites might look realistically organic, but in fact they have a similar structure to the ice crystals that build up into patterns on a glass surface. Dendritic agate is usually cut as slices and polished to be made into pendants and brooches. The more attractive and detailed the scene is, the more it costs.

Here, the milky chalcedony frames the dendritic tree perfectly.

MOSS AGATE

Moss agate gets its name from the black or brown manganese or green chloride mosslike inclusions that lie within the translucent, milky agate. The material is usually sliced quite thin to show off the mossy patterns.

The large moss agate is set with Madeira citrine and a citrine crystal in reticulated silver and hung on carnelian beads.

FIRE AGATE

This is a wonderfully eccentric stone, in which iridescent "oily" bubbles float across a rich brown body colour. The firework colours are caused by the diffraction of light through layers of iron oxide within the quartz. Careful cutting brings out the iridescent colour play and the face of the stone is often irregular where the cutter has ground away material to bring layers of colour closer to the surface.

The rich body colour in this fire agate is slightly translucent and the layered structure produces lively iridescence.

FOSSILIZED (AGATIZED) WOOD

Petrified wood occurs when sections of a buried tree transform into a mineral after centuries of immersion under extreme pressure. The wood does not actually turn into stone; instead, the shape and structural elements of the wood are preserved as the organic substances decompose and are replaced by mineral substances. The colours of fossilized wood tend to be red and reddish brown, but green also appears. It is not an expensive material.

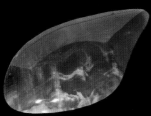

This freeform fossil wood cabochon displays the shapes and structures of wood in an earthy pattern.

FOSSILIZED (AGATIZED) CORAL

Fossilized coral is formed the same way as fossilized wood, through centuries of extreme pressure. The stones are covered in beautiful patterns created by the cross-sections of the coral branches. Colours range widely and it is possible to find delicate pinks, yellow ochres and creams as well as vibrant reds and browns. Fossilized coral is still a collectors' stone, so good examples can be expensive.

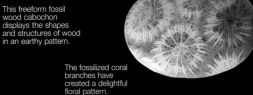

The fossilized coral branches have created a delightful floral pattern.

13/jade

Jade is a gemstone with two incarnations – one abundant, the other a rare precious gem. Yet both jadeite and nephrite gemstones possess a beautiful texture, strength and colours that range from creamy pastels to intense and earthy tones. All in all, they are a pleasure to work with.

For over 2,000 years, jade has been mined and worked throughout the world. The Chinese were the earliest users, making it part of their ancient religious cult and a symbol of high rank and authority in their society. The Natives of pre-Columbian Central America prized jade more highly than gold, while the 17th-century Maoris realized that this tough, fine-grained rock was the perfect material from which to carve their amulets and implements. It was only in 1863 that jade was finally recognized as being two distinct gemstones – jadeite and nephrite. Rather confusingly, jade remains the generic name for both!

This yellow jadeite seahorse was hand-carved by Kimi, a 16-year-old girl in Thailand.

SPECIFICATIONS

JADEITE JADE
HARDNESS 7 Mohs
SPECIFIC GRAVITY 3.33
REFRACTIVE INDEX 1.66–1.68
CRYSTAL FORM Monoclinic. Jadeite has a greasy to pearly lustre. It is found in metamorphic rocks and as alluvial pebbles and boulders. It is composed of tiny granular pyroxene crystals.

NEPHRITE JADE
HARDNESS 6.5 Mohs
SPECIFIC GRAVITY 2.96
REFRACTIVE INDEX 1.61–1.63
CRYSTAL FORM Monoclinic. It has a greasy to pearly lustre. Nephrite is found as aggregates of fibrous amphibole crystals, which form an interlocking structure making it perfect for carving. Boulders often have a brown skin due to weathering that can sometimes be seen on carvings.

SOURCES OF JADE

JADEITE JADE
Historically, Guatemala and Turkestan. Today, Myanmar (formerly Burma) is the main supplier. Also found in Japan and the United States (California).

NEPHRITE JADE
Australia, Brazil, Canada, Germany, Italy, Mexico, Poland, Siberia, Switzerland, Taiwan, United States, Zimbabwe.

Showcase

This bracelet contains Edwards black nephrite jade from Wyoming and white nephrite jade from Russia.

Black jadeite has been set with green aventurine quartz and a pyrite ammonite in 18K gold. The black jade has a great depth of colour and a beautiful satin finish.

Treatments and imitations

• A great deal of jadeite is impregnated with wax or plastic-type resins to imitate the colour of high-value imperial jade. Sometimes the dyes can fade over time. Other stones may be dyed to make them look like jade, for instance chalcedony, which because of its translucency can be made to resemble jadeite.

• Glass and plastics have been used to imitate jadeite and glued triplets and doublets have tricked buyers. Jadeite's telltale dimpled surface is visible through a loupe.

• Nephrite and jadeite jade can be confused with other materials and numerous jade misnomers exist, such as those listed below. Note that soapstone and serpentine can both be scratched easily, unlike jade.

KOREA JADE = bowenite (serpentine)
COLORADO JADE = amazonite
INDIAN JADE = aventurine
AUSTRALIAN JADE = chrysoprase
TRANSVAAL JADE = hydrogrossular garnet
HONAN JADE = soapstone

Types of jade

JADEITE JADE

Jadeite is a precious gem. In its pure form it is white, but it can also occur in a wide range of colours: green, lilac/lavender, pink, brown, red, blue, black, orange and yellow. The colours tend to be pastel and mottled; the exception is imperial jade, which is a vibrant, rich emerald- or apple-green colour. The colour derives from the presence of chromium oxide, and it sometimes contains small black inclusions. Imperial jade can be translucent to near-transparent and is highly prized and extremely valuable.

IMPERIAL JADE

Small but perfect! The colour is pure and the material is translucent.

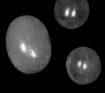

Imperial jade

LAVENDER JADE

These pieces of lavender jadeite demonstrate how purity and strength of colour affect the price. The smaller, darker cabochon is the more expensive of the two.

Lavender jade

GREEN JADE

This shows the typical mottling of colour together with jadeite's greasy lustre. This shade of green is distinctly jadeite rather than nephrite.

Green jade

BLACK JADE

Wyoming black jadeite is excellent material for carving. The colour is intense and free of any white.

MAW-SIT-SIT (CHLOROMELANITE OR JADE ALBITE)

Maw-sit-sit is a form of jadeite that has only recently become commercially available. It is composed of a mineral that is related to jadeite, combined with jadeite itself and albite feldspar. The stone has the beautiful, vibrant apple-green colour of imperial jade, with dark green to black spots or veins of chlorite. Maw-sit-sit has a similar texture and hardness to jadeite and so is durable and suitable for carving. It is found in upper Myanmar (Burma).

The strength of maw-sit-sit enables it to be cut into such slender pendeloques as these without fear of breaking.

NEPHRITE JADE

The crystal structure of nephrite jade is tougher than steel – it was once used for weapons and tools such as arrows and axe heads. The colours of nephrite jade are less delicate and pure than those of jadeite, and range from dark green (rich in iron oxide) to cream (rich in magnesium). The colours can be banded, blotchy or homogenous. The typical shade of green in nephrite jade is spinach or sage green, darker than the jadeite green. Nephrite jade that appears black is usually a very dark green. When the fibres within nephrite jade are arranged in parallel it is possible to get a cat's-eye effect that cannot occur in jadeite due to its granular composition.

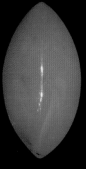

This is typical Russian nephrite material, with a bright spinach-green colour and good lustre.

Pricing jade

• The jade-carving industry is huge and the main cutting centres are China, Taiwan and Hong Kong. The fact that so many dyed and poor-quality nephrite jade goods are on sale results in its devaluation as a gemstone to be used in modern jewellery design.
• Jadeite has a considerable value, especially the pure colours such as bright imperial green and lavender. The greater the purity and beauty, the greater the price: a good colour in opaque material is worth more than a mediocre colour in translucent material. The price of dyed jade should reflect the fact it has been treated and be lower than that of natural-coloured jade.
• Colour balance and texture are also considerations when it comes to price. Jadeite has plurality of colour, meaning that often a combination of colours can appear in one mass. For instance, green might appear with lavender. Texture and faults within the mass will also affect the price, so that "clean", smooth-textured, evenly coloured pieces have the highest value.
• When judging maw-sit-sit, the considerations are similar: a bright green colour with minimal dark inclusions will increase the value. Maw-sit-sit provides very good value as it can be the colour of imperial jade but also, because it is relatively unknown, it commands a moderate price.

Working with jade

• Both jadeite and nephrite jade are used for cabochons, carvings and beads.
• Good-quality green nephrite from Siberia is readily available. It has an attractive, bright, even spread of colour and is durable and easy to cut as well as being good value for money. All of these qualities make it a great stone to design with. The jewellery designer Fabergé regularly incorporated Russian nephrite in his pieces and they were a far cry from the imported jade we see today.

14/spodumene

Spodumene is a fairly recent discovery in gemstone terms and in part still remains a collector's stone. But don't let that put you off. This species of gemstone comes in large sizes, has a wonderful lustre and attractive colours and, for the time being, is great value for the money.

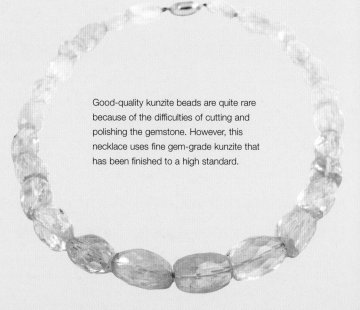

The pleochroic properties of this faceted spodumene are evident in the two colours showing.

This kunzite has a beautiful, clear lilac-pink colour. It is large (14.7 ct) and cut to good proportions without being too deep.

The gem varieties of spodumene are transparent pink, green, light yellow-brown and colourless. The crystals are pleochroic, which means that different colours or intensities of colour can be seen when the material is viewed from different angles. This pleochroism affects the way the stone is faceted – to have the strongest and best colour possible, the table facet must lie perpendicular to the main axis of the crystal. The clarity of gem-quality spodumene is excellent and once cut and polished the stones are full of life, possessing a vivid, almost iridescent lustre.

Spodumene can have quite a fibrous appearance. In the kunzite and hiddenite gems, inclusions often run parallel to each other, in the form of tubes or fractures along the length of the crystal. When the gemstones are faceted to display the best colour, inclusions will normally lie perpendicular to the table and so be minimized visually.

SPECIFICATIONS

HARDNESS 6.5–7 Mohs
SPECIFIC GRAVITY 3.15–3.21
REFRACTIVE INDEX 1.66–1.68
CRYSTAL FORM Monoclinic – prismatic tabular. Spodumene has an uneven brittle fracture with perfect cleavage and a strong vitreous lustre.

SOURCES OF SPODUMENE

SPODUMENE Canada, Madagascar, Mexico, Russia, United States.
HIDDENITE Brazil, Madagascar, Myanmar (formerly Burma), United States (North Carolina and California).
KUNZITE Afghanistan, Madagascar, Myanmar (formerly Burma), Pakistan, United States.

Showcase

The white gold ring contains a large, faceted light pink kunzite. Although the open claw setting has allowed light into the stone, emphasizing its brilliance, a closed setting would have intensified the colour of the stone.

Good-quality kunzite beads are quite rare because of the difficulties of cutting and polishing the gemstone. However, this necklace uses fine gem-grade kunzite that has been finished to a high standard.

Types of spodumene

The word spodumene is Greek for "ash-coloured," as most nongem crystals are opaque and white to yellowish grey. It was discovered that green or bluish lilac material had a tendency to turn a lilac-pink colour when exposed to sunlight. Because of this phenomenon, spodumene is frequently heat treated to improve or change the colour of the stone. The process of irradiation is also used to darken pale lilac material to a strong rose-pink colour.

Most hiddenite gemstones are pale; intensely green stones are very expensive.

HIDDENITE

This is the rarer gemstone variety of spodumene. It was discovered in the United States in 1879 by A.E. Hidden, hence its name. Chromium is the colouring agent in hiddenite, which can be found in light yellow-green, soft bluish green or bright emerald green. The latter is very scarce and commands collector prices.

Spodumene crystals often occur in large sizes; this stone weighs 31 ct. Its pink-yellow colour is natural.

KUNZITE

Kunzite is more widely available than hiddenite. It is named after G.F. Kunz, who first described the gem in 1902. Its colouring agent is manganese, which creates a range of very pretty colours: pink, bluish lilac, light violet and pink-peach. Kunzite is generally quite pale, so any naturally intense coloured stones are rare and carry a premium. To achieve more attractive pink colours, it is common for stones with brownish tones to be heated to a temperature of 300°F (150°C).

This pink kunzite cabochon shows typical inclusions and fractures but has an interesting oily lustre.

This side view shows some evidence of kunzite's pleochroism. Most importantly it shows good depth of cut, deep enough for good colour but not so deep that it is impossible to set.

Treatments and imitations

• Hiddenite could be confused with yellow-green chrysoberyl, diopside, precious yellow or green beryl, peridot or sometimes emerald. Kunzite may be offered in place of a more expensive gemstone, as it can resemble precious pink topaz, pink spinel or sapphire, morganite or rose tourmaline. It can also be confused with high-quality rose quartz or lavender (rose) amethyst.

• Synthetic corundum (sapphire and ruby) and synthetic spinel can imitate kunzite.

Pricing spodumene

Barring collector pieces, kunzite is good value as a gemstone; its moderate cost allows jewellery makers and designers to use large stones for dramatic effect without the finished piece becoming too expensive. The brilliant lustre and attractive (and popular) colours of kunzite make it an interesting alternative to the other pink gemstones traditionally used by jewellery designers and makers.

Working with spodumene

• Commercially, kunzite is much more available than hiddenite. Its cleavage makes it a difficult stone to facet and polish, however, so it is usually cut where labour costs are cheap, such as in Brazil or Pakistan.

• A step cut such as an emerald cut is frequently used with this material as it displays the colour of the stone well and ensures there are no brittle corners to worry about during setting. Check the depth of the stone's pavilion, or "belly", as kunzite is often cut very deep to improve intensity of colour and can be difficult to set in jewellery. A deep stone will sit very high on the finger, where it will be unstable and exposed to impact, or if used in a pendant could tip or rotate when worn.

• The brittleness of kunzite makes it slightly fragile for a ring stone – if hit in the wrong place the stone could chip. If your customer insists on using it for a ring, try to ensure that it has a protective mount and won't be worn on a daily basis.

• Some traders suggest that spodumene gems should be kept as nighttime stones, because of their sensitivity to sunlight and the risk of colour change.

15/zoisite

Within this species lies a gemstone of drama and intrigue that is considered, along with the sapphire, to be the finest blue stone in existence. Tanzanite, despite its scarcity, has not only gained a remarkable public awareness in a very short space of time, but has become an object of desire worldwide.

This intense blue tanzanite cabochon could be mistaken for a high-quality blue sapphire. It weighs 13.69 ct.

Tanzanite is a rare and beautiful transparent indigo-violet gemstone that is found in just one area of Tanzania – and nowhere else. It is by far the most important stone of the zoisite species but a relative newcomer to the gemstone industry, having first been recorded only in 1967. Tanzanite was recognized as a major gemstone when it was launched on the international marketplace, to great success, by the New York jewellers Tiffany & Co. in the late 1960s. In an industry where colour has become a critical factor for jewellery buyers and designers alike, tanzanite plays an important commercial role. For many people, a large blue sapphire would be too expensive to contemplate, yet a large blue tanzanite provides a colourful alternative that is much easier on the pocket.

SPECIFICATIONS

HARDNESS 6.5–7 Mohs
SPECIFIC GRAVITY 3.30–3.35
REFRACTIVE INDEX 1.69–1.70
CRYSTAL FORM Orthorhombic multifaceted prisms are rare. The material has perfect cleavage, making it soft and brittle. The visible colours of rough tanzanite crystals are ink blue, brown or honey yellow, and only when they are heated do they become the famous blue-violet colour.

SOURCES OF ZOISITE

TANZANITE Near Arusha, Tanzania.
YELLOW AND GREEN ZOISITE Tanzania and Kenya.
THULITE Western Australia, Namibia, Norway, United States.

Working with zoisite

• Care needs to be taken when polishing and soldering tanzanite jewellery as heating the stone may damage it or affect the colour. It is also very easy to remove the polish and end up with a dull patch on the crown or girdle.
• Unfortunately, tanzanite is a relatively soft gemstone that can be brittle and will chip quite easily. It is not suited to everyday wear and as a ring stone would need a protective setting on facet corners and edges. Some traders advise that tanzanite is better kept for earrings, necklaces and pendants.

Showcase

These ruby-in-zoisite beads are really unusual. The natural variation of colour and the colour distribution have been used to create striking and beautiful patterns.

These 22K gold earrings contain ruby-in-zoisite for its colour, texture and pattern. The black hornblende inclusions lend a graphic element to the design.

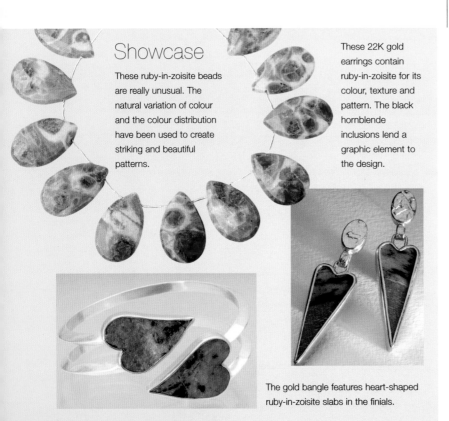

The gold bangle features heart-shaped ruby-in-zoisite slabs in the finials.

Types of zoisite

is pictured here in daylight (top) and artificial light (bottom).

TANZANITE

The colour ranges from deep sapphire blue to violet-blue to soft lavenders and lilacs. Faceted tanzanites often have violet-red or greenish yellow flashes due to pleochroism, in which different colours and intensities of colour can be seen when the material is viewed from different angles. The stone is traditionally heat treated to produce a more attractive and intense blue colour and to lose any greenish tones. Tanzanite can exhibit a slight colour change: in daylight, good-quality material will take on an ultramarine to sapphire-blue colour; in artificial, incandescent light it will appear to be more of an amethyst-violet colour.

Common inclusions in tanzanite are tiny crystals in various colours that look like spots, as well as clouds of miniature particles, fine hairlike needles and larger rods of different crystals. The hairlike inclusions give an unwanted hazy appearance to the stone and can cause damage during heating, so faceted tanzanites should ideally be "clean".

Cut is an important factor. The material does not have the brilliance of a sapphire and so faceted trillion, cushion and brilliant cuts make the stone appear more showy and bring out the hot pink highlights. Baguette and emerald cuts (step cuts) require material that has a very good colour and clarity, so that the stone does not look pale or dull.

Green or chrome tanzanite has been discovered, the colour ranging from yellowish green to grey-green to bluish green. The availability of this material is poor; it is not commercially viable.

Typical tanzanite inclusions are needles that make the stone cloudy.

THULITE

Thulite is a dense, opaque pink to red variety of zoisite that is coloured by manganese. It is normally cut as cabochons or beads or used for carvings. It has a low commercial value, and may be confused with rhodonite.

Ruby-in-zoisite faceted drop displays pale pink thulite, green anyolite, and deep pink rubies.

ANYOLITE

Discovered in Tanzania in 1954, this opaque, green zoisite rock contains black hornblende inclusions and large, low-grade, opaque rubies (called ruby-in-zoisite). It has an attractive colour contrast that works well in carvings, beads and cabochons. Despite containing rubies, it is only of moderate value.

Ruby-in-zoisite

Pricing zoisite

• Initially the supply of tanzanite was too unstable for commercial use and the market was limited to collectors. In the 1980s there was a surge of material from the Tanzanian mines, which resulted in greater recognition and appreciation of the stone. Supply and demand were high, which kept prices reasonably low and enabled buyers to choose the best-quality colours. Natural and political events have occasionally influenced interest and availability, but tanzanite's value is up and will remain high so long as only one source exists in the world and demand and interest continue to grow. Concerns that the stone will eventually become mined out will no doubt lead to a rise in prices.

• The pricing of tanzanite is based on intensity of colour; an intense blue stone will be valued higher than a purple-violet stone. The high price of intense colours has meant that more pale lilac and lavender material is being seen and used – to great effect. The gentler colours of tanzanite are not only cheaper to buy but offer designers a more versatile material to work with; they mix well with other gemstones and are just as popular with buyers.

These baguette-cut tanzanites show different colours because of the stone's pleochroism.

Treatments and imitations

• The secret of tanzanite's success lies in its dramatic colour transformation when heated and its remarkable pleochroic properties. Rough tanzanite crystals display three colours when viewed from different angles (axes), and this pleochroism influences the final colour of the stone after heating. Tanzanites have to be faceted as stones prior to heat treatment, in order that the angle of the table lies in the direction (colour axis) that will produce the best blue. Heating is then performed in a special furnace, where the cut stones are placed in layers of sand or white cement and heated to temperatures of 900–1250°F (480–680°C). Darker and larger stones require higher temperatures for longer periods of time. The brown and honey-yellow tanzanites turn into blue-violet stones, and stones that were originally ink blue become the most expensive intense blue.

• Tanzanite could be confused with other gemstones, such as amethyst, iolite, sapphire, spinel or synthetic corundum.

• The popularity of tanzanite has led to the production of very convincing glass imitations and doublets. Either glass stones are given a tanzanite crown or two colourless synthetic spinels are glued together with tanzanite-coloured glue. Other imitation tanzanites on the market go under the names of forsterite, chortanite and cortanite.

• If you are buying a tanzanite of an expensive colour it is important to have the gemstone tested by a laboratory or use a reputable dealer who will give you a written guarantee and receipt.

Beads often have pale colour or, in this case, inclusions.

16/peridot (olivine)

When peridot is good, it is very good, but when it is bad . . . There is so much pale and lacklustre material around it is easy to forget that, with good colour and cutting, peridot can be a truly impressive and important gemstone.

Prismatic peridot crystal from Pakistan containing acicular inclusions

The birefringence of peridot has been used to good effect in this buff-top cut. This is a gemstone of exceptional depth and life.

Peridot only ever comes in green – pale yellowish green, olive green, bottle green or intense, vibrant apple green (the latter being the most desirable). The best cutting material comes from Pakistan, close to the Afghan border. The large fine Kashmir peridots possess a beautiful intense colour and sell for high prices.

Peridot is an idiochromatic gemstone, which means that the colour comes from the basic chemical composition of the stone itself (iron) and not from the impurities that normally colour gemstones. The material is transparent but can contain a wide selection of inclusions; the most common are "lily pads" and "fingerprints" made up of tiny drops of silica glass. You will also find dark brownish yellow leaflets of biotite mica, small crystals of pyrope garnet and spinel, small black inclusions and "silk" (a reflection of fibrous inclusions creating a silk-like appearance). Peridot does not possess great brilliance, and the lustre ranges from vitreous to greasy. Very occasionally, cat's-eye and star effects occur.

SPECIFICATIONS

HARDNESS 6.5–7 Mohs
SPECIFIC GRAVITY 3.27–3.37
REFRACTIVE INDEX 1.64–1.69
CRYSTAL FORM Orthorhombic. Peridot appears as flat prismatic crystals with distinct striations along the length. The gemmological name is olivine.

SOURCES OF PERIDOT

Australia, Brazil, China, Egypt (St. John's Island), Myanmar (formerly Burma), Pakistan, South Africa, United States (Hawaii, Arizona), Zaire.

This peridot crystal comes from Pakistan. It displays the black needlelike chromite inclusions that are sometimes called Ludwig needles.

Treatments and imitations

- Peridot can resemble green tourmaline, green zircon, green apatite and possibly green sapphire.
- Peridot may be oiled or opticoned to reduce the visibility of flaws. Opticon is a polymer filler that is frequently used to enhance emeralds.

Pricing peridot

The high cost of bigger, intensely coloured stones reflects not only the difficulty of finding large, "clean" rough material, but also the length of time it takes to cut and polish peridot. Peridot is readily available in paler colours, which are moderately priced.

Working with peridot

- Peridot has indistinct cleavage and a conchoidal, brittle fracture. The tensions that exist within a crystal can be considerable due to the many inclusions. The characteristic "lily pads" are difficult to see and can act like cleavage planes, making faceting problematic. If the lily pad is close to the surface, the peridot may break while it is being cut and polished. If it lies well within the stone it shouldn't be a problem, and if kept parallel to the table won't be too visible.
- Check the cutting of any stone as peridot has high birefringence (the light bends at slightly different angles as it enters the crystal) and it may be possible to see a doubling of the back facets. If the material isn't oriented properly, the reflections and facet junctions will appear fuzzy as you look through the table, and the stone will lose brilliance.
- Peridot is traditionally faceted as a step cut or mixed cut in order to obtain the best colour and to reduce the risk of breakage. It can be difficult to polish and will pick up scratches relatively easy, so it is important to keep a stone set in jewellery clean and looking its best.
- Peridot is quite sensitive to heat and is easily attacked by sulphuric and hydrochloric acids, so avoid steam cleaners and chemicals. It is best not to solder or polish jewellery with the stone in situ.

Showcase

This Art Nouveau pendant combines faceted peridots with natural pearls in an organic design that contains flowing lines and delicate wire work.

17/prehnite

Prehnite only fully reveals itself as a beautiful gemstone once it has been worked. The rough material hides its potential until the polishing process brings out the distinctive pearly lustre and translucent colour that give this stone a near-luminous quality.

These cabochons have a silky translucency that makes them appear to glow.

Prehnite derives its name from Colonel von Prehn, who discovered the gemstone in South Africa in 1788 and introduced it to Europe. It appears in yellow to mint green, pale yellow to light brown, bright yellow, grey, white and colourless. Individual gem-quality transparent crystals are rare and usually small, so remain in the domain of collectors. A fine green translucent prehnite has been marketed under the name (or misnomer) of Cape emerald.

The majority of prehnite on the market occurs naturally as a translucent mass formed as a crust or a nodule (typical of the botryoidal habit). Yellow fibrous material is also found and displays chatoyancy (a cat's-eye effect) when cut as a cabochon. Very occasionally prehnite is pleochroic; this phenomenon is rare and increases the value of the stone. While some prehnite is translucent and clean, other material can be full of flaws and inclusions such as fractures, black tourmaline acicular (needle) inclusions and bright copper specks.

SPECIFICATIONS

HARDNESS 6–6.5 Mohs
SPECIFIC GRAVITY 2.82–2.94
REFRACTIVE INDEX 1.611–1.669
CRYSTAL FORM Orthorhombic. Individual tabular or pyramidal prismatic crystals are rare. Prehnite is found in basaltic volcanic (igneous) and metamorphic rocks.

SOURCES OF PREHNITE

Australia, Canada, Germany, India, Namibia, South Africa, United Kingdom (Scotland), United States (Michigan).

These faceted beads display the fresh minty green colour typical of prehnite.

Treatments and imitations

The fine green prehnite is similar in appearance to nephrite jade and jadeite jade. It could also be confused with serpentine, apatite, chrysoprase and peridot.

Pricing prehnite

Faceted stones are still viewed as collector pieces and until they become commercially available there will be no set prices. Prehnite beads and cabochons are inexpensive and readily available.

Working with prehnite

• Water is lost if prehnite is heated, and cannot be replaced. Avoid using steam cleaners and remove the stone from jewellery before soldering. Care should also be taken not to overheat the stone during polishing. Hydrochloric acid turns prehnite into a jellylike substance, so avoid contact with any chemicals.

• The cleavage of prehnite is good in one direction, and the cleavage surfaces are curved. The uneven fracture of prehnite makes it slightly brittle, so take care when setting. A ring stone should have a protective setting and its edges should not be left exposed. Prehnite is considered a good carving material, as it is soft enough to work with but can withstand reasonable wear and tear.

Showcase

This multirow necklace shows the distinct (and attractive) soft green colour of prehnite. Black tourmaline needle inclusions appear in the faceted beads; they frequently occur in this gem material.

18/feldspar

Despite being the most common rock-forming minerals at the earth's surface, the stones in the feldspar species give jewellery makers some of the most visually fascinating material available. The feldspars have gained tremendous popularity with jewellery buyers, and thanks to their dramatic optical effects, demand for these stones continues to remain high.

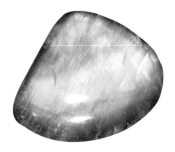

Rainbow moonstone
freeform cabochon

Labradorite rough material displays uneven, splintery fracture and the iridescence appearing from the different layers within it.

Feldspar is a very appealing species of stones. It provides a great choice of natural colours, comes in large sizes, is good value for money and has beautiful optical effects that you will never get bored with. The feldspars are often described as having a schiller, opalescence or adularescence. These terms all refer to the shimmering effect that appears to sit just below, or above, the surface of the stone when it is placed or moved under a light. Moonstone is well known for this special optical effect, in which reflected light causes a blue or white schiller. This internal reflection of light, or "interference", also produces an effect called iridescence; an example is the rainbow of colours in labradorite. The feldspar group is subdivided into two distinct varieties: the orthoclase (alkali) feldspars, which include moonstone, orthoclase and amazonite, and the plagioclase feldspars, including labradorite and aventurine feldspar.

This amazonite pebble demonstrates the irregular colour distribution and silky appearance of the material.

SPECIFICATIONS

HARDNESS 6–6.5 Mohs
SPECIFIC GRAVITY 2.56–2.62
REFRACTIVE INDEX 1.52–1.53
CRYSTAL FORM Triclinic and monoclinic. Deposits are found as water-worn pebbles and in igneous rocks. The feldspar species has perfect cleavage and an uneven, splintery to brittle fracture. The lustre is glassy (vitreous) to silky.

SOURCES OF FELDSPARS

MOONSTONE The best blue moonstones come from Madagascar, Myanmar (formerly Burma), and Sri Lanka. Moonstone is also found in Australia, Brazil, India, Mexico, Tanzania, United States.
ORTHOCLASE Yellow and colourless orthoclase occurs in Madagascar, Myanmar (formerly Burma), and Sri Lanka.
AMAZONITE The main source is India. Also found in Brazil, Canada, Namibia, Russia, Tanzania, United States (Colorado).
LABRADORITE Canada, Madagascar, Mexico, Norway, Russia.
SUNSTONE Canada, India, Norway, Russia, United States.

Treatments and imitations

• Glass imitations of sunstone and blue moonstone exist.
• Yellow orthoclase could be confused with pale yellow citrine, topaz, prehnite or yellow beryl.
• Amazonite could be confused with green jade, chrysoprase or turquoise.

Pricing feldspar

• Rainbow moonstone is much cheaper than blue moonstone. Good crystal-clear green moonstone is moderately priced; it is more expensive than rainbow moonstone but does not reach the price of clean blue moonstone.
• Sunstone is probably the most expensive form of feldspar. With Tiffany & Co. featuring this material in their jewellery range, it is possible that the stone will gain a popularity and demand similar to tanzanite's.

Types of orthoclase feldspar

Orthoclase derives its name from the Greek word for "break straight". This refers to the gemstone's perfect cleavage, breaking smoothly at nearly 90 degrees (perpendicular) to the crystal face.

MOONSTONE

Moonstone is the opalescent variety of orthoclase. Traditionally thought to be a good-luck stone and an arouser of passions, it was often offered as a gift between lovers. Moonstone can be transparent with a strong blue schiller on the surface; it can be translucent or milky with the appearance of an inner light; or it can have a striking cat's-eye or star effect. The schiller is the result of light reflecting off alternating layers of albite and orthoclase feldspar; the thin albite layers produce the blue colour and the thick orthoclase layers create the white schiller.

Insectlike inclusions are common in moonstone. They are actually parallel cracks caused by internal strain or pressure, a fact that jewellery makers need to be aware of when working with the material. Moonstone comes in a range of colours and can possess many different qualities.

BLUE MOONSTONE

Transparent and crystal clear with a floating blue schiller on the surface, this is the most valuable type of moonstone. The more intense the blue schiller, the finer and more desirable the stone. The best and largest stones have traditionally come from Myanmar (Burma), but it has become much harder to find good stones and consequently the price has steadily increased. Blue moonstone is occasionally faceted but care needs to be taken when working with it, as the material is rather brittle and prone to breaking under pressure.

African blue moonstone. The same stone shown on a black background above and a grey background below.

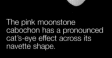

RAINBOW MOONSTONE

Rainbow moonstone has a patchy, milky appearance, which comes from the white orthoclase layers and inclusions. When the stone catches the light, the reflection off the layers and inclusions produces a rainbow effect. The colour play has made this a very popular stone with buyers and it frequently appears in silver jewellery. Unfortunately, there is a great deal of poor-quality material on the market that has virtually no colour play and is full of cracks and chips, so one has to look pretty hard for good examples.

The rectangular rainbow moonstone clearly shows the internal layered structure and cleavage planes.

GREEN MOONSTONE

Green moonstone is not as well known as rainbow or blue moonstone as it doesn't have the colour play, but it is still a beautiful stone. It usually has a clear or slightly hazy appearance and a pale yellowish green colour, and when you look down at the stone you will see a light emanating from within, like a full moon. It is often cut with a high dome to accentuate this optical effect and frequently a star of light will be visible on the top of the dome.

The elongated oval green moonstone has a fantastic clarity and silver-green colour.

PINK MOONSTONE

The term *pink* covers colours from beige to peach to honey, ranging from translucent to opaque. The stone should have a white schiller, or sheen, and is often found with a cat's-eye or star effect. This type of material often appears in rows of multicoloured beads.

The pink moonstone cabochon has a pronounced cat's-eye effect across its navette shape.

The tricoloured moonstone beads show the typical moonstone colours; greenish white, pink and grey.

ORTHOCLASE

Orthoclase is a moderately cheap transparent stone that is colourless or pale yellow and can have a bluish white schiller, or sheen. The colourless variety is called adularia, as it was found at Mount Adular in Switzerland, and it is from this name that the term *adularescence* derives. Orthoclase is usually faceted as a step cut because of its fragility, and for this reason it is not widely produced or used.

The faceted yellow orthoclase has a pale yellow colour and good clarity. It is bought mainly by collectors.

AMAZONITE (MICROCLINE)

Amazonite is an attractive opaque stone that, due to the presence of lead, is either striped blue and white or a solid blue-green colour. The colour distribution tends to be irregular, even with the solid-colouring material. Amazonite can also occur in yellow, pink, red and grey, but blue-green is the most popular and widely seen. The stone usually has a vitreous lustre, but can also possess a lovely "silk" or sheen. It can be sensitive to pressure and slightly brittle, so normally appears in bead form.

This amazonite has a vibrant green colour but is striped with white, which will bring down its value.

Showcase

Labradorite and jet suspended from a black and white ribbon create a striking neckpiece. The intense blue schiller of the labradorite forms a pleasing contrast with the black jet.

The ring below features bezel-set white moonstone.

The gold brooch is cast in a tactile sun design with a single peachy pink moonstone cabochon set in the centre.

Faceted rainbow moonstone briolettes form a ruff to catch the light and produce colour.

Rough, unpolished labradorite segments and handmade gold beads of the same shape contrast nicely in this necklace.

Types of plagioclase feldspar

LABRADORITE

This fascinating and colourful stone, which offers a range of colours and optical effects, has become a firm favourite with jewellery buyers and makers. It is named after its source in Labrador, Canada. Labradorite displays a metallic rainbow effect similar to that of black opal except with larger colour spots – the effect is called labradorescence. As with moonstone, the colours are produced by the interference of light at the junctions of internal structures. The material can be transparent orange, yellow, colourless and red, and may be cut into a faceted stone. Alternatively, labradorite can have a semi-opaque grey-black to grey-brown body colour with iridescent flashes of blues, yellows, greens and oranges that appear when it is moved in the light. This material is the most popular with buyers.

Madagascan labradorite is nearly transparent with a pale grey tint. It contains sparkling mica inclusions and has a beautiful colour play in peach, turquoise blue, yellow and pink.

Unfortunately, as in the case of rainbow moonstone, a great deal of poor-quality labradorite is being produced in bead and cabochon form. This rather murky grey-green material has very little colour play, and is full of cracks and is scuffed where the stones and beads rub against each other.

SPECTROLITE

This is the trade name of Finnish labradorite. Its properties are the same, but it tends to have a dark, opaque colour with a schiller in pink, blue, orange or yellow. The most popular material has an electric blue schiller. Spectrolite can also have a cat's-eye effect.

Cleavage planes are visible within this labradorite freeform cabochon.

Spectrolite can produce an electric blue schiller.

Madagascan labradorite is almost transparent. It contains metallic pyrite inclusions and has a strong and colourful schiller.

The best sunstone gem material is transparent and has a hot red-orange colour.

SUNSTONE (AVENTURINE FELDSPAR OR OLIGOCLASE)

Sunstone is less well known than labradorite and moonstone, although it is colourful and fascinating to design. The opaque cabochon material usually has a shimmering brownish orange to reddish orange colour and contains hematite flakes in parallel bands. Some copper-coloured stones have a metallic lustre and asterism – clear four-ray stars. Occasionally you will see clear, colourless stones with remarkable reflective inclusions consisting of red, orange and green platy crystals. The effect is quite startling as the multicoloured inclusions look like glitter – it is easy to assume that the stone has been artificially produced. Green and blue aventurine feldspar also exists.

Facet-grade sunstone is transparent to slightly translucent and ranges from a soft pinky orange colour to a fiery bright red. Initially, this was a collector's stone, but it is now appearing on the market thanks to high-grade deposits found in Oregon.

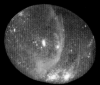

Lower grade sunstone is nearly opaque with orange and patchy colour.

This is better-grade sunstone, with even body colour and a clear four-ray star.

Working with feldspar

• The layered structure of feldspars affects their durability as well as their optical properties. Internal layers and cracks will often break through to the polished surface of the stone; rainbow moonstone and labradorite are both particularly prone to this. The perfect cleavage means that a slight blow, or too much pressure, will break a stone in two, so care needs to be taken when setting, soldering and polishing jewellery. It is probably not a good idea to use feldspars for bracelets or cufflinks. It is also important to store and protect stones, beads and jewellery properly, as they can become chipped and scuffed very easily.

• Stones that have optical effects should be set in such a way that any schiller or iridescence is fully displayed; it is worth experimenting to find the best position. Stones such as labradorite need movement in order to catch the light and flash with colour, so rings and drop earrings are better than necklaces, which are more static. A vertically hung pendant won't display a stone with a star as well as a ring on a hand that rests on the horizontal plane. Using a closed-back setting or painting the inside of the setting black will emphasize the blue schiller of a blue moonstone, displaying the sheen at its most intense. Any stars or cat's-eyes should be set straight, so that the eye or star is in the centre of the stone. To emphasize the inner light of clear stones such as green moonstone, polish the inside of the setting and make sure that no visible dirt is trapped behind the stone.

These beads show the subtle differences of colour found in sugilite.

19/sugilite

Despite the fact that sugilite has been in production for a relatively short period, there are already reports that it is nearly mined out. No other sizeable deposits of sugilite have been found, so if you haven't already done so, now's the time to check it out.

The manganese inclusions are clearly visible in this sugilite cabochon.

Sugilite, also known as sugulite, sometimes sells under the trade name Royal Azel. The first sugilite to be discovered was a tiny deposit of pink crystals found in Japan in 1944. It was not until 1973, in South Africa, that the massive form of sugilite was found, and that only became commercially available in the late 1970s.

The colours of sugilite are typically deep lavender, reddish violet and bluish purple, and a number of different hues are sometimes combined in the form of banding and mottling. Sugilite also comes in yellow-brown, pale pink and black, but these are rarely used for jewellery. The material is translucent to opaque; the gem-quality sugilite has a lovely translucency similar to fine chalcedony but is hard to source. If you're lucky you might see a drusy form (opaque material with tiny crystals embedded on the surface). Sugilite has a vitreous to resinous/waxy lustre and is often laced with manganese inclusions in the form of black, brown or blue lines.

SPECIFICATIONS

HARDNESS 6–6.5 Mohs
SPECIFIC GRAVITY 2.74–2.80
REFRACTIVE INDEX 1.607–1.610
CRYSTAL FORM Hexagonal structure. Manganoan sugilite is a massive polycrystalline rock that occurs in basic igneous rocks. It derives its colour from the presence of manganese.

SOURCES OF SUGILITE

Manganese fields of the Kalahari, South Africa. Small deposits also occur in Japan and Canada (Quebec).

Showcase

Flat slabs of sugilite bezel set in 22K gold form these earrings. The flush setting protects the slightly vulnerable material from damage. The gemstone has a matte finish, creating a natural look and accentuating the attractive purple colour.

Treatments and imitations

• Sugilite is sometimes given the misnomer purple turquoise. Natural gemstones that closely resemble sugilite include purple or lavender jadeite, charoite, amethystine chalcedony and massive amethyst.
• While no specific sugilite imitation is on the market, some unofficial imitations are available. Barium sulfate in a polymer matrix can be identified because it is softer than sugilite. Dyed magnesite has a more irregular colour distribution. Heat-treated and dyed massive beryl and quartz also imitate sugilite; the dye concentrations can be seen in fractures. Dyed quartzite, known as purple onyx, is also similar in appearance.
• When chalcedony mixes or intergrows with sugilite it becomes purple. A large amount of material labeled as sugilite is actually in part chalcedony-sugilite, which has a greater hardness and a translucency that's rare in sugilite. This is a natural occurrence, not artificial intervention.

Pricing sugilite

Sugilite is popular with jewellery makers and buyers because of its beautiful colour. The price is dependent on the intensity of colour and quality of material; vivid translucent stones are expensive. When supplies of sugilite start dwindling, the prices are bound to increase. For now, however, it is still commercially available.

Working with sugilite

• Sugilite has an irregular fracture and its cleavage is poor (in one direction). It is usually cut for cabochons and beads, but its granular structure also makes it suitable for carving and inlay work. It is fairly hard wearing, but needs to be protected from impact.
• Ultrasonic and steam cleaners should not be used. If the piece of jewellery is worn frequently, the gemstone might need repolishing over time.

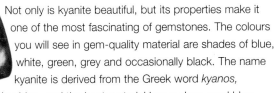

The individual crystals in this row of kyanite beads have had their corners trimmed to prevent fraying.

20/kyanite

Nearly all gemstones have a single hardness value, no matter where it is measured on the crystal. Kyanite is unique in having two hardness values. This characteristic is just one of many challenges that face a lapidary working with this gem.

Kyanite crystals are easy to distinguish; they have a characteristic blue strip running through the interior.

Not only is kyanite beautiful, but its properties make it one of the most fascinating of gemstones. The colours you will see in gem-quality material are shades of blue, white, green, grey and occasionally black. The name kyanite is derived from the Greek word *kyanos,* meaning blue, and the best material has a clear, royal blue colour that looks like sapphire. Most other kyanite has a streaky colour distribution. Gem-quality material is transparent to translucent, and the lustre ranges from vitreous to pearly. Chatoyant stones occur rarely. A great deal of bead and cabochon material contains inclusions of quartz, pyrite crystals, hematite flakes and fibres of ilmenite and rutile.

This cabochon has good clarity and colour.

Kyanite has two hardness values: 4.5–5 and 7. The lower value runs along the crystal's length, parallel to the direction of the cleavage. The harder value runs across the crystal's width, perpendicular to the cleavage. Lapidaries working with this stone have to constantly adjust their pressure and speed so that they make progress grinding the harder areas yet avoid overcutting the softer areas. Kyanite has a moderate birefringence (double refraction) and is strongly trichroic, showing colourless, violet-blue and cobalt blue.

SPECIFICATIONS

HARDNESS 4.5–5 or 7 Mohs
SPECIFIC GRAVITY 3.55–3.69
REFRACTIVE INDEX 1.712–1.734
CRYSTAL FORM Triclinic system. It has characteristic elongated, flattened prismatic crystals. Kyanite occurs in quartz-vein kimberlite pipes, alongside pyrope garnet.

SOURCES OF KYANITE

Australia, Brazil, European Alps, India, Kenya, Myanmar (formerly Burma), Russia, United States (North Carolina, Georgia).

Pricing kyanite

The availability of kyanite is good and there is a wide choice of quality and prices in bead form. The better quality is not particularly cheap, but the colour and clarity more than compensate for the price.

Working with kyanite

• Kyanite has an uneven, splintery to fibrous fracture and a perfect cleavage; it is full of small internal stress cracks that occur as the crystal forms at high pressure. Its low cohesion means that horizontal striations commonly run parallel down the broad face of a crystal, and the strong cleavage plane causes tiny cracks to form along the crystal's length. This makes kyanite a rather brittle gemstone that is susceptible to splitting. It requires careful handling, so any polishing should be done at low speed and ultrasonic and chemical cleaners should not be used. However, kyanite is not sensitive to heat.

• Cutting is limited by the nature of the material: sharp corners tend to fray, so angular or geometric shapes are not really suitable. Lower-grade kyanite beads need to be checked for any scuffs, splits and damaged drill holes or corners.

• Although kyanite poses some problems for lapidaries and jewellery makers, it should not be automatically rejected for use as a jewellery stone. There is some beautiful faceted kyanite that has been set into pendants and earrings. Natural blue gemstones are rare and gem-quality kyanite gives the colour of sapphire without the price. The higher-grade material, which is less flawed, is a safer jewellery stone.

Showcase

These good-looking earrings use long, navette-shaped kyanite cabochons. They are window set in white gold to allow light to pass through the gemstone and show off the intense blue colour.

21/opal

Precious white opal and fire opal in matrix

Mexican fire opal rough material

Opal has been attributed with various qualities over the years, from bringing misfortune and hardship to the wearer to possessing therapeutic properties for diseases of the eye. However accurate these associations may be, one fact remains true: opal might be easy to damage and demanding to work with, but it is impossible not to be seduced by its sheer celebration of colour.

The vibrant colours that appear on an opal result from the diffraction of light off tiny, closely packed silica spheres inside the stone. This is why the colours change when the opal is viewed from a different direction. The larger and more ordered these spheres are, the greater the range and intensity of colours produced. This interference of light is called colour play or iridescence. The term *opalescence* shouldn't be used to describe opals, as it actually refers to the bluish white shimmer, or schiller, on gemstones such as moonstone.

Faceted semi-black jelly opal – this is an unusual way to cut opal.

While most gemstones are cut, or faceted, to calibrated sizes and shapes, opals are frequently cut as cabochons with freeform shapes. This is accepted practice and simply a result of the cutter wanting to maximize the opal and the colour play found on the rough material. The irregular shapes make each opal unique and the stones often bring creativity to jewellery design.

This specimen is blonde Andamooka border opal. The colour play has an excellent range showing lilacs, reds, yellows and blues.

Seascape opal with dendritic inclusions

SPECIFICATIONS

HARDNESS 5.5–6.5 Mohs
SPECIFIC GRAVITY 1.98–2.50
REFRACTIVE INDEX 1.37–1.52
CRYSTAL FORM Opal is amorphous and can be found filling cavities in sedimentary rock, such as ironstone and sandstone, or running as a vein through igneous rock. It is composed of hydrated (hardened) silica gel that has a water content of between 5 and 30 per cent. Opal also acts as a petrifying agent, replacing organic matter such as shell, wood and bone.

SOURCES OF OPAL

Czechoslovakia was the main producer until the end of the 19th century, but today the biggest source is Australia. Also found in Brazil, Ethiopia, Honduras, Indonesia, Japan, Mexico, Peru, Russia, and the United States (Nevada and Idaho).
PRECIOUS BLACK OPAL Australia (Lightning Ridge, New South Wales).
PRECIOUS WHITE OPAL Southern Australia (Coober Pedy and Andamooka).

Types of opal

PRECIOUS WHITE OPAL

White opal has a light base and can have a strong colour play. Both of these stones are good quality but, like many white opals, can look rather pale and insipid. They require the closed-back bezel settings to maximize their iridescence.

Two admirable white opal gemstones

PRECIOUS BLACK OPAL

Black opal has a dark background, which can be dark grey, dark blue, dark green or grey-black – the darker the background, the greater the value of the stone. Black opals are rarer than white opals, so they have a higher carat price.

Black opal gemstones

PRECIOUS JELLY OPAL (SEMIBLACK OPAL)

This is a semiblack or "jelly" opal. It has a transparent blue-grey base with an amber-orange body color that can produce a wonderful blue-purple iridescence. The rub-over window setting protects the opal; if it had been claw set, the corners would have been vulnerable to damage. Jelly opals are good value for money, but it is not always easy to find stones with a strong colour play such as this.

This pendant displays the beautiful iridescence of jelly opal.

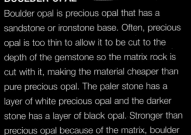

BOULDER OPAL

Boulder opal is precious opal that has a sandstone or ironstone base. Often, precious opal is too thin to allow it to be cut to the depth of the gemstone so the matrix rock is cut with it, making the material cheaper than pure precious opal. The paler stone has a layer of white precious opal and the darker stone has a layer of black opal. Stronger than precious opal because of the matrix, boulder opal is an easier stone to work with and suitable for use in a ring.

Boulder opals

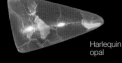

OPAL MATRIX

Some opals have a banded growth of precious opal with matrix rock, and there can also be inclusions of matrix within the opal. The resulting patterns are highly decorative and colourful, the deeper ones allowing you to look right inside the opal. The more complex pieces of opal matrix can be expensive.

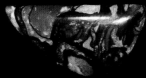

Opal matrix

FIRE OPAL

The colour of fire opal can range from yellow to red, with orange to red the most usual and red the most desirable. Fire opal usually has little colour play so the iridescent cab shown here is quite rare. Good-quality stones should be transparent with a vitreous lustre; they should not be milky or opaque. Unlike other types of opal, fire opals are often faceted like the stone below. Large transparent faceted stones with a good colour have increased in value recently, but fire opal does not realize the prices of precious opal.

Fire opals

HARLEQUIN OPAL

Harlequin opal is transparent to translucent precious opal with mosaiclike patches of colour. It is one of the most desirable and expensive types of opal. This stone displays a mosaic pattern in blue and green.

Harlequin opal

CRYSTAL OPAL

Crystal opal is completely transparent and should have good colour play over the glasslike surface. Pieces with both these qualities are rare and can be expensive. A crystal opal set in a pendant is pictured on page 94.

ANDEAN OPAL

Andean opal has become very popular because of its bright turquoise colour. It is usually opaque, occasionally translucent. There have been reports that Andean opal can change colour after contact with air, so the material is often "fixed" with a type of glue that coats the exterior, making it tougher and preserving its colour.

Andean opal

ETHIOPIAN OPAL

Ethiopian opal has a wonderful golden honey body colour and can have superb iridescence. It is quite expensive, however, and is not easy to source at this time.

OPAL CAT'S-EYES

It is possible for opal to have chatoyancy, a cat's-eye effect that is caused by the reflection of light by parallel fibres or channels. It is quite a rare phenomenon in opal, and large stones are valuable.

Opal cat's-eye

COMMON POTCH OPAL (HONEY OPAL)

Honey opal has no colour play and can be translucent or opaque. It is inexpensive and often used in bead form.

Honey opals

COMMON OPAL (PRASE OPAL)

Common (prase) opal

Prase opal possesses a pretty green colour due to the presence of nickel. It usually has a cloudy appearance and could be mistaken for chrysoprase.

COMMON OPAL (SEASCAPE OPAL)

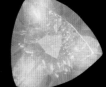

Seascape opal has an attractive blue-green colour that varies in intensity and can contain dendritic inclusions. The briolettes shown here use the material in an effective way, but would only be suitable for a necklace because of the stone's softness.

Common (seascape) opals

Opals in jewellery

Jewellery makers of the Art Nouveau period rebelled against the conventional forms of the late Victorian era and began producing "organic" pieces that contained inexpensive, colourful cabochons. Opals were used extensively; they fitted in perfectly with the insect motifs and their colour play matched the beautiful enamel work. They proved to be a versatile and popular gemstone.

The handcarved crystal opal in this pendant has a gentle translucency and colour play, harmonizing with the iridescent luster of the organic pearls and delicate colouration of the willow jasper cabochon.

An opal is everything that a diamond is not, yet they make a winning combination. The brilliance and fire of small faceted diamonds complement the more subtle colour play of the opal cabochon. The diamonds also form a protective barrier around the opal, receiving (and surviving) any accidental impact while the fragile opal remains undamaged.

Traditionally, fire opal has been cut into faceted beads and strung in graduated colours. It is now possible to find other types of opal in bead form, including precious opal (black and white), boulder opal and Andean opal, as well as cheaper varieties of common opal.

This Art Deco precious opal ring is surrounded by small diamonds. The opal is slightly dehydrated.

Pink opal chunky beads

Australian precious opal beads

Treatments and imitations

• Opal doublets and triplets are synthetic composite opals. In a doublet, the top section of the stone is precious opal, but the base is common potch opal. A triplet has three layers: a base of common opal, a thin middle layer of precious opal and a protective top dome of rock crystal. These stones are easy to spot if you look at them side-on through a loupe.

• Imitation Gilson opals were developed in the laboratory in 1973. They had a good iridescence, but the patterning of colour identified them as imitations.

• In the United States, John Slocum developed opals made of tough glass. They lacked the texture of genuine opal and appeared crumpled under magnification.

• Polystyrene latex opal beads and stones are widely available. They have a milky bluish sheen that can be spotted easily.

Synthetic latex beads

Side view of triplet opal

Pricing opal

• Opals are all about colour: the better and more even the colour, the higher the value of the opal. To assess evenness of the colour play, rotate the opal through 360 degrees. A good stone should have colour spread across the entire surface with no "dead" patches.

• The most expensive colour of opal is red. Yellow, green and blue are more common colours and so cost slightly less.

Top view of triplet opals

Working with opal

• When designing your piece of opal jewellery, it is vital that you consider the type of background the stone will have. Check the colour play of your opal and decide on the effect you want. Different colours of metal will boost different colours in a stone and the setting will affect the strength of the iridescence.

A closed-back setting can improve the colour of a precious white opal dramatically, as can painting the inside of the setting black. Here are two identical opals, one on a black background (representing a closed setting) and the other on a white background (representing an open-claw setting).

The background color can emphasize different qualities in an opal. This "jelly" opal has a completely different feel against the darker background.

• When designing the piece of jewellery and setting the stone, keep in mind that opal is quite a soft stone and is easily damaged by pressure and impact. If opal is being used for a ring, a rub-over setting will protect it whereas a claw setting will expose the stone's edges and leave it vulnerable to damage. The softness of opal makes it suitable for carving, but care needs to be taken as it is quite brittle.

• If you plan to work on the opal using drill attachments there is a risk that any heat generated will evaporate the opal's water content, causing dehydration, cracking and a loss of colour play. Sometimes it is possible to restore the water content of the damaged opal by immersing it in water. Evaporation of water content happens naturally over time and can be avoided by storing the opal in moist cotton wool.

• Opal is sensitive to acids and alkalis. Its porous nature makes it vulnerable to perfumes, soaps and detergents, so jewellery should always be removed before washing or applying creams.

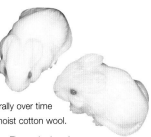

The carving of this fire opal makes the most of the ordinary light orange to yellowish material and gives the stone an extra dimension.

These mice have been carved from precious white opal, and tiny fire opals have been added for eyes. This is a fine example of the skills of German gemstone carvers.

Showcase

The pendant above features a freeform boulder opal. The vulnerable crystal opal layer is protected by the top edge of the bezel setting.

Faceted fire opals can be fragile and difficult to set. The softer 22K gold used in these earrings (right) eases the process.

Large black opals have been set in simple yellow gold settings, emphasizing the opals' spectacular colour play.

The shape and cut of this faceted Andean blue opal has dictated the ring's form. The low recessed setting protects the fragile material while the opal's intense colour and soft translucency contrast with the satin finish of the rich 22K gold.

22/hematite

This is a typical specular hematite crystal that exhibits mirrorlike surfaces.

The metallic silver-grey crystal surfaces of specular hematite are so highly reflective that they were used in the past as mirrors. It is likely that these reflective qualities and the stone's brilliant lustre were to blame for hematite's misnomer – Alaska black diamond.

Hematite is a compact form of iron oxide, or rust, and it appears red if cut into thin slices or powdered. Its name derives from the Greek for "blood". As a gemstone, hematite is opaque and it appears metallic silver to gunmetal grey when polished, and blue-black to dark brown when dull. The material can vary in compactness and form; kidney-shaped nodules and specular crystals are used for gemstones. The lustre of hematite can be dull to submetallic (brilliant).

SPECIFICATIONS

HARDNESS 5.5–6.5 Mohs
SPECIFIC GRAVITY 5.12–5.28
REFRACTIVE INDEX 2.94–3.22
CRYSTAL FORM Trigonal. The crystals are tabular with a hexagonal structure (specular). Also occurs as massive kidney ore and iridescent platy crystals. Hematite is found in igneous rocks.

SOURCES OF HEMATITE

Brazil, Canada (Lake Superior), Germany, Italy (Elba), Scandinavia, United Kingdom, United States (Arizona).

Types of hematite

The appearance of hematite varies and the stone is marketed under various names. Iridescent hematite is a hematite-rich slate from Arizona that exhibits a multicoloured iridescent surface. The effect is apparently due to long exposure on the mine dumps. Rainbow hematite is a granular specular mass with a high iridescence that occurs in the Minas Gerais area of Brazil.

These stones display the natural surface texture of botryoidal hematite. They have a slick contemporary look that would suit a minimal design.

Treatments and imitations

• In some countries, hematite is known as bloodstone. It should not be confused with the chalcedony variety of bloodstone.
• Hemalyke is the trade name of a reconstructed material manufactured in the United States. Small pieces of hematite are ground up, mixed with a binder (glue) and press-molded into shape. Hemalyke has an identical chemical composition to hematite, but is less brittle.
• Hemetine is another synthetic substance that has been used for intaglios (seal rings); it is stamped rather than carved. It has the same hardness as hematite, but may include titanium oxides or stainless steel.
• A flux-grown synthetic hematite was first recorded in 1967.

Pricing hematite

Hematite is an inexpensive material.

Working with hematite

• Hematite has a conchoidal, uneven fracture and no cleavage, but there is a natural parting on two planes. The material needs to be treated carefully during polishing as it can chip.
• The low cost of hematite makes it suitable for beads, cabochons and carvings. Its softness means that it is easy to carve and it has been used for intaglios for centuries. Sometimes hematite is faceted and the upper surface of a cabochon is cut in a similar way to a rose cut. Facet edges and surfaces lose their sharpness and polish over time, so the stone will have to be repolished at some stage.
• The specific gravity of hematite is high, which means that a row of hematite beads will feel very heavy compared to one with other gemstones of the same size.
• Hematite is soluble in acid, so avoid contact with household chemicals.

Showcase

Highly polished spheres of hematite give these cufflinks an eye-catching, contemporary look. Hematite is not the hardest of gem materials and will damage easily, so these should be worn with care.

23/tugtupite

According to Inuit legend, tugtupite possesses a special power. In the presence of lovers it will glow a fiery red from the heat of their romance and passion, and the vibrancy of the colour will reflect the intensity of their love. While most would consider this fanciful, there is actually an element of truth in it.

If you look closely, you will see the slightly mottled colouring of tugtupite and the reflective white albite feldspar.

Tugtupite really does have the ability to glow red. Under shortwave ultraviolet light, it becomes fluorescent and glows a fiery, cherry-red colour. Longwave ultraviolet light produces a softer salmon-red colour. Tugtupite is a rare stone, but its properties and good looks make it worth looking out for. Also called reindeer stone, it was officially recognized and recorded as a gemstone in 1960, named after Tugtup, Greenland, where it was found. Inuit artisans are likely to have worked with the gemstone before 1960. Not only does it fluoresce, but it is also tenebrescent, which means that the paler parts of the stone fade to white when it is placed in the dark, while exposure to sunlight or ultraviolet light restores and enhances the red colour.

Gem-quality, pure red transparent crystals are small and very rare, so remain collector stones. The translucent to opaque material is more available; this is an aggregate consisting of indistinguishable crystals formed into a large, fine-grained mass. The colours of the massive material are white, bright pink, dark red with a violet tint, and shades of orange. The pink areas can be mottled with several colours and inclusions can create a slightly spotty look. White albite feldspar frequently occurs alongside tugtupite, often intergrowing with or acting as a host for patches of massive material. Tugtupite can have a vitreous to greasy lustre, and transparent gem-quality stones can be distinctly pleochroic, showing bluish red and orange-red. The Kvanefjeld area of Greenland produces the best gem material.

SPECIFICATIONS

HARDNESS 5.5–6.5 Mohs (also recorded as 4 Mohs)
SPECIFIC GRAVITY 2.30–2.57
REFRACTIVE INDEX 1.49–1.50
CRYSTAL FORM Tetragonal. Single gem crystals occur as short tetragonal prisms. Normally found as a massive opaque material scattered in irregular hydrothermal veins and in pegmatite veins.

SOURCES OF TUGTUPITE

Canada (Mont Saint-Hilaire, Quebec), Greenland, Russia (Kola Peninsula).

Pricing tugtupite

Smaller pieces of tugtupite are moderately priced, but larger, high-quality pieces can be expensive as the stone is still quite rare and sought after by collectors.

Working with tugtupite

• The Kvanefjeld gem material is typically a bright red colour and has been used for jewellery. It can be cut as cabochons or sliced, and takes a good polish (the deep pink colour is brought out fully once the surface is polished). The fluorescence is an unmistakable bright red and could make a rather interesting design feature in any jewellery. Just in case there is any concern, tugtupite is not radioactive!

• Tugtupite has been carved by Greenlanders for many years because of its softness and fine compact grain. It has a distinct cleavage and conchoidal, uneven fracture. It would be suitable for most types of jewellery, as long as it is for occasional wear and there is little risk of impact. As a ring stone it would need a protective setting. In other words, treat tugtupite as you would an opal.

Showcase

This white gold ring displays a raspberry-pink tugtupite cabochon in a simple rub-over setting. The ring has a special feature: if worn in UV light the stone will glow a bright cherry-red colour.

24/diopside

Diopside is not really a name to attract the jewellery-buying public and it doesn't invoke the reality of this vibrant gem, with its dramatic chrome green colour. That is why efforts are being made to come up with a more tempting designation.

The asterism is a result of light reflecting off sets of parallel fibers within the cabochon; the light rays meet at one point and form a star.

Diopside comes in a number of saturated colours: bottle green, brownish green, light green, brown and purple. The gem is highly refractive, so faceted transparent stones appear lively and brilliant with a vitreous lustre. Sometimes diopside can be virtually black, with fibres that lie parallel to each other and produce a distinctive four-rayed star. There is also an opaque purple to violet-blue variety called violane, which occurs in Italy and the United States.

Russian chrome diopside (Vertelite™) looks great cut as cabochons because the colour and clarity of the material is so good. These gemstones weigh approximately 3.5 ct each.

CHROME DIOPSIDE

This is the most important and valuable variety of diopside, with a vivid emerald-green colour due to the presence of chromium. Russia is the major commercial producer of high-grade chrome diopside; the Siberian mines process between 10,000 and 15,000 carats of faceted gem material per month. The bulk of this is in calibrated sizes up to 9x7-mm ovals (2 carats in weight). Larger single gemstones are also cut, but in much smaller quantities. It is rare to find "clean" chrome diopside of over 7 carats. Some chrome diopside is now marketed under the name Vertelite™.

SPECIFICATIONS

HARDNESS 5.5–6 Mohs
SPECIFIC GRAVITY 3.22–3.38
REFRACTIVE INDEX 1.664–1.730
CRYSTAL FORM Monoclinic. Gem-quality crystals are prismatic with a square cross-section. The name of diopside derives from the two-fold symmetry of its crystal structure, but it also occurs in a compact granular form. Chrome diopside is found in calcium-rich metamorphic rocks and diamond kimberlites.

SOURCES OF DIOPSIDE

CHROME DIOPSIDE Myanmar (formerly Burma), Pakistan, Russia (Siberia), South Africa.
DIOPSIDE Austria, Brazil, Canada, Italy, Madagascar, Sri Lanka, United States.

Treatments and imitations

As yet, diopside is not enhanced. It is not treated for colour and, unlike emeralds, there is no evidence of oiling or fracture-filling with resin.

Pricing diopside

The price of "clean" bright chrome diopside is moderate if you stay under 2 carats, but large stones are more expensive due to rarity. Good-quality bead material is available, but an entire row of chrome diopside beads will cost!

Working with diopside

• Diopside is sensitive to heat, so avoid soldering and polishing with the stone in situ and don't use steam cleaners or ultrasonics. Avoid any contact with bleach or cleaning liquids as acids will dull the polish of the gemstone.
• Diopside has a rough, uneven fracture and perfect cleavage in two directions at nearly right angles. Gem-quality diopside often contains flaws resulting from internal stresses and the inherent fragility of the material, which is why it is so difficult to find large, "clean" rough material. A rectangular step cut is typically used because the crystal shape is columnar, and faceted stones are usually cut slightly shallow to obtain the best colour, as the colour saturation of diopside can make a stone appear dark. However, the perfect cleavage means that diopside is vulnerable to impact or undue pressure, so an oval or round brilliant cut is much safer than a shallow rectangular cut. The prices of the "safer" cuts will be much higher, to compensate for the far greater waste (weight loss) of rough material created by an oval or round.
• Diopside is perfectly safe for jewellery as long as it is for occasional use. Faceted diopside is not ideal for a ring stone; a cabochon in a rub-over setting would be much more robust.

Showcase

The beauty of chrome diopside is revealed in this two-row bracelet; the intensity of the colour is remarkable. Small, white keshi pearls act as a buffer for the slightly fragile chrome diopside beads.

25/scapolite

Scapolite is still relatively unknown to jewellery makers and buyers, despite good design potential. Whether it is used as a transparent faceted stone or as a translucent chatoyant cabochon, its possibilities are worth exploring as it becomes more widely available.

Scapolite is an interesting stone that has until recently remained in the domain of collectors. The name derives from the Greek words for "rod" and "stone" – *scapos* and *lithos* – which quite simply describe the shape of scapolite crystals. The gemstone is also called wernerite, after the German geologist A.G. Werner.

This lively violet scapolite weighs 8.14 ct and looks very much like amethyst.

SPECIFICATIONS

HARDNESS 6–6.5 Mohs
SPECIFIC GRAVITY 2.50–2.74
REFRACTIVE INDEX 1.540–1.600
CRYSTAL FORM Tetragonal system, with the crystals appearing as tetragonal prisms that are columnar or elongated on the C axis (they resemble sticks). It can also be found in a massive form. Scapolite occurs in metamorphic rocks and pegmatites.

SOURCES OF SCAPOLITE

Brazil, Canada, Kenya, Madagascar, Myanmar (formerly Burma), Russia (Siberia), Tanzania.

Treatments and imitations

• Faceted yellow scapolite can resemble gemstones such as yellow beryl, chrysoberyl and citrine. Pink scapolite could be mistaken for rose quartz, but rose quartz doesn't exhibit chatoyancy. Purple scapolite can easily be confused with amethyst, especially as it has properties that are very close to quartz.
• Treatment of scapolite to improve or change the colour does occur, but is limited because the gemstone has yet to be produced commercially in quantity. Aside from the occasional heating of yellow material to violet (the more desirable colour), there is Brazilian scapolite on the market that has been treated to intense raspberry pink and orange-pink.

Pricing

• The availability of scapolite is increasing and prices should reflect that by dropping slightly. However, it is not a particularly expensive stone.
• The value of scapolite is dependent on the colour or the quality of colour. For instance, pink chatoyant material with a brownish beige tinge will be worth less than a stone with a clean, pure, silky pink colour. Good violet scapolite can range from a soft lilac to a velvety blackberry – lower-quality material tends to be very dark or grey in tone. Faceted yellow scapolite is cheaper than violet, as it is more common. Cat's-eye scapolite is on a par with the faceted violet material.

Working with scapolite

• Faceted scapolite is not really suitable for ring stones. Cat's-eyes cut as cabochons would be more suitable, and would look quite fascinating in a ring. They would need to be seated so that the "eye" is centered and would require a protective bezel setting, which will allow them to withstand being worn as an occasional dress ring.
• Scapolite's cleavage and brittle fracture mean that faceted stones have to be treated with care during setting and polishing. However, scapolite is by no means the worst stone for cleavage problems.

Colours of scapolite

The transparent gem material is colourless, or coloured golden yellow, light red, blue-grey, orange or violet. Yellow is the most common colour. The colours reflect the variation in composition of the crystal's impurities, from sodium-rich to calcium-rich. The material has a glassy, vitreous lustre and can contain dark mineral or tubelike inclusions.

Translucent cat's-eye scapolite can be found in pink, orange, white-grey, light red and violet; the most common colour is pink. The chatoyancy, or cat's-eye effect, can range from good to stunning, with a sharp silver-white "eye" appearing down the stone's centre.

Scapolite is fairly durable and can be found as a transparent faceted gemstone or as a translucent to opaque cat's-eye cabochon. The stone has good cleavage and a conchoidal, brittle fracture. It exhibits pleochroism, which is particularly strong in violet stones.

The colour of this cat's-eye scapolite is really pretty, pure and free of brown tones. The silvery white cat's-eye stands out clearly.

26/turquoise

For over 3,000 years, the ancient Persians exported turquoise to the world – people couldn't get enough of it. Nowadays, demand for the stone is still so high that a worldwide industry has developed not just to mine it, but also to imitate and reproduce it.

This American Sleeping Beauty turquoise cabochon contains no matrix.

This high-dome cabochon of Iranian (Persian) turquoise weighs 30 ct. Iranian turquoise is no longer mined, so this is a collectible piece. The closely knit material doesn't crumble and has no need for treatments.

Turquoise is highly prized throughout Asia and Africa, and many cultures believe it to possess therapeutic and spiritual qualities. Historically, the Arabic countries thought it was a lucky stone, protecting the wearer from evil, and a cure for many ailments. North American Natives and ancient Inca and Aztec cultures all also venerated the stone. A great deal of antique turquoise jewellery, including amulets, has been found intact in excavations.

Imitations

• A great deal of turquoise is not natural material. Turquoise can be an expensive stone, so there are numerous imitations on the market as well as treatments designed to improve its appearance.

• Glass imitations of turquoise have existed since Victorian times. They can be very difficult to distinguish from natural turquoise once set into jewellery, but sometimes it is possible to spot small telltale air bubbles near the surface. Enamel was also used to imitate turquoise; the lustre of enamel is far greater than that of natural turquoise.

• Other stones and materials have frequently been used to imitate turquoise. Howlite, fossil bone (odontolite), limestone and chalcedony are dyed or stained, and sold to unsuspecting buyers. In 1972, the French manufacturer Gilson produced imitation turquoise, even including matrix in the imitation stones to give them the popular spiderweb pattern.

SPECIFICATIONS

HARDNESS 5–6 Mohs
SPECIFIC GRAVITY 2.80
REFRACTIVE INDEX 1.61–1.65
CRYSTAL FORM Triclinic. It is found in microcrystalline massive form as encrustations, veins or nodules. Turquoise is opaque to semitranslucent and has a waxy to dull lustre. Unfortunately, it has a high porosity, which can lead to the material fading and cracking over time.

SOURCES OF TURQUOISE

Originally, Persia was the most important source of turquoise, but now the United States produces the best material. Also found in Afghanistan, Australia, Brazil, Chile, China, Mexico, Russia, Tanzania and Turkestan.

Showcase

The shanks of the rings are carved from turquoise and the gold details added as protection and decoration. The pearls have been sunk into the shank while the beads appear to secure them. The pearls are, in fact, cemented in place.

The pendant at right is hand-carved from Sleeping Beauty mine turquoise, chalcedony drusy and aquamarine.

Colours of turquoise

The traditional colour of turquoise is sky blue. This was the colour of turquoise from Iran (Persia), once considered the best source of turquoise in the world. Iranian material is virtually mined out now, and so is very rare and valuable. It is thought that the best turquoise currently comes from the Sleeping Beauty mines in Arizona, which produce very clean material with an intense dark blue colour. A great deal of turquoise originates from China, Brazil and Russia; most of it arrives in the form of beads with matrix running throughout.

The colour of turquoise can range from china blue and deep blue to blue-green, dark greeny blue and yellowish green. The impurities present affect the colour of the stone; copper gives turquoise a blue hue while iron creates a green tint. The mother stone, termed the matrix, often penetrates the turquoise in the form of black, brown and ochre veins.

This turquoise bead material comes from China. The spiderweb matrix can make the nuggets prone to breaking up if they are handled roughly.

These 10-mm beads are made of A-grade Sleeping Beauty mine turquoise with no matrix.

These beads have an attractive green-blue colour with veins of brown matrix.

Treatments

• Aside from the numerous imitations, the market is also awash with enhanced, coated, stabilized and reconstructed turquoise. The sheer number of treatments can be rather confusing to the buyer, and it is hard to know which treatment is an accepted trade practice and which is devised to deceive. Traders have a duty to tell buyers of any treatments, but may not know exactly what treatments have been applied, as material may be treated at source by the mining companies before being sold for cutting.

• **Reconstructed or pressed turquoise** Turquoise powder and small chips are bonded with liquid plastic resin, dyed and then baked. Once the material is solid, it is cut in the same way as natural turquoise and can be dyed to various colours, including the expensive dark blues and sky blues. Examining a piece of rough pressed turquoise through a loupe, it is occasionally possible to spot small particles or chips of the original turquoise. Alternatively, heating a small piece will produce the sharp odor of burnt plastic. The final indicator will be the price: reconstituted turquoise is much cheaper than natural turquoise.

• **Stabilized and coated turquoise** Turquoise can vary in porosity and fragility depending on the source. Old Persian turquoise was less porous and so less treatable, which ensured buyers were sold natural, untreated material. Today, the majority of American turquoise is very porous and quite crumbly to work with, so it is nearly always stabilized or coated in some way. This involves soaking the rough material in an artificial resin or impregnating it with wax, to improve its colour, to harden its surface for cutting or to maintain its appearance and strength over time. This type of treatment occurs at the source and tends not to affect the price.

• **Enhanced turquoise** Normally this means dyeing or staining the turquoise to improve the colour. Oil, paraffin and copper salt also improve colour and lustre, but their results tend to be temporary. One way to check for enhancement is to look inside the holes of beads or scratch the turquoise with a sharp point – the interior of the bead or scratch mark will be a lighter colour than the exterior. Turquoise that is enhanced and dyed should be much cheaper than natural turquoise.

Pricing turquoise

The quality of turquoise is based on colour, intensity and the presence of any matrix rock. A piece of Sleeping Beauty turquoise that is free of matrix and has an intense dark blue colour would be deemed the ideal material. A row of 12-mm round beads made of ideal material would cost nearly the same as a row of 4.5–5-mm faceted rubies with a decent colour and clarity. The price reflects the grade of blue, so a light blue will cost less than a sky blue and a dark blue will cost the most.

Working with turquoise

• A low specific gravity means turquoise feels light in weight, which makes it ideal for large jewellery pieces. As a softer, microcrystalline stone it can be carved and engraved; many pieces of antique Arabic jewellery have been engraved and then filled with gold leaf.

• Turquoise has a conchoidal fracture, however, which means it is quite fragile to work with and can crumble, scratch and mark easily. It requires a protective setting as a ring stone and would need to be worn with extreme care as a bracelet. When stringing turquoise beads to make a necklace, it is a good idea to knot the thread between beads so they don't rub and damage each other.

This turquoise shows discolouration.

• Unlike other gemstones, turquoise can age and become darker in colour or turn slightly green. Light, oils and a loss of its natural water content also have a negative effect on the colour and can lead to cracking. Because of its porosity, discolouration can occur on contact with detergents, grease or perspiration; turquoise rings should always be removed before washing hands and any perspiration should be cleaned off gently with water.

• If turquoise is heated it will change into a dull green colour and eventually turn brown and disintegrate. If you are soldering or polishing jewellery with turquoise, you will need to remove the stone or protect it from heating and polishing compounds. Be careful when spreading glue to attach caps and posts onto turquoise briolettes or pendeloques, as it may affect the colour of the stone.

• Turquoise jewellery should be stored in a cool, dark box in acid-free tissue paper, away from other jewellery that might damage it.

27/lapis lazuli

The lapidary has cut this lapis in such a way that the surface of the cabochon is left natural, covered by a layer of pyrite inclusions.

Lapis lazuli translates from the Arabic as "heaven [or sky] stone" – it was clearly held in high regard in ancient times. And as for its standing today, if the number of imitations is a guide to how highly we value a stone, then lapis lazuli is one of the most popular gems on the market!

A high polish works well on this pendeloque – it makes the stone look as if it has been lacquered.

Natural lapis lazuli is an intense brilliant blue, its colour deriving from the presence of the mineral lazurite. It is completely opaque and often contains small gold or silver pyrite inclusions that run through the material in veins or layers. The finest-quality lapis has an even, deep blue colour that contains a purplish tint or tone and is free of pyrite inclusions. Afghanistan is still considered to be the best source; this material has the most desirable shade and depth of blue and is the most expensive. Russian lapis from Siberia is sometimes represented as better, but it is generally paler with more pyrite inclusions.

Sometimes lapis contains prominent patches of other minerals. White calcite is often found filling the cracks and cavities within lapis, creating mottled blue-and-white material called lapis matrix. The lustre of lapis lazuli is vitreous to greasy.

SPECIFICATIONS

HARDNESS 5–6 Mohs (depending on composition)

SPECIFIC GRAVITY 2.38–3.00 (higher if the pyrite content is high)

REFRACTIVE INDEX 1.50–1.55 (depending on composition)

CRYSTAL FORM Isometric. Lapis lazuli has three main mineral components: lazurite, hauyne and sodalite. Calcite and pyrite inclusions are also found in varying degrees.

SOURCES OF LAPIS LAZULI

Afghanistan, Argentina, Canada, Chile, Myanmar (formerly Burma), Russia (Siberia), United States (Colorado, California).

Treatments and imitations

• The popularity and value of good-quality lapis lazuli has resulted in numerous imitations appearing on the market. The large number of minerals that are stained or dyed blue can all be identified as imitations by a lack of pyrite inclusions, a difference in texture and/or hardness and visible pockets of dye. Pierre Gilson of France produced an imitation with a similar composition to natural lapis, but its softness makes it impractical to use.

• A synthetic lapis was manufactured in the 1950s. It consists of a grainy blue synthetic spinel coloured by cobalt oxide, with gold flecks added to resemble pyrite inclusions. It is much harder than natural lapis and so can be distinguished quite easily.

• Reconstructed lapis lazuli is also available and is made in a similar way to reconstructed turquoise. Small chips of lapis and particles of pyrite

are mixed together with a polymer and some dye, and then press-molded, ready for cutting.

• Unfortunately, a great deal of natural lapis lazuli is dyed to even out the colour or to improve the tone of blue. Sometimes material is dyed selectively and the dye applied only to the white constituents. Dyed lapis is often waxed, oiled or coated with a polymer to improve its lustre and to cover and preserve the applied dye, which makes it much more difficult to identify. There are also reports of lapis being heated to improve the colour.

Pricing lapis lazuli

As there is so much dyed and treated lapis on the market, not always properly labelled, it is important that you buy from a reputable dealer and ask questions about the material. Natural good-quality lapis is valuable whereas dyed material is not – the price should reflect this.

Working with lapis lazuli

• Lapis lazuli is sensitive to pressure and high temperatures, so it should not be exposed to ultrasonic or steam cleaners. Avoid contact with household chemicals (acid and alkali), and always wipe perfumes and perspiration off jewellery before storing.

• Lapis has an uneven fracture and an imperfect cleavage, but its tight granular structure makes it ideal for carving or sawing into slabs for use in mosaics and intarsias. Lapis is also available in cabochon and bead form. It is a versatile material and different surface finishes can be applied: a high polish looks great with a deep blue colour, a matte finish works well with lighter shades, and for a textured appearance the surface can be left natural.

Showcase

The lapis lazuli gemstone remains in its natural form with uneven, ragged edges and an unpolished surface. It is framed by the contrasting angular metal structure to create an eye-catching brooch.

28/sphene

Sphene is highly regarded as a gemstone by collectors, but scarcity has kept it out of the commercial market until now. The discovery of new deposits should ensure that this brilliant little gem finally achieves the attention it deserves.

This yellowish green sphene is full of lively colourful fire – it is impossible for a camera to capture the dispersion completely.

Cabochons can be found as single colours or as a mixture of greens and reddish browns. This stone has a beautiful oily appearance.

Gem-quality sphene comes in a range of clear bright tones: grass green, golden yellow, brownish yellow and reddish brown. The most sought-after and expensive colour is chrome green, and there are also bicoloured stones in a mix of green and orange-brown. Sphene is strongly pleochroic, showing three different colours when viewed from different angles: colourless, greenish yellow and reddish. It is a wonderfully brilliant gemstone that possesses an adamantine lustre and a dispersion that is greater than that of a diamond. Under incandescent light the brilliance is amplified.

Sphene has a high birefringence (double refraction), which results in the doubling of the back facets. "Clean" rough material is difficult to find and it is very rare to get a clean stone over 10 carats, but faceted stones are still stunning, even with minor inclusions, due to the remarkable properties of the material. A gemstone will usually contain needlelike and rounded plagioclase inclusions, as well as veils and mistlike inclusions.

SPECIFICATIONS

HARDNESS 5–5.5 Mohs
SPECIFIC GRAVITY 3.52–3.54
REFRACTIVE INDEX 1.995–2.05
CRYSTAL FORM Monoclinic. The crystals have characteristic wedge-shaped ends and are often twinned. Gem-quality material is found in metamorphic rocks and in granite. The mineralogical name for sphene, titanite, derives from the presence of titanium in the material.

SOURCES OF SPHENE

Brazil, Canada (Ontario), India, Madagascar, Mexico, Myanmar (formerly Burma), Sri Lanka, Switzerland, United States.

Treatments and imitations

• Sphene is often heat treated to change the colour to red or orange tones.
• It could be confused with chrysoberyl, dravite (golden brown tourmaline), heliodor, topaz or zircon (which also has a high dispersion).

Pricing sphene

The availability of sphene can fluctuate slightly, but it is easy enough to get clean stones up to 2 carats in weight. The material is moderately priced at this size, but larger stones over 3 carats are harder to find and more expensive. Sphene is not available in bead form.

Working with sphene

• Sphene is a moderately soft gemstone, but would be suitable for pendants or earrings. If it were to be used for a ring it would need to be protected and kept for occasional wear only. Do not use ultrasonic cleaners and take care during polishing. Treat sphene as you would an opal.
• Cutting sphene is a considerable challenge. The material has perfect cleavage and a conchoidal, brittle fracture, which means that it chips easily. The pleochroism and high birefringence have to be taken into account when orienting the table for faceting; the best colour should be seen from the top through the table and there should be no blurring of the back facets. Round and oval brilliant cuts are more suitable for sphene as they are less likely to result in damage or chipping. The brilliant cut was designed for a gem with high dispersion, so it will make the most of sphene's brilliance and fire. Princess cuts and baguettes are not suitable.

Showcase

This dress ring features a reddish brown faceted sphene that, despite containing inclusions, will produce great fire and brilliance when worn.

29/natural glass:obsidian and moldavite

Natural glass tends to be overlooked as a gemstone because of the extensive use of manufactured glass in gemstone imitations. However, both obsidian and moldavite have interest value – the former for its patterns and optical effects and the latter for its origin in outer space.

Types of natural glass

OBSIDIAN

Obsidian is formed when molten lava cools too rapidly for crystallization to occur. It is semitranslucent to opaque and found in black, smoky brown, grey, blue, red and green. Blue and green are less common colours, and red is the rarest. The colour can be uniform or patterned, and can have twisted or straight colour bands caused by the solidification of flowing lava. It may also contain crystal leaflets or tiny gas bubbles that sparkle as they catch the light. Obsidian can be strongly iridescent, showing purple and green patterns as light reflects off its internal structure. Snowflake obsidian is well known for the white marks that resemble snowflakes, which are caused by internal bubbles or crystallites.

This is a beautiful example of obsidian. The colour banding is distinct and the shape is perfectly symmetrical.

MOLDAVITE (TEKTITE)

Moldavite, or tektite, was first discovered at the end of the 18th century in Czechoslovakia. It is thought that the material either originates from meteorites that melted as they passed through the earth's atmosphere or is a result of rock shock melting as a large meteorite or comet impacted on the ground. The colour of moldavite is light to dark green, dark brown, grey or black. It can occur as button-shaped pieces with a rough black to brown surface covered in cooling cracks, or as green translucent to transparent material with a distinctive craggy surface.

This is the green translucent to transparent form of moldavite.

SPECIFICATIONS

HARDNESS 5–5.5 Mohs
SPECIFIC GRAVITY 2.20–3.00
REFRACTIVE INDEX 1.48–1.51
CRYSTAL FORM Amorphous. Natural glass has a conchoidal fracture but no cleavage.

SOURCES OF NATURAL GLASS

OBSIDIAN Ecuador, Guatemala, Hungary, Iceland, Mexico, Russia, United States.
MOLDAVITE Australia, China, Czech Republic, Tasmania, Thailand.

Showcase

This pendant contains rough green moldavite, hand-carved lemon citrine, nephrite jade and peridot. It is strung on a necklace of dyed freshwater pearls.

Treatments and imitations

• It is impossible to distinguish between natural glass and synthetic glass, as any visual characteristic of the natural material can be readily manufactured. However, synthetic glass is easier to melt.
• Moldavite could be confused with green diopside or tourmaline, but it lacks their brilliance and dispersion. It is sometimes called bohemian or water chrysolite, but this is a misnomer as the name chrysolite is usually associated with peridot (olivine).

Pricing natural glass

Obsidian is in abundant supply and, except for outstanding mineral specimens, is inexpensive. Moldavite is not particularly rare, but is valued by collectors because of its unusual origin.

"Once cut, they have the charm and brilliance of a bit of beer bottle; best to keep them as they are found."
–Frederick Pough, gemmologist and author

Working with natural glass

• Obsidian and moldavite are fairly soft gemstones and both can be easily scratched and cracked.
• Obsidian has been used in jewellery for many years and can be found in bead and cabochon form. Clear green moldavite is suitable for jewellery, yet it rarely appears in designs; the green colour is not that attractive and the glass material lacks the sparkle normally found in gemstones. Moldavite, especially the transparent to translucent green material, is more appealing when left in its natural state, and designers have chosen to work with it in that form rather than as a faceted stone.

30/apatite

"Good things come in small packages" – such is the case with apatite. Although seldom seen in jewellery stores, and despite its small size, this stone is popular with buyers for its wonderful clarity and colours.

The fibrous nature of this greenish yellow apatite produces a sharp golden cat's-eye effect. It weighs 25.75 ct!

This faceted apatite has great colour and clarity. The material comes from Madagascar.

The Spanish call apatite the asparagus stone, for its greenish yellow colour. In fact, gem-quality apatite comes in a range of good-looking pure transparent colours, in shades of blue, greenish yellow, greenish blue, soft pink and violet. On the whole, blue is the most popular colour and sells the best. However, the recent availability of a neon blue-green apatite from Madagascar has created enormous interest, as it imitates the colour of neon paraiba tourmalines. Fine-quality pink apatite from California is on the market, and chatoyant blue and greenish yellow cabochons containing fibrous inclusions can also be found.

This is a typical apatite crystal; it is hexagonal in form with a pyramidal termination.

Apatite has medium dispersion and a glassy lustre that produces a bright, lively gemstone. However, gem material can often be marred by the presence of numerous inclusions, which typically are in the form of black carbon specks, tiny cloudlike inclusions, melt inclusions and "silk" (a reflection of fibrous inclusions creating a silklike appearance). The included parts of the rough material are cut away to obtain clean faceted gemstones, resulting in small-sized stones. Burmese blue apatite displays strong dichroism, showing two colours (blue and weak blue or colourless).

SPECIFICATIONS

HARDNESS 5 Mohs
SPECIFIC GRAVITY 3.18
REFRACTIVE INDEX 1.632–1.642
CRYSTAL FORM Crystals form hexagonal rods with hexagonal pyramidal endings; it sometimes occurs as tabular crystals. Gem-quality apatite occurs in igneous and metamorphic rocks and in iron-ore deposits.

SOURCES OF APATITE

Brazil, Canada, East Africa (Mozambique, Madagascar), Mexico, Myanmar (formerly Burma), Russia, Spain, Sri Lanka, United States (California).

• Apatite is highly sensitive to heat, so take care during polishing or soldering and don't use steam or ultrasonic cleaners. Cutting apatite is not easy as undue pressure or heat can cause a cleavage plane to run or open up. It is also a difficult material to polish; the corners can chip easily and scratches are hard to remove. Because of these problems, a well-cut and well-finished stone will be more valuable.

• Apatite appears in bead form in a range of colours and qualities. Unfortunately, the quality of the cheaper beads can be very poor, and they may be broken, cracked or chipped and often have damaged drill holes. The fragile beads are crushed beneath heavier beads during transportation and they become damaged when strands rub together as they are being viewed. Poor-quality apatite beads can also break when they are being strung; knot between each bead to prevent damage.

• It would be tempting to dismiss apatite as a jewellery stone because of the extra effort it requires. However, the purity of colour, especially of the blues and blue-greens, is difficult to find in other gemstone material. Use good-quality, well-made material and check the goods carefully before buying.

Treatments and imitations

• The name apatite, which derives from the Greek for "deceive," was given because the stone is easily confused with other minerals, such as precious beryl, topaz, zircon, tourmaline and sphene.
• Synthetic apatite has been manufactured.
• Apatite is often heat treated specifically to improve the colour and remove the silklike inclusions.

Pricing apatite

Apatite is valued in terms of colour saturation, clarity and size. The intense blues, blue-greens and violets are the most sought-after colours and the most expensive; they will be priced on a level with clean faceted tourmaline (not paraiba). Larger sizes cost more because they are rare, and natural colours will have a higher value than heat-treated stones.

Working with apatite

• Apatite has imperfect cleavage and a conchoidal, uneven fracture, making it quite brittle. It is also fairly soft, so avoid rough handling and be careful with facet edges and any sharp corners. In other words, treat it like an opal.

31/hemimorphite

Hemimorphite has an unusual characteristic: a change in temperature or pressure induces an electrical charge in the stone. The bad news is that static attracts dust and dirt, so unfortunately any jewellery will need cleaning on a regular basis.

The colour of this hemimorphite cabochon is really pure. It is translucent to opaque with an almost fibrous texture.

Also known as calamine, hemimorphite is not a new material but reaches back into ancient history. The colours are really beautiful, and soft blue-green, intense emerald green and bright cobalt blue to dark blue are the most popular shades for jewellery purposes. Hemimorphite is also found in white, colourless, brown and yellow, with the white often appearing with other colours to create a mottled look or make the colour seem pale. Well-crystallized, transparent material does occur, but it is rare and fragile. More common is the grapelike botryoidal massive form, which is found as a thick blue to blue-green crust that is translucent to opaque. Hemimorphite also occurs as a banded aggregate or mixed with dark matrix. The lustre is vitreous to silky.

Treatments and imitations

• Hemimorphite is sometimes dyed to improve or intensify the paler colours.
• Most natural hemimorphite is immersed in a very strong and permeable gluelike material to fill the hairline fractures that are nearly always found in this gemstone and to improve its stability. The process, called stabilizing or fixing, strengthens, toughens and improves the transparency of the hemimorphite, and enables lapidaries to cut larger stones. Usually, no colour is added.
• Hemimorphite could be confused with turquoise.

Pricing hemimorphite

• This is a material that is beginning to gain more popularity. A sky-blue hemimorphite necklace appeared in one of the auctions of rare gemstone jewellery held by American auctioneers Bonhams & Butterfields.
• On the whole, hemimorphite is moderately priced, except for the pure blue material and stones in large sizes, both of which are rarer.

SPECIFICATIONS

HARDNESS 4.5–5 Mohs
SPECIFIC GRAVITY 3.30–3.50
REFRACTIVE INDEX 1.612–1.636
CRYSTAL FORM Orthorhombic system. The crystals are tabular with one termination being blunt and the other pyramidal; this structure is called hemimorphism.

SOURCES OF HEMIMORPHITE

Africa (Algeria, Congo, Namibia and Zambia), Australia, Austria, China, Italy, Mexico, Russia (Siberia), United States (Arizona, Montana, New Jersey and New Mexico).

Working with hemimorphite

• A drusy type of hemimorphite is available. This is cut from the textured crust, its surface can be matte or crystallized and it comes in blue and blue-green colours. Drusy tends to be more delicate than material that is cut *en cabochon;* the crystallized or grapelike surface textures can be easily damaged if they receive an impact, and they are prone to trapping dirt and fluff, so drusy is better for earrings and pendants than for rings.
• Hemimorphite has an uneven conchoidal fracture and a perfect cleavage in one direction, making it brittle and prone to damage. It is sensitive to acids and impact, so chemical and ultrasonic cleaners should not be used. The material loses some of its water content when heated; avoid overheating the stones during polishing.
• Hemimorphite gemstones trap dirt and dust and will need cleaning with a soft toothbrush and water.

Showcase

These beads show the mottling of colour that occurs in hemimorphite. They are inexpensive as the colour is not intense.

32/rhodochrosite

Rhodochrosite is another relative newcomer to the trade, having been on the market only since 1940. It can be distinguished by its glorious colour, which is summed up by its alternative name – raspberryspar.

This slice of rhodochrosite looks good enough to eat! The distribution of colour gives it the most wonderful texture.

Gem-quality transparent rhodochrosite crystals have a vivid pink colour. They can be faceted, despite their softness, but are normally bought by collectors as they are rare. The translucent form of rhodochrosite is more suited to jewellery work. It comes in watermelon pink to grapefruit pink – the aggregate structure of the material really does create the appearance of grapefruit flesh! Opaque rhodochrosite usually has distinct banding in shades of rose-pink, red and white, which can be serrated, straight or curved in a pattern of alternating colours.

Rhodochrosite has a vitreous to pearly/resinous lustre, depending on the type of material and the finish. Clean stones are rare; veils and planes of fingerprintlike inclusions frequently occur, together with inclusions of black manganese. While the oldest mines producing pink-and-white banded rhodochrosite are in Argentina, the prime commercial source of gem-quality material is the Sweet Home mine in Colorado.

This is a fine example of gem-quality rhodochrosite in a translucent form. It measures 1½ x ½ in. (41 x 15 mm).

SPECIFICATIONS

HARDNESS 4 Mohs
SPECIFIC GRAVITY 3.45–3.70
REFRACTIVE INDEX 1.600–1.820
CRYSTAL FORM Trigonal. Individual crystals have a rhombohedral shape but rhodochrosite is usually found as a compact aggregate. The colour is due to the presence of manganese.

SOURCES OF RHODOCHROSITE

Argentina, Canada, Mexico, Namibia, South Africa (Kalahari), United States (Colourado).

Working with rhodochrosite

• Pink and black accessories became fashionable for a while in the 1950s and the jewellery designers of that time used a combination of pink gem-quality rhodochrosite and black onyx in necklaces and bracelets. Rhodochrosite would have been very new to the market at that point.
• Rhodochrosite reacts to acids, so any contact with chemicals should be avoided. It is best not to use ultrasonic and steam cleaners, just in case the material has been stabilized or impregnated.
• Rhodochrosite has a conchoidal, non-uniform fracture and perfect cleavage in three directions, forming a rhombohedron. It is a soft material, but the colour is so glorious that it would be a shame not to use it as a jewellery stone. A fine-grained rock, it is tough enough to be carved, sliced into slabs, cut as cabochons or formed into beads. There are jewellers in the United States and Europe who are currently using rhodochrosite in their earring and pendant designs. The cabochon form removes some of the risk factor as it is less prone to breaking than a faceted stone.

Showcase

Made from silver and 18K gold, the choker is set with a large, buff-top rhodochrosite cabochon.

Treatments and imitations

• It is possible that individual lapidaries have tried treating rhodochrosite. The material could be impregnated with a polymer resin to make the stone more durable and less brittle.
• Rhodochrosite could be confused with other natural gemstones such as rhodonite, tugtupite and fire opal. Dyed banded calcite is the only known imitation, but it is softer than rhodochrosite.

Pricing rhodochrosite

The pink-and-white banded form of rhodochrosite is in abundant supply and inexpensive. Better, gem-quality beads and cabochons are more expensive as the material is rarer.

33/fluorite

It requires enormous skill to carve a matching pair of briolettes such as these out of fluorite. The lapidary is based in Idar-Oberstein, Germany.

The combination of large sizes, beautiful colours, plentiful supply and value for money makes fluorite a very tempting stone to use in jewellery. But beware: this is a gemstone that's fraught with problems and one that needs to be used wisely.

Fluorite's name derives from the Latin for "to flow"; it melts more easily than other minerals and was once used as a flux. It comes in a variety of pretty transparent to translucent colours: bright golden yellow, bluish green, rose-pink, blue, green, purple and colourless. The stone has a glassy, vitreous lustre and takes a high polish.

SPECIFICATIONS

HARDNESS 4 Mohs
SPECIFIC GRAVITY 3–3.25
REFRACTIVE INDEX 1.434
CRYSTAL FORM Isotropic. The typical crystal shape is cubic. Fluorite occurs in hydrothermal or sedimentary deposits.

SOURCES OF FLUORITE

Argentina, Austria, France, Germany, Myanmar (formerly Burma), Namibia, United Kingdom (Derbyshire), United States (Colorado, Illinois).

Treatments and imitations

• Fluorite is often irradiated to deepen the colour, and pale stones are sometimes heated in oil for the same purpose. The cleavage of fluorite means that it is rather fragile for use in jewellery, so it is often impregnated with a resin or polymer to strengthen the material and make it less likely to break along its cleavage planes during carving, cutting or polishing.
• Fluorite cabochons are sometimes capped with rock crystal (clear quartz) to prevent the stone from being scratched or damaged.
• Calcium fluoride is fluorite simulated in a laboratory. Doping synthetic fluorite with different elements permits its manufacture in any colour.

Pricing fluorite

Fluorite is an abundant, inexpensive material.

Working with fluorite

• Fluorite has traditionally been used as a material for carving decorative objects rather than as a gemstone for jewellery. Its softness makes it particularly suitable for carving cameos and intaglios.
• Fluorite has a conchoidal fracture and a perfect octahedral cleavage with four easy cleavage planes, which make it prone to breakage. The ease with which fluorite cleaves is remarkable. If it is heated the material will expand and split along the cleavage planes – there are reports of this happening in bright sunlight! Faceted fluorite is aimed at collectors only, as it is too fragile for jewellery. Beads and cabochons are less brittle and can be used, but they are not suitable for jewellery that might receive an impact, such as a ring or bracelet.
• When you purchase fluorite it is vital that you check its quality, especially if you are buying beads. Friction against other beads can easily cause chipping and scuffing and dull the polish. Fluorite should be stored on its own and rows of beads should be wrapped separately to protect them. When stringing fluorite beads, try to knot between each bead so that it doesn't rub against its neighbour.
• A customer might return fluorite jewellery if a stone breaks or becomes damaged. Warn buyers that the material is delicate and inform them that the intense colours of fluorite can fade with extended exposure to sunlight.

Showcase

Fluorite nuggets and handmade silver beads form a tactile necklace. The unpolished fluorite produces a natural look and accentuates the soft green and purple colours.

Types of fluorite

A transparent emerald green fluorite from Namibia called African emerald is one of the most popular colours. It is also an interesting gemstone that often has many colours in a single crystal, with stripes, patches and spots that subtly merge together or stand out in sharp contrast to each other. Fluorite also occurs as an opaque mass.

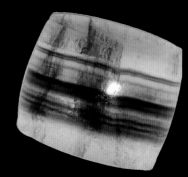

Here is an example of the multiple colours that commonly appear side by side in fluorite.

34/malachite

How tastes change. Malachite was so popular in the 19th century that the Russian royal family panelled whole rooms with it, and the Victorians loved it so much that they always set it in gold. Today, when we choose to value the rare rather than the commonplace, malachite usually appears in cheap silver jewellery.

Malachite commonly occurs as a microcrystalline aggregate with a lumpy botryoidal habit such as the material illustrated here.

Malachite is usually collected as a sideline to copper mining; it is the presence of copper that creates the popular green colour. The material is normally found as an opaque green mass, as any crystals are too small for faceting. It is marked with bands, or concentric stripes, of different widths, in contrasting shades of green. The lustre ranges from vitreous to dull.

SPECIFICATIONS

HARDNESS 4 Mohs
SPECIFIC GRAVITY 3.8
REFRACTIVE INDEX 1.65–1.90
CRYSTAL FORM Monoclinic. Malachite is described as a secondary mineral because it is created by a chemical reaction between minerals that have already formed.

SOURCES OF MALACHITE

Australia, Namibia, Russia (Siberia), United States (Arizona, North Carolina, Pennsylvania), Zaire.

Treatments and imitations

• Malachite could be confused with natural green agate and aventurine quartz. Pseudoemerald and silver peak jade are both misnomers used for malachite. As with lapis lazuli, imitation malachite is made from other materials and then dyed green.
• Synthetic malachite has been manufactured despite the fact that malachite is a natural mineral in abundant supply. The synthetic malachite comes from Russia and is virtually indistinguishable from natural malachite.
• Lower-quality, less compact malachite can be stabilized with plastic resins or given a surface polish with wax. It is commonly treated with oil, epoxy or wax to enhance the colour. Resin-bonded or plastic-impregnated malachite consists of fragments glued together with resin. Malachite has a natural variation in hardness between layers; occasionally the variation is too great and the material is put through an impregnation process to make it easier to cut.

Working with malachite

• Malachite effervesces in acid, so should be kept away from chemicals; ammonia-based products will strip the stone of its polish. It needs to be treated carefully as its rough fracture and perfect cleavage make it somewhat brittle. The material is sensitive to heat, so should not be used in ultrasonic or steam cleaning. It is not suitable for jewellery that gets rough handling, such as bracelets or rings, but would be fine for earrings, tie pins, brooches and pendants.
• Because of its softness, malachite is easy to carve and shape. It is readily available in bead form and as cabochons and slabs (for inlay work).
• The copper content of the dust released during the grinding of malachite is toxic. If you intend to work with malachite, use protective respiratory gear and keep the rough material wet as you grind.

Types of malachite

Other malachite-based gemstones are available. Azurmalachite is a mixture of malachite and azurite. Calcomalachite is a malachite and calcite mix, found in Arizona. Malachite matrix is largely malachite, but also contains very small amounts of other copper minerals. Plissovy is a Russian malachite that exhibits radiating fibres. Prase malachite is chalcedony that is naturally impregnated with malachite. Star malachite is chalcedony with inclusions of malachite in the form of a star.

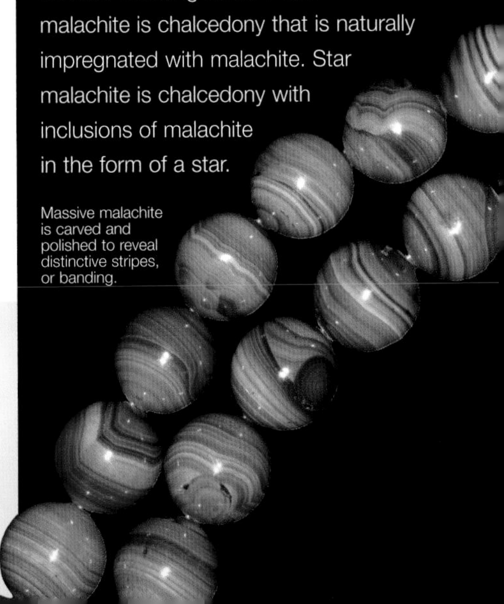

Massive malachite is carved and polished to reveal distinctive stripes, or banding.

Pricing malachite

Malachite is an inexpensive material.

Showcase

These pretty silver earrings are inlaid with malachite so that it lies flush with the surface of the metal. The earrings are double-sided so the gemstone can be seen from the back as well as the front.

35/diamond

Advertising tells us that a diamond is a rare and valuable thing to possess. While it cannot be disputed that white diamonds remain the most important gemstone within the jewellery industry, it is worth bearing in mind that diamonds are mined throughout the world on a massive scale. The only restriction to the supply comes in the form of the cartel that controls it. As for the high price, it is the result of a careful marketing strategy, not rarity.

Cubic diamond crystals from the Congo are normally used for industrial purposes.

The diamond industry works quite separately from the coloured gemstone market; it has a culture and structure that doesn't exist anywhere else in the gemstone business. Not only do diamonds dwarf the trade in other gemstones by being the most mined of gems, they are also the most carefully classified and tightly controlled. Unlike coloured stones, a detailed grading system based on carefully guarded master samples ensures that the factors used to dictate quality and value remain constant.

It is essential for jewellery designers and makers to have a good knowledge of the diamond industry and its systems so they can inform their customers wisely and make sound business decisions. The value of diamonds is so much greater than other gemstones that the risk of deception for uninformed buyers is high, and mistakes can be very costly.

Natural yellowish brown marquise-cut diamond (2.12 ct)

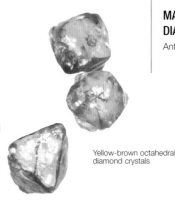

Yellow-brown octahedral diamond crystals

SPECIFICATIONS

HARDNESS 10 Mohs
SPECIFIC GRAVITY 3.417–3.55
REFRACTIVE INDEX 2.417–2.419
CRYSTAL FORM Diamond crystals belong to the cubic or isometric system and their chemical composition is crystallized carbon. Diamonds are formed at very great depth (up to 280 miles/450 km) and at high temperature and pressure. They come to the surface with rising magma in volcanic eruptions and are found in kimberlite pipes, which are mined through underground tunnels, and also as alluvial deposits in river gravels.

Diamond crystals are normally well-formed and range from transparent to opaque. The common shapes of rough gem diamonds are octahedra, cubes, rhombic dodecahedra and macles. Diamond has a strong adamantine lustre.

MAJOR SOURCES OF DIAMONDS

Angola, Australia, Botswana, Namibia, Russia, South Africa, Zaire.

MAJOR CUTTING CENTRES OF DIAMONDS

Antwerp, Bombay, New York, Tel Aviv.

Rough diamonds are selected at a mine's sorting house.

Diamond economics

About half (in terms of value) of the world's gem diamonds comes from African mines that are either owned or co-owned by De Beers. The company has signed agreements with all the other major diamond-producing countries so that its Central Selling Organization (the CSO) is responsible for sorting and selling their rough gem material as well as its own. In addition to this, De Beers has control of the marketing of cut diamonds for the diamond industry, operating across 28 countries.

De Beers was by no means the first to recognize the economic potential of diamonds. About 2,500 years ago, India was the major producer of gem-quality diamonds and records show that production was carefully regulated even then. The Golconda mines are famous for some of the finest diamonds ever found, including both the 108-carat Koh-i-Noor and the 45-carat blue Hope diamond.

Nowadays, most diamonds are sorted for selling in the De Beers CSO offices in London. Only accredited De Beers clients can purchase the diamond "lots", and the number of lots offered for sale is dictated by price trends and consumer demand. Rough diamond material is held back when consumer demand is weak, and increased when demand is strong. This single-channel marketing system maintains the high price of diamonds and ensures that they remain an attractive investment. The resale and division of lots occurs in diamond exchanges (clubs or bourses in diamond trading locations). Diamond traders refer to monthly pricing indexes, such as the Rapaport (Rap), which set the current prices of white diamonds by colour, clarity and weight, effectively fixing a top price.

This silver-gilt Deccan pendant (top left and detail at left) was made in the 19th century using Golconda diamonds, natural pearls and red glass beads. The necklace that holds the pendant features cultured pearls (visible top left).

The history of the brilliant cut

Diamonds were first cut to improve their look in the 13th century. Prior to that, the rough edges of diamond crystals were simply smoothed down and the flat surfaces polished. The cut used was the extremely basic table cut, in which an octahedral crystal was given a flat surface on top (called the table) and a smaller flat surface underneath (called the culet). In the late 1400s, the cutting wheel appeared and diamonds started to get their rounded outline.

Widely used from the early 1600s, the rose cut was an economical way to cut flat diamond rough with little wastage. The stone had a faceted dome and a flat base under which gold or silver foil could be placed to reflect light, giving diamonds a soft lazy fire that drew the eye into the stone. This method of cutting and setting diamonds had been used in the Far East for centuries; in Asia, simply cut kundan stones were set, like cabochons, with pure gold foil, and flat, angular diamond crystals were used with coloured gemstone beads and natural pearls.

At the end of the 17th century a Venetian cutter, Vicenzio Peruzzi, created what is known as the old cut. Although more irregular in shape, it is viewed as being closest to the modern brilliant cut. The old cut enjoyed considerable popularity; its 58 facets gave it life and fire, while the overall proportions brought a subtlety and depth to the gemstone.

This octahedral crystal would be suitable for cutting – it is free of yellow or brown tints and has reasonable clarity.

Pear-shape crown rose-cut diamond (3.54 ct). The facets radiate from the centre of the stone, creating the appearance of a rosebud, hence the name. This old stone shows the grade of material that was typically used.

The modern brilliant cut was introduced in 1919 and was viewed by the industry as the ideal cut. It was very popular with jewellery makers and buyers alike because it made the most of the gem's naturally strong light dispersion, resulting in tremendous brightness and fire. The brilliant cut became the standard for the trade.

Fancy cuts

If a diamond is not a brilliant cut, it is called a fancy cut. This category includes baguettes, pear shapes, heart shapes and marquises. Fancy cuts are not produced in large quantities and often have a higher carat price because they entail more wastage of rough material. A baguette- or emerald-cut diamond has a slightly lower brilliance than a brilliant-cut diamond because the step-cut style was primarily intended for coloured gemstones, the large table facet showing off the colour and the step-cut pavilion facets allowing light into the back of a stone. Modern cutting technology has brought us many new fancy diamond cuts; the Asscher, Trilliant, princess and baguette cuts have all been adapted from the brilliant cut.

These 19th-century silver-gilt Deccan diamond earrings demonstrate the simple cutting style that was used with Golconda diamonds and its similarity to the rose cut.

The 18K yellow gold brooch at left is set with three 1 ct brilliant-cut diamonds.

Amsterdam Asscher-cut diamond set in white gold ring (fancy light yellow diamond, 3.22 ct). The Asscher cut was one of the first square cuts to be developed and it has inspired a 74-facet contemporary version called the Royal Asscher. It has large angular corners, a small table, high crown and an open square culet. It produces more fire than a step-cut octagon.

Diamond cuts

TABLE CUT

The table cut was used until the early 1700s. It relied on cleaving the crystal to shape. It was based on trial and error because it could break the stone. The top and bottom of an octahedral crystal were cleaved to create a flat table and a smaller flat culet.

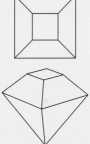

ROSE CUT

The rose cut dates from the early 1600s; its principal feature is the flat back, which allows it to be set like a cabochon. It can be simple, with three or six facets, or more complex, with facets radiating in multiples of six. It can be shallow or deep, oval or pear-shaped.

OLD CUT

In 1700, the old cut arrived, with 58 facets. It often had a cushion shape and proportions following those of the octahedral crystal. The main features were a large visible culet, a small table, a deep pavilion and a high crown. It has less brilliance than a modern brilliant cut but more fire.

BRILLIANT CUT

In 1919, Marcel Tolkowsky published his calculations for the modern brilliant cut. His specific angles and proportions produced a stone visibly shallower than the old cut: the pavilion and table were shallower, the outline was fully rounded and the culet face much smaller. The cut produced maximum fire and brilliance and could be adapted to different shapes, all with 58 facets.

Baguette-cut diamond (0.75 ct). New baguette cuts such as the Princette and bagillion have been gaining popularity because they are faceted to produce greater brilliance than a traditional step cut such as this.

Calibrated diamonds

The bulk of small diamonds are round brilliant cuts, but other calibrated shapes such as princess cuts are also produced. The stones are sorted into carat groups that equate to a particular size, which is why they are termed calibrated. Round calibrated diamonds can measure between 1.3 mm (0.01 carat each) and 3.8 mm (0.20 carat each), but they are often referred to by their point size. For instance, 1.3-mm stones are known as one-pointers and 1.8-mm stones are three-pointers. Set weights make it possible to work out how many diamonds there are per carat. Small diamonds are also graded for colour, assigned a G/H or J/K/L banding.

Diamonds that are calibrated for weight will have a slight variation in size: one-pointers generally measure between 1.2 mm and 1.4 mm. If you are planning on using pavé setting in your design and don't wish to upset your stone setter, you will need to buy diamonds that are calibrated to one size, for instance 1-mm rounds. They will have a slightly higher carat price than stones that are graded for weight because the sorting process involves more time and labour.

Calibrated black diamonds have been pavé-set to add a contemporary feel to the eternity ring design.

The design of diamond jewellery

VICTORIAN ROSE CUTS

Made in the 1880s, this Victorian ring is set with a beautiful marquise-shaped rose cut that has been foil-backed to reflect the light and produce a bright lustre. The flat base of the rose cut allows the ring to sit low on the finger. Made in gold with silver inlay, the shank has decorative work and was probably cast. It is a particularly nice rose-cut diamond; it has a fine colour and clarity with a good outer shape, and the faceting has been done with care. Rose cuts often used slightly yellow or brown material and were often very shallow with simple faceting and an irregular outer shape.

OLD CUT DESIGNS

Old cuts were used to great effect by Victorian and Edwardian jewellers. This ring is dated around 1900 and is made from white gold. It holds a large old-cut diamond weighing 3.73 carats. The diamond is slightly yellow with a distinct rounded cushion shape and a very visible open culet. It has a lazy brilliance, good depth and real charm. Old-cut diamonds were often set in closed-back claw bezel settings so that pieces of foil could be hidden behind the stones to increase their brilliance.

EDWARDIAN DIAMOND-SET JEWELLERY

The influx of South African diamonds in the late 19th century created a huge demand for diamond-set jewellery among those who were keen to show off their status and prosperity. This Art Nouveau pendant would certainly have been used as a statement of wealth. The central light cognac, natural coloured diamond is cushion cut and weighs between 5.5 and 6 carats. It is framed by numerous white old-cut diamonds that are set in delicate bezels with millegrain edges. The piece is made in gold and silver, with a background of black enamel. A large, perfect, natural drop pearl is suspended from the main pendant.

ART DECO DESIGNS

This platinum ring is set with a white pear-shaped old-cut diamond and a bright Colombian emerald cabochon (also pear-shaped). Made between 1910 and 1920, the striking asymmetrical design uses nonstandard shapes and mixes two very different stones. Art Deco jewellery designers were eager to use the new cuts and shapes of gemstones that were being brought out at that time and commonly used coloured gemstones such as sapphires, emeralds, opals, rubies and black onyx alongside diamonds to give the jewellery colour and drama. The jewellers were also keen to design with the newly developed synthetic sapphires and emeralds.

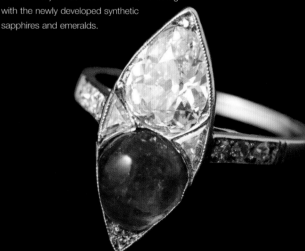

DIAMOND JEWELLERY OF THE 1950s

This white gold ring uses a large faceted demantoid garnet (3.37 carats) together with 2.5 carats of white diamond baguettes. It is a fine example of jewellery construction; the flowing design of the diamond baguettes would have required considerable setting skills. The demantoid garnet is rare for its size and is a beautiful and unusual choice of gemstone. It contains typical fibrous asbestos (horsetail) inclusions. From the early 1950s the jewellery industry began to boom around the world, and the recovery of national economies after World War II gave people increased spending power. There was a renewed interest in fashion and accessories as dressing up for the evening was back in vogue. Extravagant, adventurous jewellery that combined different coloured stones became the rage.

TIFFANY DESIGNS

Established in 1837, Tiffany & Co. was instrumental in the development of art jewellery that broke with tradition. It contained organic motifs of flora and fauna and used gemstones in unusual materials and cuts. Tiffany was also heavily linked with diamond jewellery, and the development of the Tiffany setting led to the creation of the solitaire engagement ring. The company revived many antique jewellery making techniques: filigree work, granulation and enamelling. This necklace was made in 1870. Enamelled gilt has been set with white diamonds and the pieces contain intricate filigree detail.

MODERN DIAMOND DESIGNS

This pearl and diamond necklace contains a staggering 83 carats of brilliant-cut diamonds including a natural yellow diamond. The focal point is a large mabe pearl. Despite the quantity of diamonds used in this piece, they do not dominate the design, as is often the case with diamond jewellery. Instead, the diamonds are scattered in an irregular pattern acting as highlights within the richness of the gold and complementing the pearl. They are one part of a highly complex design that uses layering, granulation and texture to draw the eye across the piece.

BACK TO BASICS

This is a pair of 22-karat yellow gold drop earrings with rough octahedral diamonds. Some modern jewellery designers have rejected the traditional faceted brilliant-cut diamond in favour of the uncut rough diamond. The natural adamantine lustre that diamond crystals possess makes them an attractive and unusual focal point. This type of rough diamond is not easy to source, as most are kept by the diamond trade for faceting, which makes them quite rare. The gold disks have been pierced so that the diamonds protrude on both the front and the back.

POLKI DIAMONDS

This is one of a pair of modern Polki diamond earrings made in Jaipur, India. *Polki* is a vernacular term describing a flat, cheaper cut of diamond that is traditionally kundan-set into jewellery. Kundan is a closed setting that uses compressed 24-karat foil to hold the stone in place. The Polki diamonds might not have the brilliance of a Western brilliant cut, but their subtle light and simplicity suit this style of jewellery and balance with the emerald beads, seed pearls and decorative enamelling. This type of diamond costs a fraction of the price of a brilliant-cut diamond.

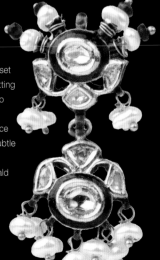

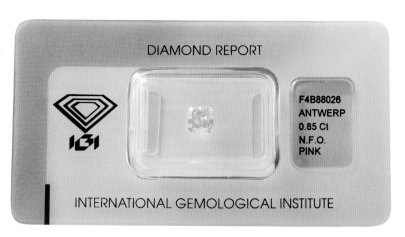

An IGI-certified pink diamond. The package containing the diamond is sealed to prevent the stone being changed or swapped.

DIAMOND REPORT

F4B88026
ANTWERP
0.85 Ct
N.F.O.
PINK

INTERNATIONAL GEMOLOGICAL INSTITUTE

Pricing diamonds

All diamonds marketed by De Beers are classified, or certified, into various standards of quality or grade, which directly affect the price. A certificate proves that a stone is genuine, sets out its individual characteristics and indicates quality and value. It is useful for insurance purposes and essential if you are planning to sell the diamond at a later stage. A certificate adds to the cost of a diamond, but buying a diamond without a certificate carries a significant financial risk.

Read the certificate carefully. If it doesn't come from one of the main diamond certifying bodies (listed at right), then contact the laboratory, quote the certificate number and check the details. Make sure that the certificate states that the stone is actually a diamond and gives a full description. If the date on the report is more than 10 years old it is worth getting a new certificate made.

Laser inscriptions

To protect consumers and laboratories, the certificate number can be inscribed by laser onto the girdle of the diamond, where it will be visible only with a 10x loupe. This won't harm the diamond or affect the clarity or colour grade. The inscription can only be removed by polishing, which would probably result in weight loss and a change of diameter.

RECOGNIZED LABORATORIES AND GRADING ORGANIZATIONS WORLDWIDE

CIBJO The World Jewellery Confederation
CSA Jewellery Council of South Africa
DPL Diamant PrufLabor, Germany
EGL European Gemological Laboratory
GIA Gemological Institute of America
HRD Antwerp World Diamond Centre
IGI International Gemological Institute

Colour grading scale

D E F	G H I J	K L M	N O P Q R	S T U V W X Y Z	FANCY LIGHT	FANCY	FANCY INTENSE
COLOURLESS	NEAR COLOURLESS	FAINT YELLOW	VERY LIGHT YELLOW	LIGHT YELLOW		YELLOW	

Clarity grading scale

FL	IF	VVS-1 to VVS-2	VS-1 to VS-2	SI-1 to SI-2	I-1, I-2, I-3
Loupe clean (flawless)	Internally flawless, minor surface blemishes	Very, very small inclusions	Very small inclusions	Small inclusions	Inclusions visible to naked eye

Grading factors for diamonds

CLARITY

The clarity grade will identify how clean a diamond is as seen through a 10x loupe. Tiny cracks that look like feathers, microscopic diamond crystals and carbon deposits are common in diamonds and generally won't affect the brilliance. They will, however, affect the price.

COLOUR

Colour is best observed by examining the stone through the pavilion, with the table upside down on folded white cardstock. If the stone is viewed through the table, the brilliance will hide the colour. Grade D carries a significant premium, yet you will be unlikely to see any difference between Grades D and E, and the price difference could pay for a larger diamond with better clarity.

WEIGHT

Diamonds are weighed to one-hundredth of a carat and are priced according to their weight. To compare the prices of two diamonds you refer to the carat price. There are 100 points to a carat and 75 points equals 0.75 carat (three-quarters of a carat). Weight also relates to size. For instance, a 1-carat brilliant-cut diamond should measure 6.5 mm in diameter. If the stone is cut slightly shallow, the diameter will be larger; if it is cut too deep, the diameter will be smaller.

Old-cut diamond –
2.76 ct cushion cut

PROPORTIONS AND FINISH

In a brilliant cut, the crown (the top portion of the stone) should measure one-third of the depth of the pavilion (the distance from girdle to culet). Good proportions create brilliance by allowing light to be reflected up through the stone's table. The proportion of table width to stone width determines a stone's fire: a smaller table produces more fire while a bigger table produces more brilliance. Poor proportions can lead to a dark bow-tie or butterfly effect across the centre of the stone in ovals and fancy cuts. This diminishes the beauty of the stone and devalues the diamond.

FLUORESCENCE

A stone that produces a colour reaction when exposed to ultraviolet light is described as having fluorescence. If a diamond fluoresces a blue colour, it will appear whiter in daylight, masking any yellow tint it may have. This is useful if the diamond has a low colour grade, but a white diamond that fluoresces yellow will have a yellow tint in daylight – not what you want in a fine white stone!

CUT AND SHAPE

The cut, also called the make, includes proportions and symmetry and has the greatest influence on the brilliance of a diamond. Poor cutting, such as a thin girdle, will affect the durability of a diamond, making it more susceptible to breaking or chipping. A sloping table, misaligned facets or poor symmetry will prevent light travelling through the stone properly and so affect the brilliance. Cutting faults will also cause significant problems when it comes to setting the diamond.

Natural coloured diamonds

Yellow, orange, brown/cognac and black are the most common natural diamond colours and easy to find. Pink, light green and lavender are rarer, but can still be sourced without too much effort. Deep blue, red and dark green are extremely rare and seldom seen; they are the most expensive of the natural diamond colours and fetch high collector prices.

The intensity, purity and uniformity of colour is critical to the price as many coloured diamond crystals have an uneven, patchy spread and cut stones often end up with the colour concentrated in one area. A stone with a muddy colour or a mix of colours will be priced lower. If you intend to buy a natural coloured diamond it is vital that the stone has a certificate from a respected laboratory. If it doesn't, the sale should be dependent on a report that verifies the colour as natural.

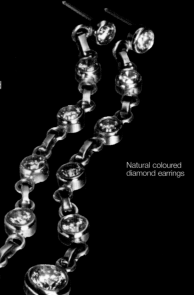

Natural coloured
diamond earrings

COGNAC DIAMONDS

Brown- and cognac-coloured diamonds are still very good value and the range of colours is beautiful. The colours range from light golden copper to fiery orange to deep cognac to dark brown. They look fabulous when set in high-karat yellow gold.

Natural cognac
brilliant-cut diamond

Pair of natural green-brown
brilliant-cut diamonds

YELLOW DIAMONDS

Yellow diamonds are slightly rarer than cognacs, with an intense canary yellow being the most expensive shade. Light fancy yellows can sometimes look like capes (diamonds of a low-grade colour). The diamond in the photo has a radiant cut, which is a brilliant version of an emerald cut. A radiant cut can be square or rectangular.

Fancy intense yellow
diamond, radiant cut
(1.57 ct)

PINK DIAMONDS

The vivid pink diamond produces stunning orange highlights. It is unusual to see a natural pink diamond of this intensity (they commonly have a pastel colour), so the gemstone has a significant premium on its price. Pink diamonds have become very popular (and very expensive) thanks to the shopping habits of celebrities and their appearance in the collections of leading jewellery designers.

Fancy vivid pink oval
diamond (0.31 ct) and
fancy pink cushion diamond
(0.28 ct).

BLACK DIAMONDS

Although black diamonds occur naturally, they do not achieve the price of other coloured diamonds. They have traditionally been used for industrial purposes. Opaque black bort (or boart) diamonds derive their colour from black mineral inclusions, the polycrystalline structure or cracking. The material is often fibrous in nature and is notoriously difficult to cut and polish; the girdle and facet edges often become chipped. A great deal of black diamond material for sale is actually treated; it is irradiated or heated under very high temperatures.

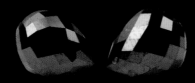

Black diamond
briolettes

BLUE DIAMONDS

Blue diamonds are rarely bright blue; the stones typically have a greyish blue tone caused by boron. A treated blue diamond has quite a different colour that is closer to greenish blue. Natural blue diamonds are considerably more expensive than pink, yellow or cognac diamonds. The blue Hope diamond pictured here is a famous stone bought by the banker Henry Philip Hope in the 1830s. It now resides in the Smithsonian Institution in Washington, D.C. The antique cushion brilliant cut weighs 45.52 carats and, unusually, it phosphoresces a bright red colour under shortwave UV light. The gem is graded as a fancy dark greyish blue and the clarity is VS-1 (it has whitish graining common to blue diamonds). The Hope diamond pendant is surrounded by 16 white diamonds and suspended on a chain that contains 45 white diamonds.

Natural blue
6.74 ct diamond

Blue diamond set in ring

The Hope diamond,
below, weighs 45.52 ct.

Treated diamonds

If your budget doesn't stretch to natural fancy colours you could always try using treated coloured diamonds in your designs. Fluorescent yellows, electric blues, magenta, coral pinks, chocolate browns, blacks and occasional greens are all available in small sizes. The manufacturers heat and irradiate inexpensive brownish to yellowish diamonds in order to obtain fancy colours that sell better. They are far cheaper than their natural counterparts, but the difficulty of the treating process can still make them pricey. Heating and irradiating have uncertain results and it is sometimes hard to achieve certain colours or produce a batch of stones with a consistent colour.

Treated blue diamond (0.32 ct). Treated coloured diamonds often contain inclusions as lower-grade, inexpensive material is used for irradiation purposes. This diamond is a good example of a treated diamond; it has a good clarity and cut with a clear, attractive colour.

Numerous techniques and treatments have been developed to improve the look of white diamonds; some have been deliberate attempts to deceive buyers. The process of using a laser to vaporize black inclusions leaves a fine white thread that starts at the surface and travels into the stone. The treatment is permanent and should be disclosed on any certificate. Fractures and cracks can be filled with a glasslike substance that is visible only under magnification. It is not a permanent treatment and bad care or handling can loosen the filler or change its colour. Certain types of yellow-tinted diamonds are put through a high-pressure, high-temperature (HPHT) process to make them colourless. The results are permanent and irreversible, but the treated diamonds can be identified by a laboratory.

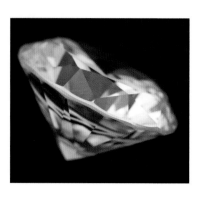

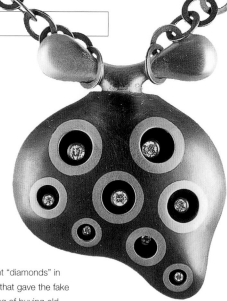

This oxidized silver and gold pendant contains synthetic stones in place of diamonds, probably to keep the piece affordable.

Diamond imitators

Many years ago, the unscrupulous used to present "diamonds" in closed-back settings that concealed the silver foil that gave the fake stone the brilliance of a diamond. If you are thinking of buying old diamond-set jewellery, check the stones with a loupe. Diamond is so hard that facet edges should stay sharp and the surfaces will withstand scratching. Glass and colourless gemstones such as zircon, white topaz or rock crystal are much softer, so their facet edges will round off and flat faces will become scratched over a short period of wearing. These days, synthetic stones are used to give the effect of diamonds; they are cheap, hard wearing and they sparkle. From time to time, synthetics deceive buyers, so it is useful to know their properties.

CUBIC ZIRCONIA

Cubic zirconia is one of the best diamond simulants created so far; it has more fire than a diamond and is almost as brilliant. However, cubic zirconias are nearly 75 per cent heavier than diamonds and, unlike diamonds, they can be scratched with a fine carbide scriber.

SYNTHETIC DIAMOND

Synthetic diamond is not identical to natural diamond and can be identified in a laboratory. It is possible to buy synthetic diamonds of up to 2 carats in weight in a range of colours. However, because production costs are so high, they remain commercially unviable.

YAG

YAG (yttrium aluminum garnet) is used extensively in jewellery because it is hard (8.5 Mohs) and wears well. However, it has a low degree of dispersion and produces virtually no fire.

STRONTIUM TITANITE

This stone is also known as fabulite. It is quite soft (5 to 6 Mohs), so scratches and chips easily, but it has the highest display of fire seen in a stone.

MOISSANITE

This stone can fool electronic diamond testers that measure thermal conductivity. It has a greater brilliance and degree of dispersion than either a diamond or a cubic zirconia and is extremely hard. It costs approximately one-tenth of the price of an equivalent diamond.

Cubic zirconias can create a blanket of light very similar to that created by diamonds.

This white gold ring contains a marquise-cut moissanite. The manufactured stone appears slightly lacklustre, not displaying the brilliance or dispersion of a faceted white diamond.

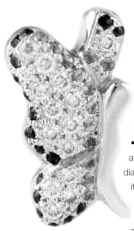

Pavé settings require well-calibrated stones of consistent size. Colour must also be consistent, because variations in whiteness will be obvious.

Working with diamonds

• The colour of the stone setting can affect the perceived colour of the diamond. A very white diamond will look its best set in white metal; a yellow gold setting will reflect a yellow tone into the same diamond, making it appear slightly tinted. However, if the diamond already has a yellow tint, an 18-karat yellow gold setting will make the stone appear whiter in contrast. For this reason it is better to have diamonds unset for certification and insurance valuation.

• Having a hardness of 10 Mohs gives a diamond longevity. Ideally, the piece of jewellery a diamond is set into should be capable of surviving as long as the gemstone. Gold is soft and wears thin. Eventually gold claws break, and at best they need retipping. At worst the diamond falls out and is lost. Platinum is a much more durable metal and enables designers to use settings that are barely visible. In fashionable modern tension settings the stone is secured to the shank at just two small contact points, exposing the diamond's girdle and pavilion. Only platinum has the strength to hold a stone this way for any length of time.

• Diamonds are insensitive to chemicals but high temperatures can cause etchings on the facets. If you solder with the diamond in situ, take precautions to protect the stone. If the diamond has been heat treated, it would be better to remove the stone before soldering.

• Diamond has perfect cleavage, which means that it can be damaged. If the side of a diamond is hit against a hard surface it will probably fracture. If too much pressure is placed on the edge of the stone during setting, the girdle might break.

The handling of diamonds

• Diamonds are always weighed on carat scales that are calibrated to either one-hundredth or one-thousandth of a carat. For accuracy, make sure the scales are completely level. Putting the lid down over the pan prevents any breeze from affecting the reading.

• Diamond dealers normally use a Leveridge gauge rather than callipers to measure diamonds; it is accurate to one-tenth of a millimeter.

• Using tweezers with fine serrated tips prevents the diamond from becoming greasy. Hold the stone by the girdle using a relaxed, even pressure. If you squeeze too firmly it will jump out of the tweezers across the table (or floor).

• Grease adheres to diamonds, affecting their colour and brilliance. Fatty deposits from dishwashing and cosmetics can lower the colour of a diamond by several grades. The simplest way to clean a diamond is to sit it in hot water with a drop of dishwashing liquid and gently brush it with a soft toothbrush. Alcohol also removes grease and dirt.

• It is better to use diamond papers for storage than plastic bags. Faceted diamonds are very sharp; they will puncture a bag and escape.

Conflict-free diamonds

The downside of diamonds is the conflict and misery that they can cause. Currently the Congo, Sierra Leone, Angola, Russia, Liberia and the Ivory Coast are suffering from diamond-funded corruption or internal upheaval. The diamond industry is using the term *conflict-free diamonds* to reassure consumers that their diamonds are "clean" and not funding someone's army. Whether this is a real attempt to stop the misery that diamonds cause, or just a marketing ploy to sell more diamonds, remains to be seen. Perhaps if more people started asking about the origin of their diamonds, the diamond industry would be encouraged to use its considerable weight to ensure that "conflict-free" meant exactly that.

The princess cut is effectively a square brilliant cut. It is ideally suited for channel and rub-over settings. The Quadrillion is a trademarked version of the princess cut that is designed to produce maximum brilliance.

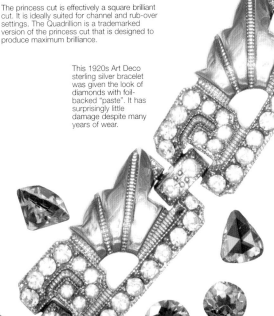

This 1920s Art Deco sterling silver bracelet was given the look of diamonds with foil-backed "paste". It has surprisingly little damage despite many years of wear.

The ring at right places a beautiful pink diamond front and centre.

ORGANICS

This section deals with gemstones that have an organic origin yet have acquired certain gemstone qualities and characteristics. The organics are an important part of the gemstone trade and, particularly in the case of pearls and coral, can have considerable value. This section includes the most popular and widely used gem materials and those most suitable for use in jewellery making: pearls, amber, coral, and shell. Although ivory and jet also belong to the organic group, they are not discussed here. The trade in elephant ivory has been banned worldwide since 1989 and it is now rarely used in jewellery. Jet is not really suitable for jewellery because of its fragility and limited availability.

36/pearl

Created naturally by a living creature over many years, every pearl is unique in its colour, lustre, size and shape. Pearl is one of the most beautiful and surprising gemstone materials available to jewellery makers. The design opportunities for pearls are limitless and, unlike some other gemstones, their flexibility and timeless appeal have earned them an enduring and worldwide popularity among jewellery buyers.

These decorative pieces have been made by piercing mollusc shells that have tiny blister pearls attached.

The beautiful Mississippi River angel-wing pearls are natural, not cultured.

These pearls have the appearance of keshi but are from China rather than Japan. They are freshwater pearls, which are much cheaper than saltwater keshi.

Buying pearls for the first time can be a confusing business: you will be confronted by hundreds of different varieties at an enormous range of prices. The two most important distinctions are the pearls' habitat (saltwater or freshwater) and how the pearls have been grown (are they natural or cultivated?).

Saltwater pearls come from oysters and mussels in oceans, seas, gulfs and bays. They are usually high quality and more expensive than freshwater pearls. Freshwater pearls are found in molluscs in rivers, lakes and ponds. They are generally more irregular and varied in shape than saltwater pearls.

SPECIFICATIONS

HARDNESS 3–4 Mohs

SPECIFIC GRAVITY
Natural (oriental) pearls 2.68–2.74
Japanese cultured pearls 2.72–2.78
Australian cultured pearls 2.70–2.79
Freshwater pearls 2.68 (average)

REFRACTIVE INDEX 1.53–1.68

CRYSTAL FORM Orthorhombic

SOURCES OF PEARL

NATURAL PEARLS Persian Gulf (off Bahrain), Gulf of Manaar, Red Sea.

CULTURED PEARLS Japan, China, Polynesia, Australia, the Cook Islands.

ABALONE MOLLUSC Off the coasts of New Zealand, United States (California, Oregon, Alaska), Mexico, Japan, Korea, South Africa, Australia.

MEASURING PEARLS

The standard system of measurement for pearls is the millimetre. This is the agreed indicator of pearl size and means of comparison around the world.

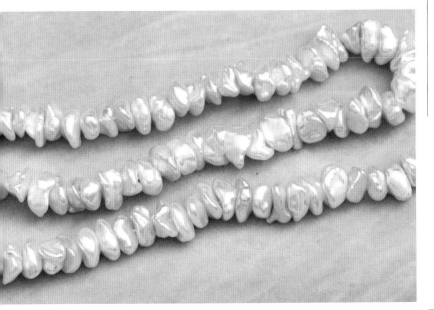

This row of Biwa pearls is exceptional for its size. The pearls measure 18 mm in diameter.

Natural pearls and cultured pearls

Sadly, our love of pearls and desire to follow fashion has greatly reduced the number of natural pearls available in the world. The constant demand for natural saltwater pearls over the last 150 years led to the overfishing of the natural pearl beds and many of them were lost for good. Natural freshwater pearls suffered the same fate. Angel-wing pearls from the Mississippi River and nearby lakes were very popular with Art Nouveau jewellers in the 1900s, but these days they have all but disappeared from the waters. Natural pearls have become very expensive.

In this Victorian gold ring, two rubies and three natural pearls sit in a protective recessed setting.

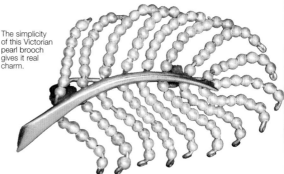

The simplicity of this Victorian pearl brooch gives it real charm.

Keshi pearls like these usually measure between 2 mm and 3.5 mm.

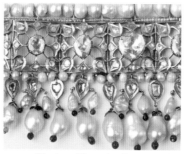

This piece of Deccan jewellery was made in the 1800s. It features baroque-shaped natural pearls, Golconda diamonds and emerald beads.

As the supply of natural pearls dwindled, the need to develop affordable cultured pearls became essential. The Japanese were the first to develop a reliable process, in which the mantle (outer membrane) of a three-year-old saltwater oyster is cut open and between 1 and 20 round mother-of-pearl beads implanted. The bead, or nucleus, stresses the oyster, which, to isolate the irritation, deposits nacre over it, creating a pearl. In cultured pearls the nucleus is large so that the time required for a pearl to develop is reduced – it takes three years for just 1 mm of nacre to form.

These tricoloured akoya pearls have an even, consistent shape.

Round mother-of-pearl beads are used as nuclei for cultured pearls.

Sizes of pearl

Round and semiround pearls are usually sorted by size, drilled, strung onto silk thread and sold as 16-inch (40-cm) rows. They can also be sold as pairs and singles.

FRESHWATER PEARLS start at about 2.5 mm and increase in 0.5-mm increments to 9 or 10 mm. The largest freshwater pearls are 10–12 mm.

This rare freshwater pearl measures 16 mm in diameter.

SOUTH SEA AND TAHITIAN PEARLS in rows start at 8–9 mm, with a maximum size of about 14 mm. The price of a row of Tahitian pearls is high, reflecting the difficulty of finding and matching enough pearls of the same shape, size and colour. Black South Sea baroque pearls measure between 9 mm and 20 mm.

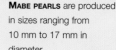

These South Sea baroque-shaped black pearls are "circled" and have green and silver overtones.

AKOYA CULTURED PEARLS are also graded by size: a diameter of 2–5 mm is small; 6–7 mm is average; 8 mm is large; 9–11 mm is very large and the maximum size possible from akoya oysters. The prices jump up with each increase of size.

MABE PEARLS are produced in sizes ranging from 10 mm to 17 mm in diameter.

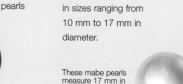

These mabe pearls measure 17 mm in diameter.

AKOYA PEARLS

These come from the akoya oyster and are typically round in shape. The natural body colours range from light pink to white to pale yellow, and include green and blue-grey tones. Akoyas are normally associated with Japan, especially if they measure over 7 mm. China, Korea, Hong Kong and Sri Lanka produce akoya pearls in smaller sizes.

White akoya pearls, 6.5 mm in diameter

Dyed akoya pearls with green overtones

Baroque-shaped akoya pearls with natural colour

SOUTH SEA AND TAHITIAN PEARLS

These pearls are cultured in the large mussel *Pinctada maxima* and usually require a longer growing time in the shell than do akoya pearls. They can be white with a rose or green tint, green, blue-grey, golden or pale yellow in colour. The lustre on light-coloured South Sea pearls tends to be less intense than on the dark pearls. Vibrant golden-coloured South Sea pearls are very popular and command a high price, as does the white-rose colour. South Sea pearls are the largest cultured pearls of all and as their size increases so does the price. Round pearls are the rarest and most expensive shape.

Sea pearl, intensity of colour influences price more than size does.

Large Tahitian pearls with excellent lustre and attractive silver overtones

BLACK PEARLS

Tahitian pearls from the black-lip mussel *Pinctada margaritifera* are the only natural black pearls that exist; all other black pearls are dyed. The "black" colour can vary from silver to dark grey and may have pink and green overtones. Black pearls can look almost metallic.

This valuable pearl is classed as black but is actually dark grey.

Small baroque South Sea pearls are great value and have wonderful lustre.

KESHI PEARLS

Keshi are tiny pearls that form spontaneously when a much larger nucleated pearl is cultured in the akoya oyster. As keshi grow without a nucleus, they are, in effect, "natural" pearls. They have the same colouring as akoya pearls. South Sea and Tahitian pearl molluscs also produce keshi, but in a much larger size. These can exceed 10 mm in length and are often used in jewellery because of their interesting shapes.

Keshi pearls are not easy to source.

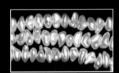

These keshi pearls measure from 3 to 4 mm in length.

Colours of pearl

It can be hard to distinguish natural colours from enhanced colours, and it is not always easy to get precise information from the dealer when you're looking at the pearls. The colour of the pearl depends on the variety of mollusc it comes from and on the type of water habitat. Pearl colour is a mixture of body colour and lustre (also called overtone). For instance, a "black" pearl could have a dark grey body colour with green or pink overtones. White-rose (white with rose overtones) is the rarest and most desirable colour of akoya pearls, and therefore the most expensive. Natural coloured pearls always have a higher value than dyed and irradiated pearls (see "Treatments and imitations", page 129).

Tahitian pearls can be found in delicate "sorbet" colours.

Baroque-shaped Biwa pearls display a range of colours.

This abalone mabe pearl has a subtle mixture of bronze, pink and blue colours.

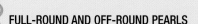

Shapes of pearl

Pearls come in a large variety of different shapes, making them fascinating to work with. The shape of a pearl depends on the type of mollusc it grew in, and on how the mollusc reacted to the nucleus.

These off-round pearls have natural colour.

This string of full-round white akoya pearls has rose overtones.

Pairs of baroque-shaped pearls do not usually match precisely.

FULL-ROUND AND OFF-ROUND PEARLS

If the irritant in the mollusc stays unattached to the shell, a nearly spherical or off-round pearl can develop. Perfectly round pearls are very rare.

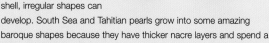

BAROQUE PEARLS

When an irritant, or nucleus, becomes attached to the shell, irregular shapes can develop. South Sea and Tahitian pearls grow into some amazing baroque shapes because they have thicker nacre layers and spend a longer time growing in the mollusc. The irregular surface generally emphasizes the pearl's lustre and iridescence. Keshi pearls also have baroque shapes and they can be bought singly or as a row.

This leaf-shaped pearl grew alongside a nucleated Tahitian pearl.

DROP PEARLS

Drop pearls are nearly as difficult to grow as round pearls. As a rule, the more symmetrical the drop shape, the more expensive the pearl. Drop pearls need evenness, symmetry, good proportions and balance. Smaller drop-shaped pearls are relatively easy to find, but sizes from 8 mm are rarer.

The circles (ringlike furrows) on this pearl drop will reduce its value, despite its good proportions.

These white pearls are more oval than drop-shaped.

These have an even, balanced shape and well-matched body colour.

FANCY PEARLS

Multiple and twin pearls occur when two or more pearls accidentally join or fuse together; sometimes a specially shaped nucleus is used. Bicoloured pearls are also described by this term. Fancy pearls are great for one-off designed pieces as they are relatively rare.

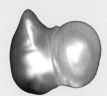

Four nuclei fused to form this pearl.

This pink triple pearl would make an interesting focal point in a design.

The colours of this fancy pearl are completely natural.

POTATO AND RICE PEARLS

These Chinese freshwater pearls are grown at great speed. The wrinkled irregular appearance of the rice pearls is a direct result of their very short cultivation period. Potato-shaped pearls can be large in size, but their lustre tends to be poor. They are often circled (with rings around them) and can be pitted.

Rice pearls are inexpensive because of their short growing time.

If a mollusc is overcrowded with nuclei, it won't be able to turn the pearls and this can result in irregular shape and size.

BUTTON PEARLS

These are grown in a similar way to mabe pearls. They are generally used for earrings and are supplied with a drill hole to accommodate a metal post for fixing. Button-shaped pearls also come as a row.

These pearls are side-drilled like coins.

Button pearls are shaped similarly to cabochons.

MANUFACTURED SHAPES

Three-quarter pearls and half-pearls are produced specifically to be mounted on ready-made stud earrings or rings. When they are set onto the metal fittings the pearls often appear to be full-round in shape.

This black akoya pearl has been trimmed to a three-quarter pearl and half-drilled ready to mount on a post.

Types of freshwater pearl

BIWA PEARLS

Lake Biwa is Japan's largest lake and was the first freshwater culturing site. Biwa pearls are noted for their good quality, smooth surface and high, even lustre. They don't normally have a nucleus as the mussel won't accept one, and as a result some bizarre shapes can occur. The colours range from creamy white to white-rose, salmon-orange, dark wine red and violet. Many freshwater pearls on the market are called Biwa pearls, despite being cultivated in China. This is probably done to impress or reassure customers, and to increase price.

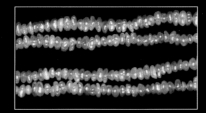

These pink pearls originate from Lake Biwa.

These Japanese Biwa coins have superb lustre

CHINESE FRESHWATER PEARLS

Chinese freshwater pearls resemble Japanese Biwa pearls, but they use a nucleus. Instead of a round mother-of-pearl bead, mantle tissue from another oyster is cut into the desired shape and implanted. The colours are wide-ranging, but include rose, white, green-white, green-rose, salmon-orange, wine red and violet.

Although labelled as Biwa pearls, these freshwater cross-shaped pearls were produced in China.

MABE PEARLS

Mabe pearls are cultured by gluing a half-bead nucleus against the inside of the shell. When the hemisphere pearl is covered in nacre it is cut out, the nucleus is removed and the hole is then filled and the pearl backed with mother-of-pearl. Because mabe pearls are constructed they are not as durable as other types of pearl, and over time the nacre coating can either lift off, become damaged or sometimes discolour. If a mabe pearl has a rim around it, making it look like a fried egg, it is called a blister mabe.

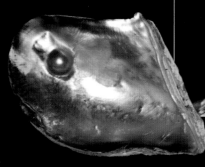

A hemispherical nucleus was attached to the interior of the mollusc's shell to produce this mabe pearl.

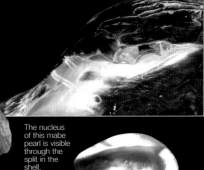

The nucleus of this mabe pearl is visible through the split in the shell.

A blister mabe pearl is the same as another mabe except for the rim around it.

BLISTER PEARLS

These pearls grow attached to the inner surface of the shell rather than loose in the mantle. They have the same iridescent nacre as the inner surface of the shell and the back is flat, without any pearly coating.

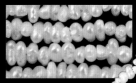

This baroque Tahitian blister pearl is backed with mother-of-pearl.

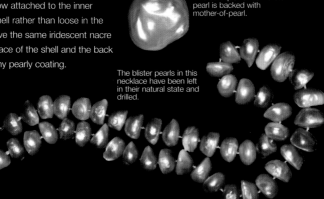

The blister pearls in this necklace have been left in their natural state and drilled.

SEED PEARLS

Seed pearls are small natural pearls that measure 2 mm or less. Because of their size, they are usually drilled and strung in a country where labour is cheap. People often choose not to restring seed pearls as they are so small and fiddly to work with.

Each tiny seed pearl has to be drilled and strung; these are less than 2 mm in size.

Pricing pearl

• **Lighting and background** To judge the colour and lustre of pearls, you will need to see them in diffused natural daylight. Never assess them in artificial light. Place the pearls on a neutral medium-grey surface rather than a bright white or black background.

In artificial light, the pearls have a much warmer colour and pinker tones.

In natural light, on a mid-grey background, the true body colour and overtones of these akoya pearls are visible.

• **Size and shape** Check your row of pearls for consistency of size and shape. Off-round pearls are more readily available and affordable than full-round pearls, and when the row of pearls is being worn it is very hard to tell the difference.

Lilac-coloured akoya pearls, although off-round, look full-round when viewed like this.

• **Lustre** Put simply, lustre is the sharpness and intensity of images that are reflected in the pearl's surface. The small ridges on the pearly nacre break up the light, giving the pearl iridescence (also called orient). Check for an evenness of lustre by looking for dull, pasty areas on the pearls. Comparison with other strands will indicate the quality of the lustre.

• **Nacre thickness** The thickness of the nacre and its quality will dictate the longevity of the pearl. High lustre generally means that the nacre layer is thick and the pearls will last. Occasionally, the nacre layers don't crystallize properly, and no matter how thick the layer is, the lustre will always be poor.

• **Surface quality** Different molluscs create different surface qualities, from smooth to grainy. Surface defects can include spotting (depressed or raised dots), raised bands or ridges, bumps, growths, splits and colour spots. They will always lower a pearl's value.

These grey freshwater pearls are uneven in shape and have poor lustre. However, they are a good size for freshwater pearls.

• **Colour** The body colour of a pearl should be even, without any mottling or discolouration. The overtones should be distinct; you should be able to see the pink tint on a white-rose pearl or the green tint on a dark grey Tahitian pearl.

• **Make** The term *make* describes the overall quality of a row of pearls. To check this, lay the pearls out on a flat surface and see if they all sit neatly, side by side in a row. If any pearls project out to one side, then they haven't been drilled centrally. The drill holes should all be the same size; if they aren't the pearls will be difficult to string. Look for any chipping or damage to the nacre around the holes.

These semiround freshwater pearls have a poor make.

• **Compromise** Most jewellers have to work within a budget. Much as we'd like to use the best, reality means compromising on either shape, size, lustre, surface quality or make. With a string of pearls, shape and size are usually less critical than lustre and surface quality. Tahitian pearls, however, are often chosen for size and shape.

The 13-mm silver-grey Tahitian pearls above are worth less than the 10-mm dark grey Tahitian pearls at right. A combination of shape, smooth surface and lustre make the smaller pearls more valuable.

Pearls produced by snails

ABALONE PEARLS

The abalone is a large snail that produces pearls. The shape of abalone pearls is irregular and their colour is a wonderful combination of green, blue, pink, purple, silver or occasionally white. The pearls are highly prized, whatever the size, as they are very rare; the odds of finding a pearl in an abalone shell are estimated at 1 in 50,000. Abalone blister pearls are cultivated.

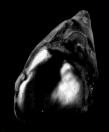

Two exotic abalone pearls feature the colours seen in abalone shells.

These rare conch pearls have exceptional colour and lustre. They deserve to be set with diamonds!

CONCH PEARLS (PINK PEARLS)

The pink conch pearl is as rare as the abalone pearl. It can be found in the great conch, a large marine snail that lives in the Caribbean. The pearls have an irregular shape with a surface that looks like porcelain. Ideally, they should be symmetrical in shape with a strong pink/peach colour and a distinct flamelike pattern. In terms of price, the rarity of these little conch pearls puts them on par with a large, perfectly round Tahitian pearl.

Treatments and imitations

It is possible for pearls to be treated in order to change their appearance but, unlike the heat treatment of nonorganic gemstones, these processes cannot be classed as routine. Any of the following treatments should be disclosed by the dealer.

• **Silver nitrate** Pearls are soaked in silver nitrate to make them appear black. This weakens the pearls, making them easier to damage.

• **Bleaching** Chinese freshwater and low-grade akoya pearls are often bleached after drilling to make their colouring look lighter and more even. If the process is done badly it can soften the nacre and shorten the lifespan of the pearl.

• **Buffing** This process is performed to improve the lustre of the pearl and remove any superficial scratches. Chemical polishes or beeswax are generally used; beeswax wears off fast and chemical polishes eat away the nacre of the pearl.

• **Coating** Occasionally, thin plastic coatings are applied to darken the colour of pearls. It can be detected by touch and over time the coating will wear away, leaving bald patches.

The permanent colour enhancement on this string of pearls was skillfully done. The pearls have retained their lustre and the quality of colour on individual pearls is good.

• **Dyeing** The dyeing of pearls has been practiced since the 1930s and is accepted in the trade as long as the buyer is informed. White pearls are sometimes soaked in pink dye to give them a desirable pink tint. Check the inside of the drill holes for a telltale change of colour.

These dyed grey freshwater pearl drops are dull with flat colour and poor lustre.

Golden Tahitian pearls are sometimes dyed to a darker golden colour to increase the price – a lab test can check for colour treatments.

Most black and grey pearls are dyed. An iridescent peacock colour also indicates treatment. If pearls have an irregular shape or surface, dye concentrations will show in pitted areas. If all the pearls on a strand have an identical colour, it indicates that they are dyed; natural coloured pearls never look exactly the same. Some dyed pearls will fade over time if the dye is unstable or the process is done badly.

Copper-coloured Biwa sticks have obvious pockets of dye residue. The colour is too intense and even to be natural.

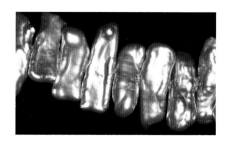

• **Irradiation** This treatment works best on freshwater pearls. It involves bombarding them with gamma rays to blacken the nucleus, in order to darken the nacre. Some pearls are dyed and irradiated. The irradiation gives pearls an iridescent blue-green-grey colour. If the pearl has pits or blemishes in the nacre you can see the blackened nucleus.

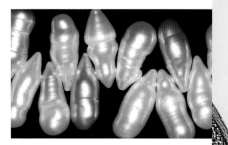

These freshwater pearls were marketed as Biwa pearls but are actually from China. The lustre is fine, but it doesn't compare to that of actual Biwa pearls.

An unusual mabe pearl dominates and illuminates this brooch.

Working with pearls

• **Stringing** Pearls are traditionally strung onto silk thread, which should be thick enough to prevent the pearls from sliding up and down and the knots from disappearing into the drill holes. Knotting between each pearl stops them rubbing against each other and damaging the nacre. It also limits the loss of pearls if the necklace breaks.

• **Drilling** Pearls can be drilled easily with a high-speed twist drill bit or a pearl-boring bit that clears the hole of debris as it is drilled. Make sure you drill slowly to avoid overheating the pearl, as this can cause cracks. If possible, drill the hole where there is a pit or blemish as the metal fitting will help conceal the flaw. If you roughen the drilling area, the drill bit will be less likely to slip and damage the nacre. Using a new sharp drill bit will prevent the nacre around the hole from being chipped. Small pearls can be drilled top to bottom in one pass, but it is more practical to drill larger pearls from either end and meet in the middle. If you intend to string the pearl, the hole should be small (0.3–0.5 mm). If the pearl is to be fixed to a metal post, the hole needs to be bigger (0.8–1 mm).

• **Fixing** Metal posts should measure half the diameter of the pearl and fit tightly into the drilled hole. Placing a metal cap on top of the pearl hides the drill hole (and any blemishes) and gives the metal fitting extra grip when it is glued. Always use good pearl cement, such as an epoxy resin that is mixed with a catalyst, and apply it with a pin accurately and cleanly. Any excess glue should be wiped away or gently removed with a blade. Instant adhesives are not really suitable as they harden off so quickly that no repositioning can be done and in the long term they become brittle.

• **Care** As pearls are organic, they are affected by heat, alcohol in perfumes, creams and detergents, which cause them to lose their beauty and diminish their lifespan. Perspiration is acidic and will also damage the pearls' nacre and lustre, so should be cleaned off before the pearls are put away. Acid-free tissue paper is perfect for storing pearls, as is a cloth pouch, but plastic bags will cause condensation and don't really protect the pearls from impact.

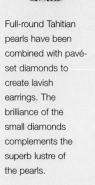

Full-round Tahitian pearls have been combined with pavé-set diamonds to create lavish earrings. The brilliance of the small diamonds complements the superb lustre of the pearls.

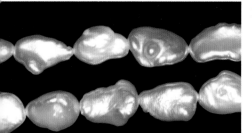

Genuine Japanese freshwater Biwa pearls have a high lustre.

A delicate pattern of wirework and granulation has been combined with the silver-white pearl drops. The gold design does not diminish or overpower the pearls, yet can still be appreciated in its own right.

The pearl locket at left is made from textured silver overlaid with 24K gold. The pattern is based on Indian fabric and is mirrored in the mixing of the pearl colours with the polished beads.

The simplicity of this design makes the earrings suitable for everyday wear. The colour and texture of the gold complements the freshwater pearls.

The late-Victorian gold star brooch above and right features seed pearls in clawed-bezel settings and bead settings. The pearls are well matched in colour and lustre, and the smallest is just 1 mm in diameter.

Natural pink and silver-white Biwa pearls have been combined in this pretty necklace. The strange shapes give the design an organic quality and the high lustre draws the eye.

37/amber

It is easy to see why amber, once called the gold of the north, was so highly prized. Remove the crusty, weathered outer layer and you will discover a stone that is warm and silky to the touch and rich to the eye. Amber has been worked and appreciated since prehistoric times, making it one of the earliest-used gem materials.

The polished slice is a mix of transparent yellow and opaque white amber.

Amber is the hardened, fossilized resin of pine trees that existed over 50 million years ago. Its appearance can vary from transparent to virtually opaque and it has a resinous lustre. Amber often contains insects and lichens that were trapped when the resin was still sticky. It also has "lily pad" inclusions, created by trapped air. (Lily pad inclusions can also indicate amboid; see Treatments and imitations on page 133.)

Until the beginning of the 20th century, amber had significant value as a gemstone, but it lost its popularity with the arrival of synthetic ambers. Recent years have seen a rise in the status of natural amber and it has regained some importance as a gemstone. This has been reflected by the continuing rise in price.

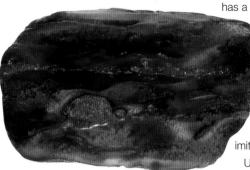

Amber is normally found in a weathered state. Once the crust of this Baltic amber is ground away and the surface polished it will reveal its full colour and beauty.

SPECIFICATIONS

HARDNESS 2–2.5 Mohs
SPECIFIC GRAVITY 1.05–1.09
REFRACTIVE INDEX 1.54–1.55
CRYSTAL FORM Amorphous. Small, irregularly shaped masses with a cracked and weathered surface.

SOURCES OF AMBER

The most famous amber comes from the Baltic region (Poland, Russia). It can also be found in the Mediterranean near Sicily and in Norway, Denmark, northern Myanmar (formerly Burma), Romania, Dominican Republic, Mexico, France, Spain, Italy, Germany, Canada and the United States.

This yellow amber cabochon displays typical "lily pad" inclusions.

This white amber has a rough, yellow-brown exterior crust.

Amber can have a fascinating inner world – it can contain particles of plants, small pyrites and, occasionally, insects. Amber specimens with large insects are collectable and more costly.

Colours of amber

YELLOW AMBER

Bright transparent yellow is considered to be the most desirable and expensive colour of amber. However, many jewellery buyers prefer the spangled effect caused by inclusions.

Yellow amber

COGNAC AMBER

Cognac amber can cover a range of shades from mid-golden brown to deep brandy colours. The polished amber segment here contains a mixture of rich tones.

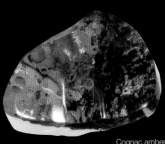
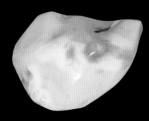

Cognac amber

GREEN AMBER

Green amber is always popular, but it is not easy to source.

VIOLET AMBER

Violet amber is extremely rare and not commercially available.

RED AMBER

Red amber occurs naturally but is quite rare. Most red amber in jewellery is imitation, often cognac amber backed with red foil.

WHITE AMBER

Only 10 per cent of Baltic amber production is white. It is sometimes called bone amber and is full of small bubbles. It ranges in colour from pure opaque white to pale cloudy cream. It often occurs alongside yellow amber material, and fabulous swirling patterns can result where the two colours meet.

White amber

BLACK AMBER

Like violet amber, black amber is so rare as to be considered a collector's gemstone that is not commercially available.

Treatments and imitations

• Copal resin is often sold as amber (for amber prices). It is actually a resin produced by a type of tropical tree.

• Ambroid is a composite amber that is created by heating small pieces of real amber at a high temperature and compressing them together. It is often dyed and is much stronger than natural amber. Ambroid usually has a misty look and will frequently contain trapped elongated air bubbles that can be seen through a loupe.

• Use a hot needle to distinguish amber from synthetics. Real amber will produce smoke that smells a bit like incense, while plastic will melt and show a black mark.

• Poland is one of the main sources of high-quality amber, which has been classified by the government as part of the country's national heritage. As a result, Polish dealers need a license to manufacture and export amber. A useful way to check that the amber you buy from a Polish dealer is genuine is to ask to see this license.

The lariat-style necklace appears to use genuine amber beads but they are in fact synthetic material. It is an easy mistake to make, so buyers should be careful.

Pricing

Amber is a low-priced stone and the different colours have only minor variations in cost.

Working with amber

• Amber can be cut and carved with ordinary steel blades or abrasives. Gently shape it on a whetstone or different grades of abrasive paper.

• If you look closely at amber you will see small tension fractures, which make the material slightly brittle and tricky to drill. To avoid problems, use a very small, high-speed twist drill bit for the initial hole and then gradually increase the size of drill bit. To avoid splintering around the hole, drill in from either side and meet in the middle.

• Amber produces a negative electrical charge when rubbed and, if the amber isn't cooled sufficiently during polishing, this electrical charge can cause it to "explode". The most suitable polishing compounds are

Amber is a difficult material to facet, but these beads have an even, consistent shape.

chalk and tin oxide. Use felt or flannel polishing wheels and finish by rubbing the amber with vegetable oil.

• Never immerse amber in a plating bath or use jewellery cleaners on it. Amber is very sensitive to acids, caustic solutions, gasoline and alcohol, which can be absorbed into the resin and will affect the lustre and the look of the stone.

• Don't leave amber near heat sources as it will dehydrate and crack. Try to avoid wearing amber jewellery in bright sunshine or hot weather.

This necklace design has made a feature of the different amber colours and has been cut in an unusual overlapping bead form.

This sweet little bee brooch has combined an amber cabochon with white gold and pavé-set diamonds.

The intense yellow colour and the brilliance of the faceting in these briolette earrings make them really eye-catching. They are also light and comfortable to wear compared to earrings made of denser gem materials.

Showcase

The silver bracelet below is set with freeform amber cabochons. The large, high-cut stones show off the beauty of the material while its organic nature keeps it lightweight.

38/coral

Its colour and rarity once gave coral the same status as diamonds, emeralds, sapphires and rubies. In recent times, coral's popularity has varied as concerns about environmental issues made buyers of jewellery opt for a different stone. Environmental laws now control the harvesting of coral, protecting reefs from long-term damage, so maybe it is time to reconsider this precious gem.

Corals are small marine animals called polyps. They live in colonies, either in reef systems in warm, shallow water or in deep sea colonies. They build on the calcified skeletal remains of their dead, forming treelike structures. Coral "branches" are found in a variety of colours depending on the coral type, its location and the depth of the water.

There is a great deal of misinformation on the environmental damage that occurs as a result of coral harvesting. Of the 2,000 types of coral in existence, only certain varieties are at risk of extinction and the main threats to those do not come from the jewellery industry.

This necklace uses red sponge coral with distinct orange vein-like markings. Silver and gold metal segments intersperse the barrel-shaped beads. The patinated and textured surface of the metal echoes the markings on the sponge coral.

SPECIFICATIONS

HARDNESS 3–3.5 Moh
SPECIFIC GRAVITY 2.68
REFRACTIVE INDEX 1.49–1.66
CRYSTAL FORM Trigonal and microcrystalline. Has a banded structure similar to a tree trunk.

SOURCES OF CORAL

RED, PINK AND WHITE CORAL Western Mediterranean and African coast, Red Sea, Malaysian archipelago, Japan, Hawaii.
BLACK AND GOLDEN CORAL Coast of West Indies, Australia, Pacific Islands.

Three-quarters of all harvested coral is processed in Torre del Greco, Italy.

Showcase

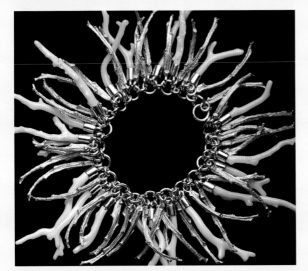

Slender branches of white coral have been set into polished gold caps and interspersed with cast branches of gold to make a delicate bracelet full of movement.

Red coral and green nephrite jade have been inlaid into thin white jade and riveted on a post with white pearls. It is the similarity in the qualities of jade and coral that has made these mismatched earrings so successful.

Carnelian, coral and gold have been combined in a classic design. The bright red carnelians match the multistrand red coral necklace that is twisted into a bunch.

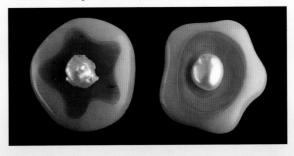

White noble coral is less valuable than the pink or red varieties and is often dyed. It is possible to see pockets of dye residue in these inexpensive pink coral twigs.

Bamboo coral, which is not endangered, is often shaped into beads and dyed pink or red.

Reef coral (including precious noble coral as well as blue, golden and black coral) and deep sea corals are the most threatened, primarily by the fishing industry, the rise in water temperature from global warming and deep sea oil and gas development.

Australia, New Zealand, Canada and Norway have all taken steps to change their fishing practices and so protect both deep sea coral forests and reef corals under their jurisdiction. Pressure is being applied to other countries to restrict their fishing methods and so protect coral colonies within their waters.

Treatments and imitations

• Porcelain, stained bone, glass, plastic and synthetics have all been used to imitate coral. Synthetic coral can be carved, polished or made into beads just like the real thing, and it can be stained to any of the noble coral colours.

• Rarely showing a completely even spread of colour, natural coral usually has pale or white patches. Synthetic coral has an even colouration and is often an unnatural orangey red. Natural coral is sometimes dyed to improve its colour, in which case it will have a much lower value than coral with the natural colouring.

Pricing coral

• The pricing of noble coral depends on its quality, colour, shape and size. It is always sold by gram weight.

• Coral twigs are much cheaper than round beads, and beads over 7 mm in diameter jump up in price because more rough coral is needed to make them. Large single pieces of coral are rare and expensive.

Working with coral

• As coral is a soft stone it should be used with care, but its softness makes it an excellent material for carving. Coral can be easily shaped and cut by files and abrasives.

• Be careful that the coral doesn't become too hot as the colour will fade and the material degenerate. The colour of coral can fade naturally over time; you will see evidence in antique jewellery.

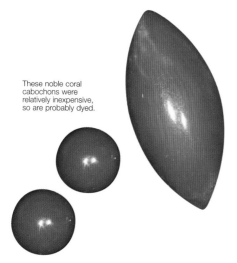

These noble coral cabochons were relatively inexpensive, so are probably dyed.

These pale carved beads have small areas of pink on them. The carving is mass produced, but the coral is natural and not dyed. It comes from Japan.

Types of coral

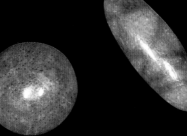

Sponge coral is lightweight compared to gemstones of the same size.

SPONGE CORAL

Sponge coral is often attached to reefs but is not a rare or valuable form of coral. The plentiful supply means that sponge corals have a very low extinction level and so have not been included in international preservation programs.

Sponge coral is colourful and inexpensive; it occurs naturally in reds, purples and yellows but is also dyed or stained.

NOBLE CORAL

Precious noble coral occurs both in deep sea colonies and in coral reefs with warm shallow water. Turning raw, harvested noble coral into a polished gemstone is a labour-intensive process, which adds to the high cost of precious coral.

The white areas in these Momo beads indicate natural colour.

SARDEGNA CORAL

This coral is very popular for its medium red colour. If you see bright red colour, it is dyed, not natural Sardegna coral.

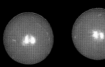

The Sardegna coral cabochons are natural; they have a slightly uneven colour.

MOMO CORAL

Momo coral has a beautiful light red to salmon colour, often mottled with white areas.

MORO CORAL

Moro coral has a darker, oxblood colour. It is the rarest and most expensive variety of noble coral and comes from the seas around Italy. Its rarity is a result of the damage caused to the reefs by overfishing and pollution.

JAPANESE RED CORAL

Some gem dealers consider Mediterranean red coral to be of higher quality than Japanese red coral because Japanese material often contains white patches.

The white areas on these large pendeloques indicate the source is Japanese, but they don't spoil the appearance or intensity of the colour.

The consistent colour of these red twigs suggests that they have been dyed.

ANGEL SKIN CORAL

Angel skin coral is a pretty rose-pink colour with whitish or light red spots. Angel skin is a popular type of coral for jewellery and more readily available than Moro coral.

This exceptional piece of angel skin coral has an even colour except for a small white patch on the back.

BLACK CORAL

Black coral is not considered important by the trade and is inexpensive. It is thought to be coral in an early stage of decay.

BLUE CORAL

Blue coral looks wonderful as a decoration, but has little value as a stone. It is thought to be in the first stage of decay.

GOLDEN CORAL

Like black coral, golden coral consists of the hornlike substance conchiolin. It is found in the coastal waters of Hawaii and has a resinous or lacquered lustre and texture.

The blue coral beads are large (25 mm in diameter), and the weight of this strand is considerable.

39/shell

You can saw it, file it, carve it, drill it and engrave it: shell is one of the easiest of materials to work with. Beauty, flexibility and value for money make shell extremely popular with creative jewellery makers and jewellery buyers alike.

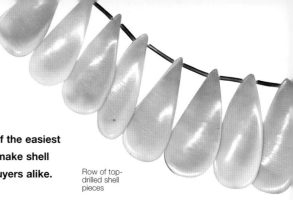

Row of top-drilled shell pieces

Large pearl oysters, abalones (paua) and topshells (*Trochidae*) are all prized for their iridescent, smooth mother-of-pearl shell linings, which can be used for jewellery, inlays and beads. These mother-of-pearl linings consist of pearly nacre. This is the same substance that covers natural and cultured pearls, yet mother-of-pearl sells at a fraction of the price of pearls.

Pieces of paua shell

Row of white shell beads

Pink potamilus purpurata

SPECIFICATIONS

MOTHER-OF-PEARL (NACRE)
HARDNESS 3.5 Mohs
SPECIFIC GRAVITY 2.65–2.78
REFRACTIVE INDEX 1.57
SHELL
HARDNESS 2.5 Mohs
SPECIFIC GRAVITY 1.30
REFRACTIVE INDEX 1.53–1.69

SOURCES OF SHELL

OYSTER SHELL Northern Australia.
ABALONE SHELL Off the coast of the United States and South Africa.
PAUA SHELL New Zealand.
CONCH SHELL Indo-Pacific inshore sands.

Showcase

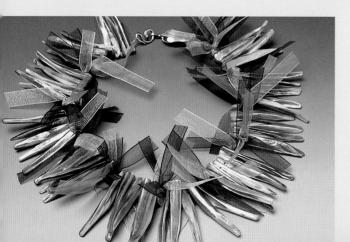

The delicate shell bracelet at left combines pink and white ribbon with pink shell beads.

Gold foil has been applied to drilled mother-of-pearl discs to make a delicate multistrand necklace.

Types of shell

CONCH SHELLS

These shells are built in pink and white layers. They have traditionally been carved into intricate cameos, which command high prices. The shells originate in the Bahamas, Madagascar and the Maldive Islands.

PEARL SHELLS (MOTHER-OF-PEARL)

Most mother-of-pearl comes in flat sheet form, but some pearl shells produce a layer of nacre up to ¾ inch (2 cm) deep, which can be machine-carved into spheres, drilled and made into beads. The usual colour is pale, but the mother-of-pearl that comes from Tahitian and South Sea molluscs is dark.

Mother- of-pearl slab

Mother-of-pearl oval beads

PAUA SHELL (ABALONE)

Mother-of-pearl that comes from the paua shell (the abalone mollusc) has a stunning blue-green iridescent colour play, which is why it is also called sea opal. Paua cannot be carved into beads but is cut into double-sided flat beads, low cabochons and slabs for inlay work.

Paua shell beads

Rectangular river shell beads

RIVER SHELL

Most river shell on the market is in bead form. Its colours are neutral – grays, browns and some blacks – but there is a colourful iridescence on the surface.

Pricing shell

Shell is an inexpensive material with little variation in price.

Mother-of-pearl carved beads

Working with shell

• Mother-of-pearl is soft enough to be cut with a jewellers' saw and filed down using abrasives, yet the structure of the shell is tough enough to resist cracking and splitting. It can be put on a "dop" stick and polished with Tripoli and rouge, just like a cabochon. It can be tumbled, drilled, sanded and acid-etched. The material can also be engraved and the engraved areas filled with coloured resin.
• Sharp steel gravers with different cutting edges can be used on shell to create cameos and carvings, as can small diamond wheels or power-driven carbide abrasives mounted onto a power rotary tool.
• Mother-of-pearl cabochons and polished slabs can be set in bezel

or prong settings. In the case of inlay work, the polished slabs can be cemented into place with epoxy resin (the glue that you would use for pearls).
• Mother-of-pearl retains its lustre and polishes well. If the surface becomes scuffed or damaged by alcohol, acid perspiration or detergents, it can be repolished using tin oxide, Tripoli or rouge. If the damage is bad you might need to file or sand off the top layer before repolishing the surface.
• If shell jewellery becomes wet, any cemented inlay work could loosen or fall off. Make sure the jewellery wearer knows to avoid contact with water.

Mother-of-pearl donut

Mother-of-pearl cabochon

designing with gemstones

This section explores the qualities that gemstones bring to jewellery design and shows how these qualities are used by jewellery makers and designers. These pages emphasize the use of stones as a design tool, investigating the possibilities that arise from themes such as colour, texture, scale and groupings, as well as considering the treatments of precious natural forms and organic materials. It reviews the various systems of setting gemstones and discusses how they might be adapted to incorporate stones more fully into a design.

settings

A stone setting is more than just a means of securing a gemstone. It plays an important part in the design of a piece of jewellery and needs to be considered from an early stage, in light of the piece's proposed usage. The setting can also bring a gemstone alive – or kill it dead. While the gem material will partly determine the type of setting you use, there are always opportunities for modification, decoration and trying something new.

The designer has used a claw setting for the diamond, but has given it a modern look by creating claws that have a strong architectural feel.

Talk of the trade

As with the cut of a gem, a stone setting is described with specific terminology, which you will need to know if you are to brief another goldsmith or stone setter about a design.

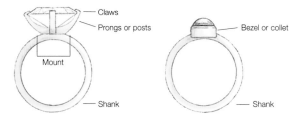

Claws
Prongs or posts
Mount
Shank
Bezel or collet
Shank

Stone settings are sometimes pigeonholed as having either a traditional or a modern look, which can inhibit jewellery designers from trying something new. A claw setting can certainly have a traditional feel when it is made of thin round wire and has a plain single bezel, yet changing the format slightly, for example by making the prongs heavier and the profile square and removing the bezel, can give the setting a much more contemporary appearance.

Designing or adapting a stone setting requires consideration of the type of gemstone material, the size and weight of the stone and the usage the jewellery will receive. Tension setting might look very impressive and have a contemporary edge, but if you wear a tension-set ring every single day the stone will fall out. Design and practicality have to be balanced, and finding the means to achieve a concept is a challenge of gem-set jewellery design.

Tension-setting rough diamonds and an emerald in these gold and steel rings has provided an open view of the gemstones.

This brooch has grain-set small diamonds and a single bezel-set diamond. The grain setting follows and emphasizes the curved lines of the design.

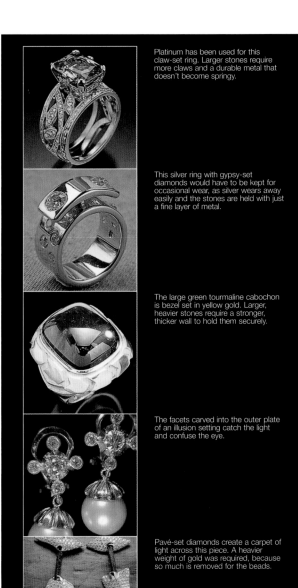

Platinum has been used for this claw-set ring. Larger stones require more claws and a durable metal that doesn't become springy.

This silver ring with gypsy-set diamonds would have to be kept for occasional wear, as silver wears away easily and the stones are held with just a fine layer of metal.

The large green tourmaline cabochon is bezel set in yellow gold. Larger, heavier stones require a stronger, thicker wall to hold them securely.

The facets carved into the outer plate of an illusion setting catch the light and confuse the eye.

Pavé-set diamonds create a carpet of light across this piece. A heavier weight of gold was required, because so much is removed for the beads.

Types of setting

CLAW SETTING

The claw setting is commonly used with transparent faceted stones as it elevates and displays the stone while keeping the surrounding metal to a minimum. The prongs are attached to a bezel to maintain shape and stability, and at least four claws should hold the stone. Decorative detail can be added, such as splitting the prongs to create forked claws or setting small diamonds into the top of the claws.

GYPSY/INVISIBLE SETTING

Gypsy setting is popular because of its clean minimal look. Faceted stones are sunk into the metal so that the girdle is flush with the surface and the metal is then burnished over the stone's edge. Cabochons with good angled sides can be recessed and the metal pushed over to meet the stone, leaving no evidence of a setting.

BEZEL/RUB-OVER SETTING

This is one of the most secure types of setting and can be used on both cabochons and faceted stones. The top edge of the bezel or collet can be decorated with a beadlike pattern that is created with a millegrain tool. The bezel setting lends itself to high-karat golds, as they are soft enough to burnish over the edge of the stone.

GRAIN/BEAD SETTING

A grain or bead setting can be used for cabochons, faceted stones and full or half pearls. The stone is recessed slightly and held in place by a number of tiny beads. These are made by chiselling up metal chips and then shaping the chips into rounded beads or grains with a beading tool. This type of setting is best carried out with softer, higher-karat gold.

PAVÉ SETTING

This type of setting also uses bead or grain setting. Small stones are arranged very close together (with tiny gaps) and secured by beads that are carefully raised by chiselling up metal. Pavé setting requires great skill and many jewellery designers use specialized setters for the work. A similar effect can be produced with prongs instead of beads.

CHANNEL SETTING

A channel setting is used for securing rows of square or baguette step-cut stones. Ledges are cut in the edges of the channel and metal is folded over to grip the girdle of the stones on two sides. This allows for gems to be butted up, giving a continuous effect. The setting demands accuracy as the stones have to match in colour and be a calibrated size. A channel setting is traditionally used for eternity rings.

TENSION SETTING

This relies on the tension of the shank to keep a stone in place with just two points of contact securing it. Tension-set stones frequently fall out, so the setting is not suitable for an expensive diamond ring. It can be made more secure by filing a ledge in the two sides of the shank to seat the girdle and then pushing metal over the edge of the stone. A tension setting works best with platinum, which is malleable but not springy.

ILLUSION SETTING

An illusion setting is designed to make a stone look larger than it really is. It consists of a white gold or platinum disc with a hole in the centre into which a small stone is fitted. The stone is traditionally bead-set or grain-set and the chiselled beading creates carved facets on the disc, which enhance the stone and confuse the eye.

PEGGED SETTING

A pegged setting allows for close groupings of cabochons or rose cuts, with the stones touching each other. The stones need a flat base and well-angled sides. Tiny pegs or pins are fixed in the spaces between the stones and then pushed down so they thicken and spread, gripping the surrounding stones.

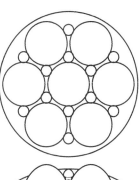

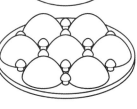

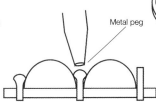

Metal peg

colour

The most crucial factor in assessing coloured gemstones, colour is also the most important consideration when designing jewellery with coloured stones. Hue, intensity and tone are all relevant to a design, whether they are used to create a focal point, a contrast to the colour of the metal or a subtle tonal effect. Colour also has a vitality that relates to the cut of the stone, and this too will have an impact on the design. A piece of jewellery that contains a transparent faceted sapphire will have a vibrant mood, while one that uses a translucent cabochon will possess a quieter, gentler energy.

These earrings use identical pear-shaped tourmaline cabochons of two different colours. The mismatch is playful but not extreme as the colours are balanced tonally and are of a similar hue.

Coloured stones can be used quite simply in a design. A gem with a pure intense colour will always draw the eye and become a focal point, and coloured stones can be grouped in a pattern to lead the eye across the piece. Colour contrasts can be created using the colour of the metal; a satin or matte finish will make red, yellow and green gold look richer in colour than when highly polished and will enhance intense gemstone colours. While some metal colours improve or accentuate stones, others will make them look visibly worse. Hot pinks can become orangey red when placed on or next to yellow gold, making pinkish rubies look cherry red but destroying the hot bluish pink of rubellite. The blue of aquamarine is enriched by the warmth of rose gold, but becomes grey and watery next to white gold.

Decorative finishes such as enamel work and patination are perfect for coloured stones; the colour and pattern combinations can be truly opulent and the jewellery vibrates with colour. In cooler colours, patination and metal inlay can produce very refined, subtle designs and be highly effective with stones that have a less intense colour, such as earth-toned agates or soft chalcedony and jade.

Colour is used to brilliant effect in this piece. The bands of yellow, white, red and green gold contrast with and intensify the blue of the sapphire.

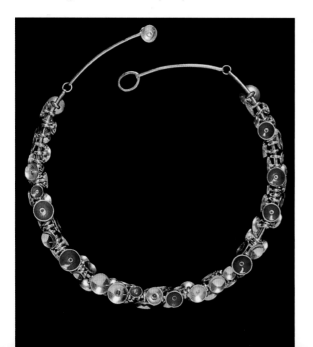

This necklace is fabricated from 24K gold, sterling silver, enamel and rubies. Some disks have pink cloisonné enamel, while others have been set with cabochon rubies or textured with fused gold. The pink colour theme has been used with restraint to draw the eye across the piece.

Decorative finishes using colour

ENAMELLING I

Photo-etched silver was used here. Cloisonné wires were placed on flux and fired. The coloured enamels were laid wet into the cloisons and fired when dry.

ENAMELLING II

The pattern was hand-engraved onto photo-etched silver, then transparent grey enamel was applied.

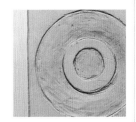

GOLD AND SILVER FOILS I

Silver was enamelled with transparent purple and fired. Silver foil was then brushed on and fired, then gently rubbed with a burnisher.

GOLD AND SILVER FOILS II

A cast piece of silver was decorated with gold foil and fused.

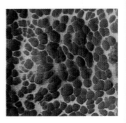

PATINATION AND OXIDIZATION I

After annealing and hammering, silver was dipped in hot potassium sulphide and then rinsed with cold water as soon as the colours appeared.

PATINATION AND OXIDIZATION II

Hammered silver was oxidized in hot potassium sulphide. The indentations held the oxidization and the relief areas were rubbed clean.

INLAY I

The circles were pierced, then the silver sheet was soldered to copper sheet and put through a rolling mill for inlaying. Next the texture was applied.

INLAY II

Here 18K white gold sheet and 18K red gold sheet were inlaid and soldered and then domed.

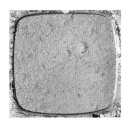

The colours of the semiprecious cabochons and enamel mix well in this silver brooch.

This necklace and earring set uses red coral, carnelian and gold. Rich, hot tones are always appealing – the carnelian has an unusually fine colour that matches the coral.

This simple yellow gold bangle has an eye-catching hexagonal, flat-cut blue sapphire as its focal point.

These brooches are made of mill-pressed gold and silver. The cabochons are used as small bright highlights, contrasting with the delicately coloured background.

This exotic pendant uses coloured gemstones in a highly decorative way, mixing different hues and shapes. The colours are reminiscent of antique Asian jewellery.

texture and lustre

Decorative surface textures and coloured gemstones enhance one another, and their combination results in cohesive designs in which the impact of stone and metal is balanced. Decorative techniques such as granulation, texturing and fusing can produce beautiful effects that are similar to a gem's optical property of lustre, and when combined with a stone lend a design depth, sensuality and richness.

Fused gold wires and a stamped pattern enliven this silver locket and set off the tourmaline stones.

In the same way as the colour of metal interacts with a coloured stone, the texture of metal also influences the design of gem-set jewellery. Just like the gemstone, gold can be admired for its qualities of colour and lustre, and the two materials can be combined to create some exciting effects. Granulation produces a rich golden texture that sits beautifully with the smooth lustrous nacre of a pearl or the clear liquid colours of a cabochon. Fused and textured surfaces offset the brilliance of a faceted stone; sparkle and fire are enhanced by gentler, unpolished surfaces. Conversely, the drama of a perfect high polish suits the duller "greasy" lustre of carved jade or natural, unfinished lapis lazuli.

If a gemstone possesses an optical effect it needs to be set sympathetically, so that its iridescence or colour play is emphasized. Decorative or satin finishes are less likely than a high polish to compete with the stone, and the surface texture will provide visual interest when the colour play can't be seen. Designing and making jewellery such as this is highly rewarding, as by virtue of the creative process each piece is individual and unique.

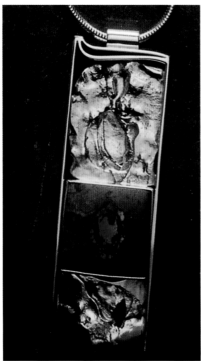

The incredible texture and colour of the fused gold in this pendant balance the texture and colour of the opal slab. The fused gold also illuminates the opal's dark areas.

Carved jade brooch with small diamonds. The colour distribution of the jade and the carving draw the eye into the frame of yellow gold. The high polish on the gold contrasts with the lustre of the stone.

This ring uses strips of gold that have been reticulated and wrapped. The labradorite cabochon has a blue schiller and sparkling inclusions that catch the light when the hand is moved. The gold's texture matches the lustre and texture of the stone.

These simple diamond stud earrings have been textured by mill pressing. The convex textured frame gives the illusion that the diamonds are larger than they are. Studs should not tilt away from the ear, so the post needs to be soldered a little higher than halfway.

The texture of the granulation in these gold Celtic crosses offsets the pretty lustre of the drilled pearls.

These brooches have a subtle surface texture and pattern achieved by mill pressing. The gentle texture doesn't overpower the carefully placed single cabochon.

Decorative finishes

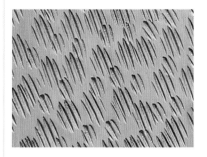

STAMPS AND HAMMERING I
A lined chasing tool has been applied to the annealed silver using a ball-peen hammer.

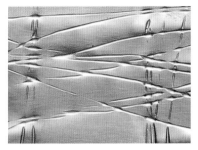

STAMPS AND HAMMERING II
The silver was annealed and wrapped in binding wire, then placed on a steel plate and hammered on both sides.

FUSING I
Thick silver was heated until the sides gravitated toward the middle.

FUSING II
Different thicknesses of 18K gold were fused to form an undulating background.

GRANULATION I
A triangular shape was engraved in silver and 18K gold balls were soldered in place by heating from underneath.

GRANULATION II
Domed circles of 22K gold were dipped in a borax solution and the piece was then heated until a granulation flash occurred.

RETICULATION I
Reticulation was achieved on silver sheet and the piece was oxidized afterward to give the blue-pink effect. The relief areas were polished with a buffing cloth.

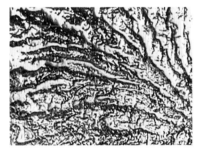

RETICULATION II
A sheet of 9K gold shows classic reticulation markings. Results can be unpredictable with 9K gold.

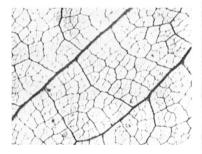

ROLLING-MILL TEXTURING
The impression was made using skeleton leaf, highlighted with a black oxide.

size

Selecting the right size of stone for a jewellery design is not just a question of proportion or impact; the decision also has implications for the structuring of the piece. Small stones demand precise planning, accuracy and setting skills, while large stones require careful consideration of weight distribution, balance and support mechanisms.

This 18K white and yellow gold ring uses a large central stone together with small diamonds set in the folds of the ring face. The structure is well balanced and sturdy – the cabochon is set low and the diamonds are protected with bezel settings.

The size of the gemstone will often be dictated by the amount and type of usage that the piece of jewellery will receive. Wearability and comfort come high on the list of design considerations, so large designs that use big stones may be considered impractical. Large rings are frequently top-heavy and rotate on the finger, or the gemstone may be exposed and become damaged. Ornate gem-set earrings look dramatic and are fun to dress up in, but they have a tendency to feel excruciating after a couple of hours of wear.

Using small stones in jewellery doesn't necessarily entail fewer technical problems. The designs and setting styles are frequently more refined than with large stones, making strength and durability important factors. Small faceted stones are secured with less metal, so settings will wear more quickly and fine jewellery will break if it is caught on hair or clothes. With careful planning, however, it is possible to address these common size-related problems and create designs that are both robust and wearable.

These earrings use 18K and 22K gold and are set with azurite, boulder Australian opal, pearls and diamonds. The stones have a low density and have been cut quite shallow, but their combined weight plus gold must still make the jewellery fairly heavy.

These gold rings use traditional bead-set graded diamonds, but challenge the archetypal ring form. The jewellery's extreme shape could make the stone settings vulnerable to sharp impact; platinum would be more robust.

Considerations of size

RINGS WITH DEEP STONES I

Pearls look great in a ring, but they tend to sit quite high and need protection. This design uses the gold weight of the shoulders to keep the centre of gravity low, while the near-vertical sides will prevent the ring from rotating on the finger.

RINGS WITH DEEP STONES II

The stone in this ring is deep, wide and heavy. The basket setting incorporates a bezel that is wider than the stone and sits close to the finger, lowering the ring's centre of gravity and preventing rotation.

RINGS WITH SMALL STONES

Rings with small pavé-set stones can be vulnerable to damage. Recessing the diamonds behind a low wall has made this ring much more durable. Platinum is required for strength.

OMEGA FITTINGS

Omega fittings are essential for stud and drop earrings with large stones. They provide a neat appearance, without stretching of the pierced hole or tilting of the earring.

PENDANT BAILS

If the pendant bail were placed centrally on the back of the disk, the pendant would rotate or tilt forward under the weight of the stone. A bail on either side will support the stone's weight and keep the pendant aligned.

TUBULAR BAILS

A tubular bail such as this suits the design and will keep the pendant from tilting. However, if the tubular bail is too short or the cord or chain too fine, the piece will swing from side to side

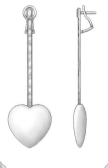

This gold and silver bracelet is set with many faceted sapphires of different shapes. The visual impact of so many small gems is considerable and brings colour and decoration to an otherwise minimal design. Rub-over settings and granulation protect the stones.

The cabochons in these simple drop earrings are fairly large, yet the elongated navette shape prevents them from becoming too heavy and keeps the appearance streamlined.

This ring takes the solitaire format to the extreme. Despite its small size, the ruby catches the eye and provides a spot of colour within the gold setting. A high-polish finish would have killed the effect.

The heavy shoulders and shank needed to secure the large cabochon in this white gold ring have been broken up visually by the addition of small gypsy-set white diamonds.

Large stones often require heavy shanks to support them on the finger. This design is strong yet has lightness and fluidity – the stone is exposed rather than encased. The high polish of the metal offsets the silky lustre of the gem.

single stones

People often assume that a single gemstone will become the dominant focal point of a jewellery design, but this isn't necessarily the case. A well-placed stone can, instead, be used to accentuate a design feature. The eye could be drawn to a surface texture or an interesting form solely by the glimmer of a 2-point brilliant-cut diamond. A gemstone can be used in many subtle ways to balance a structure, link different elements within the jewellery or bring directional energy to a design simply by being placed at a certain angle.

The brilliance of the single white diamond in this pendant draws the eye to the centre of the piece, while textured gold serves as a frame for the stone.

More often than not, a single stone will appear in a ring in a traditional solitaire format, the gem sitting proudly in the centre of the shank in either a raised claw setting or a modern rub-over collet. Yet a gemstone has so much more potential than this – it can function on many levels in a jewellery design. A single-stone ring can be transformed simply by avoiding regularity and repositioning the gem off-centre. The gemstone can also be used as just one element of a design; placing a pearl among the colour and pattern of enamel work will stop it from being the sole focal point of the piece. Using one very small stone can be as powerful as using a large stone. In the brief moment that a pure spot of colour catches the eye, the viewer will also notice the texture and structure of the surrounding jewellery. The designs and ideas featured in this chapter show some of the many functions of a gemstone and illustrate a stone's ability to give a design cohesiveness as well as beauty.

This beautiful, tactile ring was cast in silver, inlaid with gold and then patinated to complement the colour of the pearl. The pearl is not the dominant element in the ring, but one part of a complex design.

This brooch is made from sterling silver, 14K rose gold and a garnet cabochon. The stone plays a supporting role in the design, giving balance to the structure and highlighting the colours in the rose gold mokume-gane tree.

The flowing lines of this ellipse bracelet are echoed by the shape and form of the rock crystal cabochon. The large stone gives the structure solidity and its lack of colour prevents it from dominating this minimal design.

Designing with single stones

FOCAL POINTS I

Vibrant pear-shape emeralds are the focal points of these long slender earrings. They also lead the eye up the length of the swan-necked hooks. The size of the stones is important as they need to balance the elongated hooks, not dominate them.

FOCAL POINTS II

A gemstone is placed at a random point on this pendant. The shape of the single stone reflects the shape of the pendant and the etched designs and encourages the eye to explore the whole piece.

HIGHLIGHTS

The square motif of this brooch is highlighted by the setting of a single white diamond of the same size as the multiple square cutouts.

JOINING STONES I

These earrings have very clean lines with bands of inlaid silver and 18K white gold. The single small ruby cabochon that joins the two earring elements suits the minimal design.

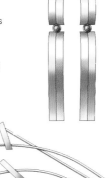

JOINING STONES II

A single small diamond joins the two sections of this brooch. The placement of the stone is crucial as it balances the piece and draws the whole structure together.

KEY STONES

These highly refined pin designs use key stones to lead the eye. The shapes and colours of the stones add interest and energy, but never dominate the structure.

Trillion lapis lazuli cabochons run as a motif across the different pieces in this suite. The bold shapes and colour dominate the design. Granulation adds texture, balance and protection.

This cast ring makes a very restrained use of the gemstone. The stone is sunk into the depth of the shank and left exposed on two sides. It will need regular cleaning.

This chased-gold pendant has an unusual engraved stone as its centrepiece. The gold frames the gemstone as if it were a classical painting – it can't fail to catch the eye.

The silky lustre of the pearls in this simple, sophisticated piece is brought out by the texture of the granulation. Never apply perfume while wearing pearl jewellery, as it will damage the luster of the pearls.

This gold chain bracelet has been kept simple with large round links, but the toggle clasp has been set with a small diamond and made a part of the overall design.

grouped stones

Stones may be grouped in traditional, formal arrangements or in a more random placement. Conventional grouped designs use small calibrated stones in one or possibly two types of gemstone material to create linear and geometric patterns. Informal groupings tend to make use of contrasts of light, lustre, size, shape and colour to lend a more organic feel to a piece of jewellery. "Scattered" stones may actually have been carefully placed to highlight design features, while combinations of shapes or gemstones may produce interesting visual and tactile qualities.

Three asymmetrically cut sapphires have been bezel-set within the gold segments of this brooch. The cut of the stones accentuates the segment shapes, creating windows of colour.

Traditional, structured groupings of stones normally use a channel setting, bead setting (pavé setting) or claw setting, so that the gems can be butted up closely to form a line or shape. The more organic designs employ a variety of setting methods. Bezel and gypsy settings are often chosen for their simplicity and clean lines; a plain bezel setting will always accentuate the shape of the stone and the gypsy setting is ideal for a minimal look as it has no metal structure.

This design is effective because of the restraint shown in the grouping of the diamonds – their brilliance is enhanced by the matte surface of the gold.

The placement of grouped stones will affect the energy of a design – a massed, even coverage will be dramatic but also rather static, while a few carefully positioned stones will create tension in the piece. Mixing gemstone materials allows a design to make use of differing lustres, textures, colours and qualities of light. The translucency of blue chalcedony contrasts beautifully with the brilliance and colour of rhodolite garnet or pink sapphire, while iridescent silver pearls look great with bluish green emeralds or smoky quartz.

This belt is made from sterling silver, 18K gold, gemstones, glass and shell. The tonally similar soft greens and blues of the cabochons produce a cohesive look, and the stones also lead the eye around the belt.

Types of multiple setting

STRUCTURED GROUPINGS

The structured grouping of the square princess-cut gemstones creates impact and gives the illusion that the stones are larger than they really are. The two-part design is highlighted by the placement of stones on two faces.

In this brooch, an organized mass of tiny round cabochons have been peg-set for closeness. The matching colour, shape and form of the stones create considerable texture and impact, despite their small size.

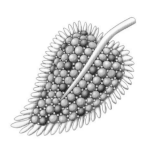

NONSTRUCTURED GROUPINGS

Careful placement of just a few stones can balance a design and add drama.

This multistone brooch uses a variety of faceted shapes in an unstructured arrangement. The gemstones all have warm colours, which gives the design cohesion.

Small white diamonds placed as an unstructured group highlight the shape of the wire frame.

ORGANIC GROUPINGS

Organic designs are effective in the way they combine different materials.

In this gold ring, a pearl, an emerald and a couple of diamonds are grouped together within a textured face. There is no sign of any structure or pattern.

This organic design uses lost wax casting. Grey baroque pearls and diamonds are set around the shank, some partially hidden. The irregular placement of the stones is matched by irregularity of form.

In this pendant, the diamonds are recessed in, and revealed from, the dark interiors of the pierced holes. The stones are randomly placed; the hole motif gives the design its structure.

This ring design places formally grouped stones along the side of a larger single stone; the small diamonds highlight and balance the asymmetric placement of the large stone on the shank.

This design of freeform geometric cabochons displays the individual stones outlined by their bezel settings, and then allows the eye to readjust and see the piece as a whole.

The traditional linear format of the eternity ring is ignored in this design. Instead, different-shaped and -sized diamonds are joined in a random pattern around the finger.

Bullet-shaped stones are grouped to accentuate the tubular forms within this design; their irregular outline pattern is displayed once the bracelet lies on the wrist.

fragile stones

Despite their beauty, softer gemstones such as opals, turquoise and the organics – pearls, coral, jet, fossilized wood, amber, shell and mother-of-pearl – are often avoided because they can be damaged by impact and exposure to heat and chemicals. As jewellery has to withstand a certain amount of wear and tear, this type of material presents designers and makers with a real challenge. How do you incorporate suitable protection for the vulnerable stone and make it an integral part of the piece's design?

The opals have been bezel-set in 22K and 18K gold. The granulation is decorative in its own right and enhances the stones, but also acts as a protective barrier.

A barrier is one of the most effective ways of protecting fragile material. For instance, granulation not only looks good, but if built up around a ring setting will take impact in place of the stone. Wirework and domed cups act in the same way. It is possible to use other gemstones to shield delicate material – white diamonds are often set around opals as they are tough and durable (as well as beautiful). Alternatively, colourful sapphires and spinel could be used.

The stone setting itself can be revised. The shoulders of the shank can be used to frame the gemstone, or a bezel could be widened out like a hat brim to provide some extra cover. Recessed settings such as the gypsy setting could be considered for delicate gemstones, as long as high-karat gold is used and care is taken when the metal is pushed over the edge of the stone.

Inlaying is another technique that could be used on soft gemstones. If the surface of the metal is flush with the surface of the stone, there will be nothing projecting to be damaged. Softer material has itself the potential to be inlaid. Pearls can be drilled with a burr to allow decorative metal work such as gold balls to be inlaid and glued into the pearly nacre coating. This technique can also be used with coral, turquoise, mother-of-pearl and amber.

These earrings feature pearl with inlaid 22K gold balls.

New technology enabled the creation of this amazing caged pearl necklace. Laser welding was used in place of soldering, which meant that the heat could be localized and the pearls left unharmed. This technique allowed the platinum and 18K gold cage links to be joined physically rather than mechanically.

The Tahitian pearl has been snugly secured in an innovative and stylish gold bezel setting.

Protecting fragile material

PROTECTIVE SETTINGS

The two extended shoulders offer extra protection to this beautiful opal.

INLAY

Inlaying has allowed opal to be used for these cufflinks, a form of jewellery usually regarded as unsuitable for delicate material.

WIREWORK

An organic wire-work design makes an effective and decorative setting for the opal.

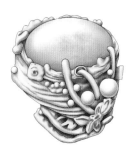

PROTECTING PEARLS

This ingenious design not only highlights the pearl as a focal point, but creates a useful barrier as the pearl is held only by a post.

DOMED CUPS

A domed cup will safely protect a delicate gemstone as long as it lies below the level of the edge. This is also an eye-catching setting for a stone.

CASTING

Lost wax casting allows the creation of designs that shield a stone yet are excitingly tactile at the same time. A single pearl nestles within this structure.

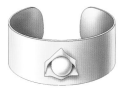

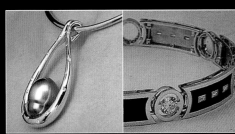
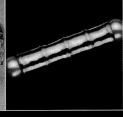

The Tahitian pearl is seated safely in this diamond-set white gold pendant. The pearl's lustre and baroque shape contrast with the high polish and clean lines of the gold.

This gold choker is inlaid with delicate organic material, probably wood. Diamonds have been set and inlaid into the wood panels. Skin oils and acid perspiration can damage organic material, so care should be taken to keep it clean.

Two pearls are set into the ends of the gold pin in a simple but pleasing combination of form, colour and texture. It is likely that the pearls have been mounted on posts, then cemented.

Pearls of different sizes secure the frayed ends of the wire-worked pin. The pearly lustre makes an effective contrast to the oxidized wire.

Organic material, probably wood, has been shaped and inlaid with forged silver. The softness of the wood makes it easy to carve, drill and inlay, and its lightness makes it easy to wear.

nonstandard gemstone forms

Nonstandard gemstone forms are stones that are neither cut to a calibrated shape, such as an oval or a square, nor cut in a recognized form such as a cabochon or faceted gem. The term also covers freeform or baroque stones and pearls, crystal forms and carved material. The unique visual qualities of this type of gem make nonstandard forms very popular, but using and securing them in a piece of jewellery requires some thought. The problem-solving process will often mean that a design has to evolve rather than be preplanned, but this can be a satisfying method of working that may result in a truly individual piece of jewellery.

The colour zoning within the amethyst slices gives a lovely texture and tone to this brooch. The setting of the asymmetric shapes within the open framework has produced a striking and original abstract design.

The description "nonstandard" encompasses most natural and organic forms, found objects and hand-carved pieces. These tend to be used in organic designs that have a less formal structure, rather than in traditional jewellery formats or standard arrangements of stones. The challenges of the design process will often entail the construction of mock-ups to find alternative means of fixing the gemstones.

The strength and durability of the gem material have to be considered because some natural forms are more vulnerable than a traditionally cut stone. Drusy and crystal slices, for example, can be fragile and will need to be handled and set with care. The method of setting has to be secure enough for the type of jewellery and must protect the material from the resulting wear and tear. There are a number of mechanisms for setting nonstandard forms, such as cages, wire-wrapping, framing, pegging and riveting. These can be adapted to suit a variety of materials and can produce exciting and unusual pieces of jewellery.

This rather witty hand-carved necklace has a fluid line and form. Rock crystal was hollowed out so that the large pieces were not too heavy to wear. The crystal was then inlaid with black jade to seal the internal space, and synthetic ruby was used for the tongue.

This stunning 18K gold brooch is set with a drilled nugget of aquamarine, which is secured by a long pin. The colour and surface texture of the gold bring out the blueness of the stone.

Securing nonstandard forms

STRIP SURROUNDS

Small crystals can be grasped in the middle by a strip surround, allowing them to be viewed from different angles and "float away" from the main structure. This type of fixing would not be suitable for jewellery that gets a lot of wear and tear.

CAPPING

A cap allows the full beauty of a belemnite opal or crystal to be seen. It needs to be fixed firmly with a good epoxy resin. Opal has a low density, which makes the material light and suitable for supporting in this way.

CAGES

Cages come in many shapes and sizes. They may wrap tightly around the stone or take a larger form, allowing the material to move around inside.

WIRING

Wire-wrapping pearls or beads to make a frame for a stone is an attractive device that looks best with smaller-sized pearls such as these. They can be secured with wire loops that thread through drill holes in the back plate.

PEGGING

This peapod brooch has used pegs to fix the row of pearls in graduated sizes. The pearl should always fit tightly onto the peg or post and be glued with a two-part epoxy resin.

RIVETING/PINNING

A riveted post enables elements of a design to be fixed when it is not possible to solder and secure several elements together centrally. The rivet is itself a design feature.

To protect it from wear and tear, the freeform boulder opal has been embedded in this cast ring. A stone doesn't need a regular outline for this setting, but the surface must be level.

The pebble-shaped boulder opal has been skewered through the centre with a post and is held by the quirky cast frog. Boulder opal is much tougher than crystal opal, but this ring will still have to be worn with care.

The gold wall around the tourmaline crystal slices allows light to pass through the stone and display its colour. The crystalline surface of the upper stone will catch the light as the earrings are moved.

The piece of meteorite has been captured in a gold ring that tapers around the finger like a shooting star. Yellow gold brings out the earthy tones and lustre of the rock, and the rough bezel setting is in keeping with the natural form.

Carefully selected pebbles have been strung together with forged silver disks for a flowing, organic design. The contours of the pebbles are matched by the contours of the silver.

beads, drops and briolettes

Beads have enormous versatility. Along with faceted briolettes and pendeloques (plain drops), they can be incorporated into most forms of jewellery, including rings and brooches. Their potential for movement and light can provide an added dimension to a design; the reflections produced by a moving cluster of brightly coloured drops can be mesmerizing. The range of bead shapes and sizes is vast. Whether they are used singly or combined with other gemstone material, beads can create a dramatic impact and produce many different looks.

The large faceted citrine briolette featured in this necklace has been fixed with a simple gold bail and suspended from green tourmaline beads.

Beads possess a strong tactile quality that combines very effectively with different coloured or textured metals; they look wonderful next to decorative surface finishes such as patination, etching and enamelling. Beads can be reworked into chain designs or threaded onto fine wire that is then twisted and knotted delicately into necklaces or bracelets.

A bead that has an interesting shape or colour can be used as a single focal point. For example, a single beautiful crystal bead could replace a traditionally cut stone and be set into a brooch or ring by an inventive method of fixing. Drilled drops look good as the central focus of a necklace and long slender pendeloques can be entwined with fine gold wire to create unusual earrings. Smaller faceted briolettes can be wired into extravagant clusters as pendants, placed with contrasting beads in a bracelet or even attached to a ring to create a fluid (and noisy) design.

Beads and briolettes must be fixed and wired carefully so the piece is durable. Fine wire must not be overtwisted as it can break. If the bead holes are very small, it is better to use platinum wire, which is stronger and more flexible.

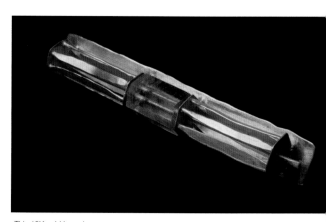

This 18K gold brooch has a wonderful simplicity of form. A single aquamarine crystal bead has been skewered by a pin through the length of the brooch. The striations of the aquamarine crystal have been reproduced in the cast gold.

This is a highly creative use of beads. There is a dramatic contrast between the polished silver pendants and the red seedlike beads, which are suspended on nylon cord to give the impression that they are spilling out of the pendants.

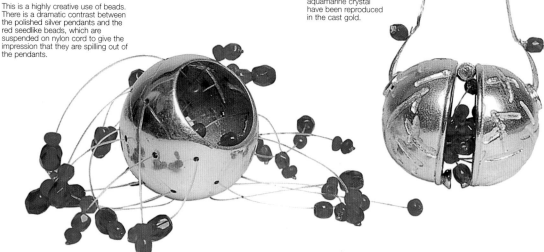

Designing with beads

The beads in this brooch have been threaded onto wire to create an unusual abacus design. The wire has been passed through drill holes and fixed at the back of brooch.

Beads and faceted briolettes are combined in a colourful, delicate bracelet that will catch the light as the arm moves. The piece is constructed using fine gold wire that is twisted into links.

Small faceted briolettes have been wired and attached to the ring mount surrounding the central gemstone. The colour of the briolettes is reflected in the central stone, and the ring's movement and sound gives the piece an added dimension.

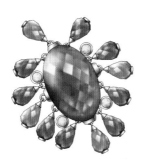

The simplicity and lightness of form of this ring give it a contemporary look. The branched arms are split into forks that are terminated by a small drilled pearl or bead.

Slender elongated pendeloques have been embellished with gold wire that twists and turns like a climbing rose and is decorated with tiny gold flowers. The drop is secured with a simple post-and-cap fitting.

The tassels of tiny beads give this necklace an Art Deco feel. Bead tassels need to be strung on silk for them to hang and sway properly. They add texture and movement to a design.

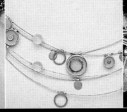

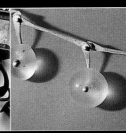

The large set stone and cluster of drops make a colourful and dramatic focal point. They contrast with the plain woven silver, the mix of colour and form adding texture and interest to the design.

This multirow necklace uses gemstone beads, inlaid mother-of-pearl and gold leaf. The beads have been positioned individually to create a larger design. The nylon cable ensures that the piece has strength as well as delicacy.

Labradorite beads are threaded through every couple of links in this silver necklace, bringing movement and colour to the piece. As the stones catch the light they will reveal their blue schiller (sheen).

Drilled crystals have been capped at either end and linked into a chain. The pale colour of the stones is offset by the stark black oxidized chain and caps. The detail of the design draws the eye along the necklace.

In this necklace, beads have been used individually in a simple design. Forged silver links secured the beads, which were then riveted in place. The subtle use of colour and texture is very effective – the frosted rock crystal is echoed by the matte surface of the silver.

the ring

A ring makes a personal statement, reflecting the character and lifestyle of the wearer. It can represent an attachment to another person, as well as signifying social status and financial achievement. Its purchase can be a celebration marking a new stage in life or simply a frivolous act of retail therapy. A ring has to mean so many different things to so many different people that the gemstone becomes an essential feature of design, without which it would be impossible to fulfill all the demands made on this piece of jewellery.

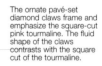

This is an elegant and wearable ring. The raised outer band of the white gold shank acts as a protective barrier to the vulnerable bead settings.

The ring is the item of jewellery most often worn by women and men and it is also the form most frequently set with gemstones. The illustrations on these pages show the impact that gemstones can have on ring design and how easily they can change the personality of a piece. By concentrating on just one form of jewellery, it is possible to focus on the common themes influencing gem-set jewellery design and to see how jewellery makers explore and work with these themes. Each ring featured here refers to one or more of the ideas discussed in "Designing with gemstones". These include the creative role of the stone setting, the use of colour and texture of both gemstone and metal, the impact of a stone's size, the placement of single or grouped gemstones and the opportunities presented by nonstandard forms and drilled beads.

Dating from the 1960s, this gold ring has an articulated shank divided into five parts. Rubies have been claw-set in raised settings.

This ring is dominated by the vibrancy of the large rubellite cabochon. A simple bezel setting and wide shank hold the stone and ring securely, and the high-polish finish gives the ring an opulent look.

The ornate pavé-set diamond claws frame and emphasize the square-cut pink tourmaline. The fluid shape of the claws contrasts with the square cut of the tourmaline.

Flat mirror-cut tourmalines and aquamarines were bezel-set to accentuate the marquise shape of the stones and offer protection from impact. The angle at which the stones are mounted creates directional energy in the rings and the finish of the metal complements the gentle colours of the stones.

Drilled aquamarines have been secured with a central pin that is riveted in place. The inclusion of plates and bolts adds decoration yet also lends an industrial quality to these witty cocktail rings.

This cast gold ring is simply set with a large heavy cabochon. The tapered band reduces the weight of the piece and keeps the ring secure. The smooth form makes the ring suitable for everyday wear.

The depth of the sapphire dictated the depth of this ring's band, which has been set flush with the stone's surface. The upper half of the ring, including the sides, has been pavé-set with small diamonds to provide contrast, while the lower half is highly polished for ease of wear.

A single faceted stone has been discreetly set into the gold band. The design is simple with clean lines, but the engraving work and colour of the gold give the ring warmth and texture and prevent it from looking austere.

Chasing and repoussé work have created a flowing linear design that wraps around the group of different-shaped diamonds. The irregular placement of the gemstones suits the organic nature of the ring.

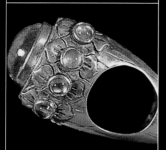

This ring has a strong form and tactile quality. Subtly coloured labradorite cabochons complement the metal's patination and texturing. The low profile of the stones protects them from impact and their placement draws the eye to the decorative work.

The line of gemstones is balanced on either side with band forms, which also protect the small rubies. The design gives the eternity ring format a contemporary edge.

The combination of a large cabochon with highly decorative granulation work and small set diamonds gives the design balance. The quietness and simplicity of the central stone are a foil to the opulence of the metalwork.

The open, fluid band structure offsets the size of the main stone, as do the small pavé-set diamonds. The sculptural approach allows the emerald to be viewed from all angles and creates the appearance of lightness. Platinum was required to give the structure its strength.

This fancy articulated ring uses a synthetic gemstone for durability – a natural stone would not withstand the movement and stresses resulting from the design.

This inventive solitaire design challenges preconceptions of form and function. The ring is designed to fit among the fingers, and titanium and aluminium provide lightness and strength.

PRACTICAL ADVICE

The following pages contain information essential to jewellery makers and designers. Tips on care and handling will keep your gemstones looking beautiful; insider knowledge regarding appraising and purchasing stones will make you a savvy shopper; and a resource list and glossary tell you where to turn and what to say. These pieces of information, and more, will help guide any jeweller towards a successful designing experience with gemstones.

Kunzite needs careful handling as it is quite fragile and at risk of chipping or breaking. If set in a ring it should be removed for household tasks and physical activities. A buildup of grease and dirt behind the setting would spoil the delicate colouring of kunzite, so it needs regular cleaning to keep it looking good.

Handling gemstones

Ideally, gemstones should be handled as little as possible; the more contact you have with them, the less good they look and the more you risk damaging them. A stone should be cleaned with a cloth prior to viewing, as grease and dirt can affect the brilliance and colour – diamonds can lose several colour and clarity grades as a result of accumulated grime. Gemstones should never be placed on a glass or metal surface because they can scratch easily there. Try to keep a white cloth handy as a protective covering – the white background will also display the full colour of the stone. Be careful when measuring stones, as they can pick up scratches from caliper and vernier gauges.

GEMSTONE CARE

All gemstones and gem-set jewellery should be stored individually in boxes or bags. If you keep stones such as tourmaline or topaz together in a bag they will damage each other. Brittle and soft stones, including organic material, require extra care – they should be stored separately away from any heat sources or chemical contact. Ideally, rows of pearls should be wrapped in acid-free tissue paper rather than in plastic bags because the organic nature of the material is vulnerable to heat and condensation. Tissue paper allows air to flow around the pearls.

Jewellery that is set with fragile stones is vulnerable to perfumes, lotions, household chemicals and detergents, so should be removed when showering, bathing or doing household cleaning. Metal polishes can also affect organic stones and gem materials such as opal and turquoise; the polish can be absorbed by the stone, which will then become discoloured or lose its lustre. Direct sunlight can inflict damage on jewellery that contains gemstones such as kunzite and amethyst and cause their colour to fade, while hot sunlight can dehydrate opal, leading to cracking and a loss of colour play.

Gemstones that are set in particular rings will need cleaning from time to time, because dirt can gather under the setting and affect the appearance of faceted stones. Simply soak the item in hot water with a dash of detergent and then clean gently with a toothbrush. Note that detergent shouldn't be used with organic and porous gemstones.

USING TWEEZERS

If you hold a stone with your fingers, not only will you make it greasy and reduce the brilliance, you'll also get only a limited view. Ideally you should use tweezers that are fine-tipped with serrated jaws; the slimmer they are, the greater the accuracy when picking up and placing the stone. The serrations prevent the stone from slipping and rotating, but don't use this style of tweezers on softer, delicate material because the rough jaws could damage the surface finish of the stone. Over time, the serrations will wear down, especially if they're used for hard gem material such as diamonds. The spring, or tension, in the tweezers can also be lost through misuse and become floppy. A temporary wedge made from folded paper will open up the jaws and bring back the tension. Always try to hold the stone by the girdle; if you hold it by the table and pavilion you may scratch the large table facet. Don't squeeze the tweezers too hard or place too much pressure on the gemstone or it will pop out (and usually end up under the table or across the room). All that's needed to keep the stone in place is a constant gentle pressure, which you will achieve with practice. In the meantime, a torch is useful for finding dropped gemstones.

USING A LOUPE

The best type of loupe is one with a triplet lens and 10x magnification. Some dealers prefer to use a loupe that has black housing around the lens rather than chrome so that the housing doesn't affect the colour of the stone.

Hold the loupe between your thumb and forefinger and bring it about 1 inch (2.5 cm) away from your eye, with your hand resting on your cheek. If using tweezers, place the stone face down on the tray, grip the girdle (outer edges) of the stone with the tweezers, and rotate at the wrist until the stone is face up. Bring the gemstone or jewellery toward the lens until it is in focus. To avoid shaking, put your elbow on the table. Illuminate the stone correctly so the light is angled into the stone and not in your eyes. Focus on both the surface and the interior of the stone.

appraising gemstones

When you are first presented with a tray of gemstones it is easy to feel dazzled and slightly overwhelmed, and to forget to look at the stones in detail. It is not difficult to miss basic faults, only to realize a couple of days later that the gemstone you purchased is not quite as good as you thought.

This chapter will guide you through the essential stages of appraisal so that you can choose a stone of quality and ensure value for money. First you need to know that you are looking at the real thing – that the sapphire really is a sapphire and not a fake. Other than going to the effort of taking the stone for testing at a laboratory, you need to choose a reputable dealer. Preferably this will be someone who is recommended by other dealers, who knows the history of the gemstones he or she is selling and who will offer you good trade prices. It's worth remembering that within the gem trade, reputation is everything – dealers who get a bad name for deceiving a customer don't survive in the business for long.

Ruby-in-zoisite cabochons

This Burmese ruby has been cut to retain as much weight as possible and is rather deep, with an off-centre culet. However, when viewed from the top the cutting faults are not evident as the colour saturation is so spectacular. The inclusions are acceptable as they denote origin. A large unheated Burmese ruby such as this has considerable value.

Do touch

Gemstones look lovely in their presentation cases, but you should never buy a stone without taking it out of its box or bag first. Boxes can hide flaws and cracks, alter the colour of the stone and disguise poor cutting. A good dealer will take the gemstone out for viewing without being asked. Many faults, such as symmetry, quality of colour, inclusions and surface damage, can be seen with the naked eye as long as there is a good light source. The light should come from above or behind you, so it shines down through the stone. Some store lighting is designed to make a gemstone look intense and dazzling; don't be afraid to ask to see the stone in daylight. A piece of white paper will also help you to judge colour properly. Hold the stone against the white background and look at it from the top and the sides, then turn the stone upside down to check for colour zoning.

If you are unpractised with tweezers then don't use them; you can lift the stone up in a tray and rotate it through 360 degrees. Balancing the gemstone on the back of your hand, with the culet sitting between your fingers, will help you to identify shallow stones and evaluate size in relation to your hand. Feel free to use a loupe, but practise before visiting the gem store. It is useful to take along a small penlight, to reveal any cracks in cabochons, and a lint-free cloth to remove grease.

Look at gemstones when you are fresh; don't view them at night or if you've been working all day. Comparison is the best means of appraisal – the more stones you look at, the quicker you will separate good from bad. Get to know the comparative carat prices of different materials. It may seem obvious, but double-check the name of the gemstone with the dealer. Misnomers are still used; for instance, citrine often gets called topaz. Finally, take account of your gut feelings – does the stone excite you? If a gemstone seems too good to be true, it probably is!

Cabochons

As with faceted stones, rarity, colour and optical effects are the main indicators of value. A symmetrical outline, flat, solid base and good finish are also important. The degree of clarity is less crucial because cabochons are typically cut from lower-grade material, but stability is important as a cracked stone might break during setting. Check for cracks by running your fingernail over the surface and shining a penlight through the stone.

Beads

Surface finish, drilling, symmetry and evenness of cutting are the prime indicators of quality in beads. Cracks, chips, wonky drilling and poor polishing are common faults.

The colour of this pink kunzite cabochon is attractive, but the cut and polish are not very good. The outline is lumpy and traces of the green polishing compound are visible on the underside of the stone. However, kunzite is notoriously difficult to cut and polish because of the gem's cleavage and fracture. The oily lustre makes the stone interesting.

The cut of these sillimanite beads is irregular, producing an uneven shape and thickness. The quality of material is also variable. However, it is rare to find sillimanite in bead form, so they have some value.

What to look for in a gemstone

RARITY

Gemstones can be rare for a variety of reasons – the type of gemstone, the origin, the colour or the size. However, rarity doesn't automatically mean that a stone is valuable as it still needs to be assessed on other criteria. Check to see if the stone has a certificate.

Most people would consider the colour of this faceted hiddenite too pale and the cut too shallow; unfortunately, the cross cut hasn't helped reduce the window effect. However, hiddenite is a rare gem and intense colours seldom occur (and when they do it is only in small sizes). Despite the delicate colour, this stone is valuable for its rarity and size.

TREATMENT

In general, treatment, whether it is heating, irradiation, staining, dyeing, fracture filling or stabilization, devalues a gemstone. Heat treatment is more acceptable than the others as it doesn't affect the future wearability of the stone. Some processes, such as irradiation, fracture filling and beryllium or diffusion treatment, are not permanent.

This Sri Lankan sapphire has a lovely colour – a pure strong pink with a blue tone – and its size and cushion shape make it instantly attractive. However, its proportions aren't quite right: the stone is shallow and the cutter has tried to disguise this with a fully faceted crown that has no table. The colour appears saturated around the outer edges of the stone while the centre looks paler; this is the effect of the "window".

COLOUR

This is the most important aspect of a coloured gemstone, worth at least half of the total value of the stone. The finer a gemstone's colour, the less impact cutting, clarity and weight will have on the value. If the colour of a stone is poor, brilliance will be an important factor. The closer the colour comes to a pure hue (spectral colour), the rarer and more valuable the stone. Intensity or saturation of colour is also an indicator of quality and highly desirable, but will be diminished by irregular colour distribution and the presence of grey tones. View a stone in both artificial light and daylight. Some gemstones, such as kunzite and amethyst, can fade naturally over time and should not be worn in direct sunlight. The style of setting can affect the colour of a gem; rub-over collets can make dark stones appear even darker or intensify the colour of pale stones.

Alexandrite, faceted cushion (1.57 ct)

Good alexandrites are not easy to source. Their most important feature is quality of colour change, which in this gemstone is excellent. The colour changes from reddish brown to a bright emerald green. It is possible to see inclusions at the bottom edge of the stone, where the cutter has hidden them under the crown facets. This would not affect the value.

HARDNESS AND DURABILITY

Is the gemstone suitable for your design? Will it survive the intended wear and tear?

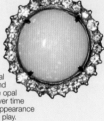

Made in the early 1900s, this ring is beautifully worked and the diamonds that surround the precious white opal are bright, lively and well matched. The opal has dehydrated over time and has a pasty appearance with limited colour play.

OPTICAL EFFECTS

The quality of an optical effect such as asterism or colour change is as important as colour or clarity, and will affect the value of the stone.

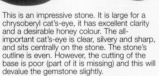

This is an impressive stone. It is large for a chrysoberyl cat's-eye, it has excellent clarity and a desirable honey colour. The all-important cat's-eye is clear, silvery and sharp, and sits centrally on the stone. The stone's outline is even. However, the cutting of the base is poor (part of it is missing) and this will devalue the gemstone slightly.

CLARITY AND INCLUSIONS

Clarity is worth approximately 20 to 30 per cent of the total value of a gemstone. Some inclusions are acceptable, as they can prove a stone's identity and origin, and will not affect the value. However, as a rule, heavily included faceted stones are not worth as much as "clean" stones, because internal flaws can spoil a gemstone's appearance and undermine its stability.

This Zambian emerald cabochon contains many inclusions but should not be criticized for that; it is very rare to find emeralds of this size that are "clean". It has a good emerald colour – grass green with a hint of blue – and does not have any brown or whitish inclusions. There is no evidence of fracture filling and no cracks on the surface. The shape is smooth and even; the stone has been cut and polished well. It is rare to see an emerald cabochon of this size and quality.

CUT

The cut accounts for 10 to 20 per cent of total value. It is less critical than colour and clarity because it can be changed. Gems that are cut very deep will be overweight (and therefore expensive) for their size and dull. A shallow stone that has a large spread might look showy, but will have little "life" and could break during setting. It may be advisable to recut a good stone to better proportions, despite the loss of weight and size.

Golden citrine princess cut (22.14 ct)

This citrine has a rather pale colour that is unevenly distributed. When viewed from the side, there is little colour in the base of stone, or culet. When viewed upside down, one side of the stone has a better colour intensity than the other. The stone is slightly shallow, but overall the cutting and finish are very good.

SURFACE ABRASIONS

Finish accounts for about 10 per cent of total value. It is reasonable to ask the dealer to polish out any abrasions, scratches or chips as a condition of the sale.

buying gemstones

Recent advances in gem treatments and synthetic stones have made buying gemstones much more of a challenge. As a consequence, finding a dealer or shop you can trust is a crucial part of purchasing a gemstone. It is also important to see the stone in person rather than in a picture – a flat, static image will never give a true representation of the stone.

Compare these three synthetic pink sapphires to the genuine Sri Lankan pink sapphire on the previous page. Aside from the fact that they have different cuts, could you tell them apart?

Reconstituted turquoise can look identical to natural turquoise. The pear-shaped cabochons above are Grade A Sleeping Beauty material and quite expensive, while the round cabochons are reconstituted turquoise and have little value.

Guidelines for buying

• Gemstone dealers are, on the whole, honest and do the job because they have a passion for gemstones. Most are not trying to dupe you, so please don't try and get a price reduction by being rude about their stones. If you denigrate their goods you will lose their goodwill and any possible discount – courtesy works better! When looking at a gem dealer's stock, don't automatically take a stone out of a box without asking. Traders have invested a huge amount of money in their gemstones, so many prefer to handle the stones themselves. If you damage or break a stone when handling it you should offer to pay for it because the dealer will have lost the money on it.

• Before you buy a valuable gemstone, try to do some homework. For instance, if you are planning to buy a quality ruby, get to know the carat prices of the different types and grades. Then you'll know if the shop or dealer you've gone to is overcharging. Bear in mind that a shop will have to double or triple the cost price of a stone to cover overheads such as rent and staffing. A smaller independent dealer generally won't have those overheads, so the prices should be lower.

• Be aware of the common gemstone treatments and get to know which gemstones are most frequently treated. Coral and jade are often dyed, while a great deal of lapis lazuli and turquoise is reconstructed. If buying a valuable gem, ask a laboratory to do a grading report on colour treatment. Get as much background information as possible from the dealer. If you don't understand what the dealer says, ask for an explanation; don't feel embarrassed.

• If you see a stone that you really like, try to camouflage your intentions and avoid becoming overeager. Wait for the dealer to offer the price first, and then wait a while before responding. It is sometimes helpful to take a disinterested third party with you when buying to make your decisions more measured. Don't feel pressured or bullied into taking a gemstone if you're not certain about it.

• Some gem dealers and shops will allow you to take a stone "on appro", in other words, to borrow the stone for a set period to show a customer or consider whether a gemstone is suitable for a design. If you take something on approval, you must return it within the specified time – don't sit on it for weeks or you will lose the goodwill of the dealer. The goods are your responsibility while they are in your possession; you will have to pay for loss or damage.

• When you purchase a gemstone, ensure that you get a detailed receipt stating exactly what the goods are: the type of material, the carat weight, whether the colour has been treated, details of the clarity or flaws, dimensions and cut. If a shop or dealer won't do this (and guarantee the goods), you should seriously consider going elsewhere.

BUYING ON THE INTERNET

The Internet might provide us with a fast, easy and private means of purchasing basic goods, but in the case of gemstones, it's far from ideal. Internet sales can lock you into a deal when you haven't had the chance to see or compare the gem firsthand, and the returns policy will often only allow you a very short period of time to inspect the goods, or the vendor might insist on an exchange rather than a full refund of your money. The Federal Trade Commission (FTC) has reported that information given in support of online gem sales is frequently inaccurate, incomplete or unreliable (bogus lab reports have been used to increase the buyer's confidence). The goods tend to be overpriced and sometimes are never delivered. The main reason for these problems is that the vendors don't usually have track records or reputations that they need or wish to maintain.

BUYING AT TRADE EVENTS

Trade shows tend to be noisy, short of space and packed with people, and they usually have appalling lighting – all of which make it very difficult to assess a stone accurately. Traders often return overseas after the event, making it difficult to return faulty or misrepresented goods. To get a good deal, you'll need to be fast and accurate at assessing a stone and be able to stand your ground with some very persuasive dealers. Gems that have undergone diffusion or beryllium treatments can be hidden easily at events like these.

BUYING FROM A REPUTABLE DEALER OR SHOP

A shop or an established dealer will give you much greater peace of mind when you buy gemstones. You'll be able to check their credentials and how long they've been in business, get recommendations from other customers and ensure that they have a fair and clear returns policy. Most importantly, a well-known shop or dealer will guarantee merchandise by stating exactly what the goods are on a receipt and will always agree to a lab report.

resources

At times all jewellery makers need expert advice regarding gemstones. Laboratory reports can be essential for verifying or certifying sapphires or diamonds, and the support of a professional gemmological assessor is important when buying an expensive gem. A jeweller might require up-to-date information on the treatments of certain types of stones and need to approach a gem trade association or, in a case of misrepresentation, might need some leverage and legal backup from a consumer rights organization.

Jewellery and gemstone trade events

Trade shows have become increasingly popular among jewellery makers as they provide opportunities to see new types of gemstones and pick up some bargains. It is possible to find out about these events on the Internet from an organization such as the American Gem Trade Association (www.agta.org). The main international event in the United States for the gemstone trade is the Tucson Gem and Mineral Show (www.tucsonshowguide.com). Traders from around the world converge on the city for six days at the end of January or beginning of February. The Tucson trade show is a huge event, and even if you don't feel confident enough to buy, it is still worth going to look.

The main event for jewellery trade in the United Kingdom is the International Jewellery London exhibition (www.jewellerylondon.com) held at Earl's Court at the beginning of September. The show has a good section dedicated to gemstones, pearls and beads with traders from around the world.

Germany has a couple of events that are excellent. Intergem (www.intergem-messe.de) occurs in September, when the famous gem-cutting town of Idar-Oberstein opens its doors to visitors. Idar-Oberstein also boasts a wonderful museum of minerals and lapidary work. In February, the Inhorgenta show (www.inhorgenta.com) opens in Munich. It is one of the major European jewellery shows and has many gemstone booths with international stone traders.

Information about several jewellery trade shows can be found at www.jewellery.reedexpo.com.

CONSUMER INFORMATION AND ADVICE IN THE UNITED STATES

Federal Trade Commission
Consumer Response Center
600 Pennsylvania Avenue NW
Washington, DC 20580
www.ftc.gov
The FTC can offer advice if you are buying or have bought a gemstone and are not happy with the conduct or practices of the shop or trader.

Jewelry Information Center
52 Vanderbilt Avenue, 19th Floor
New York, NY 10017
(646) 658-0240
800-459-0130
www.jewelryinfo.org
The centre provides information about buying gem-set jewellery.

American Gem Society
8881 W. Sahara Avenue
Las Vegas
NV 89117
(702) 255-6500
www.ags.org
The society provides information on buying gemstones.

Better Business Bureau
Local branches
www.bbb.org
The bureau investigates complaints about a firm's practices or policies.

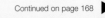

Continued on page 168 ▶

◀ Continued from page 167

Jewelers Vigilance Committee (JVC)
25 West 45th Street, Suite 1406
New York, NY 10036
(212) 997-2002
www.jvclegal.org
If a jeweller has misrepresented a stone, the JVC will
provide assistance and investigate the complaint.
The organization will take action if they believe there
was fraudulent activity.

The Diamond Registry
580 Fifth Avenue
New York, NY 10036
800-223-7955
www.diamondregistry.com
The diamond registry produces a newsletter that
includes consumer information.

International Colored Gemstone Association
19 West 21st Street, Suite 705
New York, NY 10010-6805
(212) 620-0900
www.gemstone.org
The ICA is an association for gemstone wholesalers,
gem cutters and miners. It is based in New York and
has members from 41 countries.

Polygon (internet marketplace)
Polygon Network
PO Box 4806
Dillon, CO 80435
800-221-4435
www.polygon.net
This online service for jewellery industry professionals
provides opportunities to network, buy and sell. It
gives details of supplies and services to the trade and
access to an inventory of diamonds.

GEMMOLOGIST APPRAISERS IN THE UNITED STATES

American Society of Appraisers
555 Hendon Parkway, Suite 125
Hendon, VA 20170
(703) 478-2228
www.appraisers.org
Ask for a list of master gemmologist appraisers.

American Gem Society Laboratories (AGSL)
8881 West Sahara Avenue
Las Vegas, NV 89117
(702) 233-6120
www.agslab.com
Ask for a list of certified independent gemmologist
appraisers.

Accredited Gemologists Association
888 Brannan Street, Suite 1175
San Francisco, CA 94103
(619) 501-5444
accreditedgemologists.org
Ask for a list of gem laboratories or certified master
gemmologists.

International Society of Appraisers
1131 SW 7th Street, Suite 105
Renton, WA 98055
(206) 241-0359
www.isa-appraisers.org
Ask for a list of certified appraisers of personal
property.

GEM TRADE LABORATORIES IN THE UNITED STATES

American Gemological Laboratories (AGL)
580 Fifth Avenue, Suite 706
New York, NY 10036
(212) 704-0727

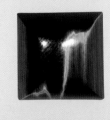

International Gemological Institute (IGI)
589 Fifth Avenue
New York, NY 10017
(212) 753-7759

550 South Hill Street
Los Angeles, CA 90013
(213) 955-0008
www.igi-usa.com

Gem Certification and Appraisal Lab (GCAL)
580 Fifth Avenue LL
New York, NY 10036
(212) 869-8985
www.gemfacts.com

Gemological Institute of America (GIA)
World Headquarters
The Robert Mouawad Campus
5345 Armada Drive
Carlsbad, CA 92008
800-421-7250
www.gia.edu

GIA Gem Trade Laboratory (GTL)
580 Fifth Avenue, Suite 200
New York, NY 10036
800-366-8519
www.gia.edu

American Gem Trade Association (AGTA)
Gemological Testing Center
18 East 48th Street, Suite 502
New York, NY 10017
(212) 752-1717
www.agta.org

Professional Gem Sciences (PGS)
5 South Wabash Avenue, Suite 1905
Chicago, IL 60603
888-292-1888
www.progem.com

European Gemological Laboratory (EGL)
30 West 47th Street, Suite 205
New York, NY 10036

EGL USA
6 West 48th Street
New York, NY 10036
(212) 730-7380

EGL USA/Los Angeles
550 South Hill
Suite 840
Los Angeles, CA 90013
(877) 893-8593
www.eglusa.com

CANADIAN GEMMOLOGICAL ORGANIZATIONS

Canadian Gemmological Association (CGA)
1767 Avenue Road
Toronto, ON M5M 3Y8
1-877-244-3090
www.canadiangemmological.com

Gem and Mineral Federation of Canada
Box 136
Slocan, BC V0G 2C0
www.gmfc.ca
The GMFC has details of lapidary societies and
mineral and gem shows including the National Gem,
Mineral and Fossil Show.

INDEPENDENT GEMMOLOGICAL LABORATORIES IN CANADA

EGL Canada
United Kingdom Building
409 Granville Street
Suite 456
Vancouver, BC V6C 1T2
(604) 630-0464

55 Queen Street
Suite 500
Toronto, ON M5C 1R6
(416) 368-1200

IGI Canada
27 Queen Street East
Floor 12
Toronto, ON M5C 2M6
(416) 594-2500
www.igi-canada.ca

Harold Weinstein Ltd (HWL)
55 Queen Street East, Suite 1301
Toronto, ON M5C 1R6
(416) 366-6518
www.hwgem.com
Qualified appraisers will provide diamond grading
reports and gemstone identification. They also
provide jewellery appraisals.

Gem Scan International Inc.
27 Queen Street East, Suite 406
Toronto, ON M5C 2M6
1-877-868-6656
www.gemscan.com
This independent jewellery appraisal laboratory will
provide gem identification, diamond grading and
related services such as laser inscription.

CANADIAN JEWELER ORGANIZATIONS
(including consumer support)

Canadian Jewellers Association (CJA)
27 Queen Street East, Suite 600
Toronto, ON M5C 2M6
1-800-580-0942
www.canadianjewellers.com
The CGA is a jewellery industry organization that has
a directory of jeweller members who abide by the
association's code of conduct.

Jewellers Vigilance Canada (JVC)
27 Queen Street East, Suite 600
Toronto, ON M5C 2M6
1-800-636-9536
www.jewellersvigilance.ca
The JVC is an independent association that handles
consumer and industry complaints and will tackle
fraudulent activity within the industry.

GEM TRADE LABORATORIES IN EUROPE

Gemmological Association and Gem Testing
Laboratory of Great Britain (Gem-A)
27 Greville Street
London, UK EC1N 8TN
+44 (0) 20-7404-3334
www.gagtl.ac.uk

German Gemmological Association
Laboratory (DGemG)
Prof.-Schlossmacher Strasse 1
D-55743 Idar-Oberstein
Germany
+49 (0) 6781-50840
www.dgemg.com

Gubelin Gem Lab
Maihofstrasse 102
CH-6006 Lucerne 9
Switzerland
+41 41-429-1717
www.gubelinlab.com

Swiss Gemmological Institute
Falknerstrasse 9
CH-4001 Basel
Switzerland
+41 61-262-0640
www.ssef.ch

Antwerp World Diamond Center (HRD)
Hoveniersstraat 22
BE-2018 Antwerp
Belgium
+32 (0) 3-222-0511
www.hrd.be

International Gemological Institute (IGI)
Schupstraat 1
2018 Antwerp
Belgium
+32 (0) 3-231-6845
www.igiworldwide.com

WORLD TRADE CENTRES OF COLOURED GEMSTONES AND DIAMONDS

AFRICA
South Africa: Johannesburg and Cape Town
Important gem-producing countries in Africa:
Kenya, Madagascar, Namibia, Nigeria,
Tanzania, Zambia

ASIA
Hong Kong
India: Jaipur and Mumbai (Bombay)
Japan: Tokyo
South Korea: Seoul
Sri Lanka: Colombo
Thailand: Bangkok

AUSTRALASIA
Australia: Sydney

EUROPE
Belgium: Antwerp
Italy: Cavalese and Milan
Germany: Dusseldorf and Idar-Oberstein
Switzerland: Basel and Lucerne
United Kingdom: Birmingham and London

MIDDLE EAST
Dubai
Israel: Tel Aviv
Pakistan: Lahore

NORTH AMERICA
Canada: Toronto and Vancouver
United States: Los Angeles and New York

SOUTH AMERICA
Brazil: Sao Paulo

index

credits

Author's Acknowledgments

Nathan Aziz and Son, Ltd.
Diamonds
Hatton Garden, London

Richard Bernhard and Co.
Gemstones
Idar-Oberstein, Germany

Yeves Frey
Colored diamonds
Hatton Garden, London

Holts
Gemstones and jewelry
Hatton Garden, London

Paul Kessler, Ospray Trading

Olivia Qizilbash

Bibliography

Dundek, Marijan, IGI. *Diamonds*. London: Noble Gems Publications, 2000.

Francis, Sondra, GG. *Gem Dealer's Secrets: Handbook for the Gem Buyer*. www.ganoksin.com

Hall, Cally, FGA. *Gemstones*. London: Dorling Kindersley, 2000.

James, Duncan. *Antique Jewellery*. Risborough, Buckinghamshire: Shire Publications, 1999.

Keller, Peter C. *Gemstones of East Africa*. Tucson: Geoscience Press, 1992.

Matlins, Antoinette, PG, and A. C. Bonanno, FGA, PG, ASA. *Jewelry and Gems: The Buying Guide*. Woodstock, Vt.: Gemstone Press, 2001.

McCreight, Tim. *The Complete Metalsmith*. Worcester, Ma.: Davis Publications, Inc., 1991.

Newman, Renee, GG. *The Pearl Buying Guide* (3rd Edition). Los Angeles: International Jewelry Publications, 2004.

Peters, Nizam. *Rough Diamonds: A Practical Guide*. Deerfield Beach, Fl: American Institute of Diamond Cutting Inc., 1999.

Schumann, Walter. *Gemstones of the World*. London: NAG Press, 1997.

Sevdermish, M., and A. Mashiah. *The Dealer's Book of Gems and Diamonds* (2 volumes). Israel: Gemology (A.M.), 1996.

Untracht, Oppi. *Jewelry: Concepts and Technology*. London: Robert Hale, 1985.

Websites

These websites were helpful to the author:

www.colored-stone.com/archives.cfm
www.cst.cmich.edu/users/dietr1rv
www.faceters.com
www.ganoksin.com
www.gemsociety.org
www.geocities.com/mineralsgems
www.gia.edu/gemsandgemology
www.mineraldata.com
www.minershop.com
www.professionaljeweler.com
www.tucsonshowguide.com/stories
www.webmineral.com

Jewellery credits

Quarto would like to thank and acknowledge the following artists for supplying work reproduced in this book:

KEY: **a** = above, **b** = below, **c** = center, **l** = left, **r** = right, **R** = row

6bl Daphne Krinos, **7al** Louise O'Neill, **8ar** Memory Stather, **8bl** Elena Tanturri, **9ar** Susy Telling, **14a** Ben Day, **14bl** Susy Telling, **14br** De Beers Images, **15ar** James Newman, **15al, 15bl** Ben Day, **15br** Boodles, **16–17, 18cr, 18bl, 19al** De Beers Images, **19bl** Scott Peterson/Getty Images, **23c** De Beers Images, **24l** Ulla Hörnfeldt, **25al** Emma Farquharson, **25ar, 25br** Tom Munsteiner, **26bl** Charlotte de Syllas, **26br** Ben Day, **30a** Louise O'Neill, **30c** Goodman Morris Ltd, **30bl** Catherine Mannheim, **32al** Jean Scott-Moncrieff, **32ac** Phebe Allen Blake, **32c** Ulla Hörnfeldt, **32bl** Jinks McGrath, **32br** Whitney Abrams, **33br** Catherine Mannheim, **35al** Charlotte de Syllas, **35ar** Rebecca Reimers Cristol, **35c** Abby Griffiths, **35br** Catherine Mannheim, **36al, 36cl** Daphne Krinos, **36cr** Dale Day, **36b** Charmian Harris, **37b** Louise O'Neill, **39al** Charmian Harris, **39ar** Catherine Mannheim, **39c** Daphne Krinos, **39bl** Memory Stather, **39br** Charmian Harris, **41a** Jutta Munsteiner, **41cl** Memory Stather, **41c** Jutta Munsteiner, **41cr** Charlotte de Syllas, **44al** Daphne Krinos, **44b** Elizabeth Maldonado, **45al** Nicola Morris, **45bl, 45br** Monica Boxley, **50cl, 50cr** Ben Day, **50bl** Louise O'Neill, **54bc** R Holt & Co. Ltd, **54br** Jean Scott-Moncrieff, **56b** Boodles, **60bl, 60br** Goodman Morris Ltd, **64bl** Ulla Hörnfeldt, **65b** Charlotte de Syllas, **66bl, 66br, 68bl** Ulla Hörnfeldt, **70br** Sotheby's Picture Library, **72c** Charmian Harris, **72b** Hana Levy, **76al** Emma Farquharson, **76ar** Memory Stather, **76b** Ulla Hörnfeldt, **78bl** Memory Stather, **78br** Charlotte de Syllas, **80bl, 80br** R Holt & Co. Ltd, **82bl, 82br** Charmian Harris, **85br** R Holt & Co. Ltd, **88al** Susy Telling, **88ar, 88c, 88bl** Lisa Hamilton, **88br, 90b** Charmian Harris, **91b** R Holt & Co. Ltd, **94al** Memory Stather, **95cl** Charmian Harris, **95c** Ben Day, **95cr, 95b** Jean Scott-Moncrieff, **96b** Boodles, **97b** Paul Kessler, **100bl** Elizabeth Lancaster, **100br** Memory Stather, **102b** Emma Farquharson, **103b** Sotheby's Picture Library, **104r** Memory Stather, **107b** Ulla Hörnfeldt, **108bl** Monica Boxley, **109bl** R Holt & Co. Ltd, **111a** De Beers Images, **112bl** Liz Tyler/Photo: Joîl Degen, **112br** Nathan Aziz & Son, **113br** Ben Day, **114, 115a** Nathan Aziz & Son, **115cl** The Bridgeman Art Library, **115cr** James Barker, **115bl** Jean Scott-Moncrieff, **118a** Ben Day, **119cl, 119c** Christie's Images/The Bridgeman Art Library, **119b** Boltin Picture Library/The Bridgeman Art Library, **120ar** Catherine Hills, **120bl** Liz Olver, **120br** R Holt & Co. Ltd, **121a** Elena Tanturri, **121c** James Newman, **121bc, 129ar** Bentley & Skinner, Bond Street, **130ar** Whitney Abrams, **130c** Susy Telling, **130br** Alix & Co/Photo: Hap Sakwa, **131ac** Jinks McGrath, **131ar** Jean Scott-Moncrieff, **131b** Monica Boxley, **134cl** Elena Tanturri, **135a** Alexander Raphaîl, **135c** Alix & Co/Photo: Hap Sakwa, **135bl** Susy Telling, **135br** Charlotte de Syllas, **138bl** Monica Boxley, **138br** Emma Gale/Photo: Graham Clark, **142a** James Newman, **142R1** Alix & Co/Photo: Hap Sakwa, **142R2** Antoine Chapoutot, **142R3** Whitney Abrams, **142R4** Liz Olver, **142R5** Tom McEwan, **142bl** Barbara Christie, **142bc** Liz Tyler/Photo: Rodney Harrigan, **144a** Louise O'Neill, **144c** Robert Feather, **144b** Jinks McGrath, **145bl** Heinz Brummel, **145bcl** Alix & Co/Photo: Hap Sakwa, **145bc** Whitney Abrams, **145bcr** Jessica Briggs, **145br** Alix & Co/Photo: Hap Sakwa, **146a** Jinks McGrath, **146bl** Jon and Valerie Hill, **146R1** Judy Diamond Designs Inc, **146R2** Ruta Brown, **146R3** Liz Olver, **146R4** Whitney Abrams, **146R5** Jessica Briggs, **148a** Peter Page/Photo: Llewellyn Robin, **148cl** Angela Hübel/Photo: Mathias Hoffmann, **148cr** Ben Dyer, **148b** Angela Hübel/Photo: Mathias Hoffmann, **149bl** Alix & Co/Photo: Hap Sakwa, **149bcl** Barbara Christie, **149bc** Manuel Vilhena, **149bcr** Antoine Chapoutot, **149br** Liz Olver, **150a** Jinks McGrath, **150c** Margaret Shepherd, **150bl** Goodman Morris Ltd, **150br** Phebe Allen Blake, **151bl** Whitney Abrams, **151bcl** Liz Olver, **151bc, 151bcr, 151br** Whitney Abrams, **152a** Catherine Mannheim, **152bl** Georgina Taylor/Photo: Georgina Taylor, **152br** Louise O'Neill, **153al** Catherine Hills, **153bcl** Phillippe Rulliere, **153bc** Chris Carpenter, **153bcr** Liz Olver, **153br** Keng Nio Lolly Ong, **154a** Linda Lewin, **154b** Antoine Chapoutot, **154cl** James Barker, **155bl** Phillippe Rulliere, **155bcl** Antoine Chapoutot, **155bc** Whitney Abrams, **155bcr** Hanne Behrens, **155br** Nichola Ballerstedt, **156a, 156bl** Daphne Krinos, **156b** Charlotte de Syllas, **157bl** Judy Diamond Designs Inc, **157bcl** Charmian Harris, **157bc** Whitney Abrams, **157bcr** Liz Olver, **157br** Kyoko Urino, **158c** Daphne Krinos, **158b** Liz Olver, **159bl** FranÂoise Montague, **159bcl** Emma Gale/Photo: Graham Clark, **159bc** Amina Kaufmann, **159bcr** Daphne Krinos/Photo: Joîl Degen, **159br** Syann van Niftrik, **160a** Teodoro Tschrepp, **160cl** Goodman Morris Ltd, **160cr** Elena Tanturri, **160bl** Daphne Krinos, **160br** Louise O'Neill, **161lR1** Ibu Gallery Edition, **161lR2** Liz Olver, **161lR3** Amina Kaufmann, **161lR4** Alix & Co/Photo: Hap Sakwa, **161lR5** Melissa McArthur, **161rR1** Phillippe Rulliere, **161rR2** Patricia McAnally/Photo: Maggie Campbell Pedersen, **161rR3** Whitney Abrams, **161rR4** Jean Christophe, **161rR5** Kim Buck, **162a, 162c** Jean Scott-Moncrieff, **162b** Charmian Harris.